TEACHING MUSIC

TEACHING MUSIC

Managing the Successful Music Program

Second Edition

DARWIN E. WALKER

Professor of Music, Emeritus
South Dakota State University

SCHIRMER

THOMSON LEARNING

Australia • Canada • Mexico • Singapore • Spain • United Kingdom • United States

Wadsworth Group/Thomson Learning
10 Davis Drive
Belmont CA 94002-3098
USA

For information about our products, contact us:
Thomson Learning Academic Resource Center
1-800-423-0563
http://www.wadsworth.com

For permission to use material from this text, contact us by
Web: http://www.thomsonrights.com
Fax: 1-800-730-2215
Phone: 1-800-730-2214

Library of Congress Catalog Card Number: 97-46175

Printed in the United States of America

Printing Number

15 14 13 12 11 10 9 8

Library of Congress Cataloging-in-Publication Data
Walker, Darwin E., 1936–
   Teaching music : managing the successful music program / Darwin E.
Walker. — [2nd ed.]
      p.   cm.
   Includes bibliographical references and index.
   ISBN-13: 978-0-02-864596-4
   ISBN-10: 0-02-864596-0
   1. Music—Instruction and study.   I. Title.
MT1.W28 1997   97-46175
780'.7—dc21   CIP
                                                                 MN

This paper meets the minimum requirements of ANSI/NISO Z39.48–1992
(Permanence of Paper).

Contents

PART THREE

WITHIN THE SCHOOL ENVIRONMENT

Part Four

Outside the School Environment

ACKNOWLEDGMENTS

I take this opportunity to express my deepest appreciation to my teachers, students, and colleagues, who through the years have all had a profound influence on the information found here.

I owe a very special debt of gratitude to Dr. John Berggren. His faith in me as a young music educator provided me with numerous opportunities for personal growth in the profession. His musicianship, knowledge, and friendship served as an inspiration for me in my formative years as a music educator. Thanks again, Jack.

To my dear friend, Barrie Wells, for his always insightful comments and suggestions. I will be forever grateful to this music educator's "music educator" for his contributions to both editions of this text.

Any individual attempting to construct a broad and comprehensive project such as this book would be remiss if he did not acknowledge all of the scholarly work that has gone on for decades that has contributed so magnificently to the body of literature supporting our profession at all levels. The many books and articles listed in the bibliography are testimony to that significant influence.

Finally, this book is respectfully dedicated (once again) to my wife, Marlenna, for her faith in me, her brilliant work as a music educator, for her assistance and advice, her support, patience, and understanding, without which this book would not have been possible.

PREFACE TO THE SECOND EDITION

If music educators are less successful in their careers than they could or should be, they are not necessarily deficient in musical skills. That lack of success can often be traced to their inability to deal successfully with the day-to-day organizational obligations that confront all music educators. This book is offered as a means of anticipating and alleviating administrative problems in music education in as practical a manner as possible.

Prospective music educators in upper-level college music education classes, as well as practicing music educators, will find the information included in this book to be extremely helpful to their efforts in performing the numerous noninstructional functions of a successful music education program. Many of the chapters will also be beneficial to musicians not directly associated with music instruction in the public schools. Church musicians, for example, will find all of the managerial chapters helpful in their profession. The chapters on the development of a teaching philosophy, leadership, public relations, music assessment, motivation and discipline, scheduling, budgeting, fund-raising, music rooms, and equipment should all hold a degree of interest for private music teachers, as well as some professional musicians. Graduate students in music education will also find this book to be a valuable supplemental text and research source.

A sincere attempt has been made to present the material in accessible language, and practicality has determined the book's scope. Far too often, books associated with music education discuss problems without offering solutions or indicate that the reader should adopt a particular concept without offering examples of the implications of that concept. The intent of this book has been to provide numerous examples as rationale for the recommendations made. When discussing the "goal and objective" process, sample goals and objectives are offered; when discussing philosophy, a sample philosophy is provided; when discussing the importance of press releases in public relations, a detailed format for a press release is presented; when discussing the budget process, a detailed sample budget is included; when block scheduling is discussed, examples of block schedules favorable to music education are offered; when the assessment and grading of orchestras, choirs, and bands are presented, valid and educationally sound sample grading plans are included. Contest and festival formats, library filing systems, a parents' group constitution, and music room specifications are just a few of the many practical examples given throughout the book. Great emphasis has been placed on the what, how, when, and why of administering a music education program.

The overwhelming popularity of the original printing of this book is what has driven this revised second edition. Many changes have taken place in just the last decade in music education. Accountability and assessment, sparked by the need for public school students to demonstrate competency in the arts as outlined in the Goals 2000: Educate America Act, has had a tremendous impact on music program evaluation in this country. National standards for arts education and strategies for assessing progress toward those national standards have highly significant implications. Alternative assessment and the process of assigning grades to performance classes (or lack of a process) has become a hot topic in music education. Block scheduling at the secondary level has sent ripples of anticipation and apprehension throughout the music education profession. These subjects, among others, make their debut in the pages of this second edition. All chapters have been updated and revised to reflect the latest needs of music students and their teachers and the trends they face as they enter a new millennium.

To facilitate use of this book as a text by college and university professors and their students, a suggested activities section has been provided at the end of most chapters. Because it is a music education book, this work will fulfill the needs of a music education methods class that involves both choral and instrumental music students. It will also stand alone as a required text for either a choral methods or instrumental methods class.

No teaching area in all of education requires the degree of administrative skills that must be developed by a music educator. It is intended that this book go a long way toward developing the noninstructional skills of prospective and practicing music educators in this country.

D E W

THE MUSIC
EDUCATOR AS AN
ADMINISTRATOR

The Role of the Music Educator

Introduction

In music education, administrative tasks can become an almost overwhelming noninstructional responsibility for music educators. Only through the development of basic administrative skills can educators become efficient contributors to the musical growth of their students.

There are sixteen administrative functions that need to be considered by any music educator: anticipating, orienting, programming, organizing, staffing, resourcing, leading, executing, changing, diagnosing and analyzing conflict, deciding and resolving, coordinating, communicating, politicking, controlling, and appraising. These functions also apply to a total education system but are adapted specifically in this chapter to the music teacher.

It is necessary for any educator to develop both long-range goals and short-term objectives for the classroom. Strategies must be developed to implement these, and a monitoring process must be put in place that will verify the level of success in achieving them. This monitoring system is perhaps the most important ingredient in attaining any goals and objectives. It is also the most frequently overlooked aspect of that process and will be dealt with in-depth in this chapter.

Although music educators need to have the ability and fortitude to identify, analyze, and resolve existing or potential problems, few are adept at analyzing them, and fewer yet can anticipate and resolve problematic situations. This chapter, as well as the rest of the book, will consider specific problems that can arise and present possible solutions.

A well-kept secret in educational circles is the amount of organizational time it takes to operate a quality music education program. There are as many types of administrative assignments in our school systems as there are classifications of administrators. By the time music educators graduate from college, they have been exposed to a variety of styles of educational administration and leadership. From the university president or chancellor to the various vice presidents and deans, department heads, and academic advisors, music educators have had the opportunity to observe a broad spectrum of educational administration. Add to that the multifaceted administrational web to which music educators were exposed as students at the public and/or private school level, and the diversity and quality of observed administrative functions can seem immense.

Through this exposure, music educators have gained insight into how the educational administration system is structured and how it functions. What they don't understand, however, is the multitude of nonmusical functions that need to be performed on a daily basis simply to make the program work. Far too many young music teachers become completely overwhelmed by myriad adjunct activities demanding efficient organization and administration. They would much rather be teaching private lessons, conducting rehearsals, and teaching music classes than administering a program.

For many teachers, the development of organizational skills becomes on-the-job training, because not enough emphasis was placed on this aspect of teacher preparation at the college or university level. These same teachers welcome and thrive on the challenge of developing and operating a smoothly running music education program in their schools.

Others become totally engulfed in the many administrative tasks confronting them and stumble through their early years of teaching, completely unaware of how a well-organized music education program functions. The teachers who fall into this category often leave teaching after a few years, citing poor pay, unruly students, or poor working conditions as the reasons for their departure when, in fact, it was their own inability to deal effectively with the day-to-day noninstructional obligations of the profession.

A third category of music educators includes those who graduated from a school system where the teachers administered an organized, well-balanced, efficient music education program. Such a program develops quality general music skills and offers satisfying, stimulating, and exciting performance opportunities for the students. There is a saying in education, "We teach as we've been taught." This adage is never more true than when applied to music education. Students who have graduated from successful school music programs will possess a distinct advantage as music educators, having experienced the benefits of efficient administration on the part of their own music teachers.

In their teacher training programs prior to student teaching, all three types of prospective music educators can benefit from a thoughtful, and above all, practical approach to the development of basic administrative skills. As part of the preparation for this book, the author personally interviewed several hundred music educators. When asked what aspect of their actual teaching experience their undergraduate training *least* prepared them for, an overwhelming number indicated music program administration.

THE MUSIC EDUCATOR AS AN ADMINISTRATOR

John F. Kennedy, in his 1961 State of the Union message, said, "The capacity to act decisively at the exact time action is needed has been too often muffled in the morass of committees, timidities, and fictitious theories, which have created a growing gap between decision and execution." Music educators need to develop the managerial skills that will enable them to promote decisive action when it is needed and avoid the administrative pitfall of making plans and decisions, then falling short of success when converting those plans and decisions into action.

A good administrator is often thought of as a person who "can really get things done." What this translates into for the music educator is the ability to identify, maintain, and utilize resources to develop a workable system that will focus energies on music education objectives. In other words, administration is not an end in itself when measuring program success, but rather a means of achieving goals and objectives associated with a quality educational experience.

The role of the music educator as an administrator includes determining the type of program, defining the nature of experiences to strive for, developing a philosophical foundation for the program, establishing teaching patterns, and creating an educational environment. All of these responsibilities can best be accomplished through an organized and thoughtful examination of the requisite administrative skills. In reality, administration facilitates successful teaching.

It is assumed that when music educators graduate from college, they possess the necessary musical competency. Exit exams administered to college graduates prior to their commencement have become useful tools (when taken seriously by the students) to measure prospective teachers' depth of understanding of the practical and theoretical aspects of their undergraduate studies. For music majors, the senior recital also serves as an indicator of personal music performance skills. However, these same potential music educators will, at best, face several difficult years in the teaching profession, unless at the undergraduate level they are adequately prepared both mentally and academically for the administrative challenges that will confront them the very first day they walk into music classrooms and rehearsals.

The discussion of the music educator's administrative functions that follows provides further insight into the need for the development of the abilities so necessary to administering a music education program as we know it today.

THE MUSIC EDUCATOR AND ADMINISTRATIVE FUNCTIONS

In a highly respected book geared primarily toward graduate students, Stephen J. Knezevich (1975) wrote on the subject of school administration. He listed sixteen upper-level administrative functions. What follows is a statement and a brief explanation of each function, along with an application of each function to music education.

ONE: ANTICIPATING
Foreseeing the future conditions that may confront the institution.

The *music educator* must plan far in advance for anticipated enrollment in performing groups, proper instrumentation in instrumental ensembles, and overall enrollment in the music program in light of possible declining enrollment schoolwide. The *general music teacher* must anticipate what changes may affect the program and investigate the latest teaching models and techniques that may be employed in the music classroom in future years. The *instrumental music educator* must look at grade school enrollment with an eye to recruitment for the program. The *choral music educator* must focus on continuity in the total choral program, which may often be adversely affected by low male enrollment, due perhaps to the adolescent voice change and competing electives in the school curriculum. Anticipating future facility and equipment needs, along with projecting future concert wear replacement, are additional far-reaching concerns of the music educator.

Accurate record-keeping of student participation in annual school music events, cost per pupil figures, and student/teacher ratio, as well as the constituency served by the program, can be of great assistance should the school district consider making staff or program reductions. Annual records that include figures indicating program growth, strength, and expected growth patterns should be kept. Proper anticipation of future conditions facing the music education program can do much to prevent organizational problems from becoming a disproportionate preoccupation, placing a physical and mental drain on the music educator's time and energy.

TWO: ORIENTING
Ensuring that objectives are generated and then used.

Any successful program, in or out of education, must include the setting of definable and achievable goals and objectives. It has been a widely accepted policy to treat the terms *goals* and *objectives* synonymously. For the purpose of clarity in this book, an educational goal will assume a meaning that is distinct from an educational objective.

Goals in music education are long-range in scope, broad in direction, and general in nature. An educational goal is a desired outcome for a student or for a program. Examples of goals in music education could be: "All graduates should be able to read music," or "All students should have the opportunity to experience making music on instruments." Both statements demand some type of support strategies or techniques in order to be realistically achievable.

An *objective* in music education is an accomplishment that is short-term in scope, is easily verified and specific in direction, and, when properly implemented, supports progress toward achieving a goal. In other words, specific objectives support and facilitate attainment of broader, long-term goals in music education.

The establishment of goals and objectives is closely tied to a music educator's philosophy. The development of a philosophy of music education will be presented in chapter 14. At this point, the focus will be on the setting of short-term, annual objectives, which are such a vital part of administering a music education program.

The setting of realistic goals and objectives is one of the most important ingredients in any successful music education program. The key word here , of course, is *realistic*. Objective setting for general music classes, as well as all performing groups, can involve colleagues, school administrators, and the students participating in those classes and ensembles.

Of a more personal nature are the objectives that the teacher sets for pedagogical improvement. The setting of these objectives is often done in conjunction with the teacher evaluation process administered each year under the supervision of the school's principal. The music teacher is usually asked to state in writing the objectives for the current year and is then asked the following year if they were met, and if so, how. These can include far-reaching program objectives, as well as more immediate personal objectives.

Specific objectives set by an experienced teacher can be quite different from those set by a first-year music educator. Also, keep in mind that specific objectives such as "Increase concert attendance" or "Increase communication with my fellow music educators" will generally be welcomed by school administrators and will be realistically achievable. The following lists show objectives for teachers holding different positions in a school district's music program.

I. Middle school general music teacher

1. Incorporate music of other cultures into classroom activities.

2. Improve personal computer literacy and investigate the latest published software suitable for use in the general music classroom.

3. Include more singing as part of the general music class offerings.

4. Increase the number of fretted instruments available for classroom use.

5. Become more active in a leadership role in the state music education association.

II. High school choral director

1. Improve choral sight reading by spending a few minutes of each rehearsal reading new material.

2. Attempt to improve the choir's unaccompanied singing by programming at least one additional unaccompanied selection for each concert.

3. Increase solo participation at music contests by twenty percent.

4. Visit middle school choir rehearsals at least once a month for recruitment and continuity purposes.

5. Recruit more tenors and basses for the high school choir by starting an all-male ensemble and encourage the middle school music teacher to do likewise.

III. High school band director

1. Establish improved criteria for evaluation and grading purposes.

2. Organize monthly, systematic cleaning and inspection of all instruments in the high school band.

3. Increase concert publicity and promotion.

4. Increase participation of instrumental students at summer music camps by twenty percent.

5. Develop a higher level of computer literacy by attending at least one workshop dealing with the use of computers in music education and research available technology applicable to instrumental music, such as computerized solo accompaniments and music composition software programs.

Note that all of the objectives set down for the three music educators are specific, easily monitored, and reasonably easy to verify.

The dangers that music educators often encounter in setting objectives is being too general. For example, one instrumental teacher's objective might be "Make the band play more musically." This is a most noble and worthy objective; however, it lacks specificity. How will the band come to play more musically? What elements of a musical performance require the most work to achieve this objective?

An objective written by a junior high choral director might be "Improve students' attitude toward chorus." Again, such a general objective is difficult to monitor and verify. The key to writing worthwhile objectives is to be practical, direct, and specific.

Another guideline to observe when establishing goals and objectives is to keep them educationally sound. They should be *educational* objectives and goals. Beware of setting goals and objectives lacking an educational foundation, such as "Win the Tri-State Jazz Festival" or "Raise $85,000 for a trip to the Macy's Thanksgiving Parade."

Other than personal goals, those goals that deal with the music education process are most often established as part of the school curriculum through the committee work of all the music educators in the school system. Music educators are encouraged to secure a copy of any formulated educational goals and, if not in agreement with them, to work with colleagues for mutual change. Progress does not always result from change, but progress is not possible without it.

THREE: PROGRAMMING
Generating alternatives or strategies that can be used to reach an objective.

Now that specific objectives have been established, the next administrative task is to plan the means to achieve those objectives.

The general music teacher in our hypothetical middle school had as her first objective "Incorporate music of other cultures into classroom activities." After having decided upon this objective, the music educator should develop the approaches or strategies he or she feels would best achieve that objective. For example:

1. When rhythms are being studied, use Native American, Latin American, or other music of diverse cultures.
2. Study the pentatonic scale with Orff instruments using music of the Orient.
3. When studying jazz, incorporate the African call-and-response technique.
4. Invite foreign exchange or university students to visit class.
5. Plan a unit on folk songs from different countries.

The first objective listed by the high school choral director was "Improve choral sight reading by spending a few minutes of each rehearsal reading new material." Some possible strategies to reach this goal are:

1. Purchase a choral sight-reading group method book.
2. Sing with syllables during a portion of each rehearsal.
3. Count and clap rhythm patterns.
4. Devise interval and pitch matching studies.
5. Investigate available technology designed to assist music educators in pitch testing, measurement, and improvement.

The band director who was concerned about evaluation and accountability listed as the first objective of the program "Establish improved criteria for evaluation and grading purposes." Five steps designed to assist in achieving that objective are:

1. Use music achievement tests to determine musical progress.
2. Administer written tests based on music in the folders.
3. Develop a means of allowing extra credit for participation in musical activities in addition to band work.
4. Investigate available computer software that can simplify record-keeping, organization of library files, and numerous other music administration areas that make demands on valuable teaching time.
5. Develop an improved and more organized rehearsal atmosphere to allow adequate time to aid the evaluation process.

As the year progresses, each music educator will develop substeps in conjunction with the strategies supporting each objective. Through this organized approach to setting goals and objectives, a music educator creates an administrative setting that promotes success.

FOUR: ORGANIZING
Creating the structural framework required to satisfy the objectives.

The organizational framework required for music educators to properly and efficiently run their programs is vast as well as diverse. At this point, a legitimate question might be "Do our colleges and universities, as part of their music teacher training programs, accurately present to their students in a practical manner the challenges to be faced by their graduates upon entering the profession?"

Take, for example, the novice teacher who is placed in charge of a school's music program, grades five through twelve. Besides daily class and rehearsal planning, this teacher will more than likely be in charge of curriculum decisions as they affect the general music portion of the program, deciding which books or methods to use throughout the program, arranging for the procurement and spending of funds, organizing the dispersal and collection of band and choir music, and maintaining the instrument inventory. Additionally, he or she is in control of the lesson and sectional schedules and the concert scheduling of two high school choirs, one high school band, two grade school bands, and two general music programs. This particular educator may also head fund-raising projects, schedule students for the annual solo, ensemble, and large group contests, host a music festival in his or her own school, organize a music booster organization, and design a new uniform for the band. He or she will likely be involved in community activities—

such as directing a church choir, becoming involved in a local service club, and assisting with the scouting program—all the while being solely in charge of public relations for the school music program.

It should be perfectly clear at this point that this music educator must have well-defined goals and objectives and must function in a well-organized instructional atmosphere in order to achieve a high level of cohesiveness and continuity in the music education program.

FIVE: STAFFING
Assigning human resources needed to pursue an objective and fulfill program demands.

Normally, a young music educator is not in a position to delegate responsibility to other full-time music staff members for the simple reason that he or she is likely to be either part of a one- or two-person music department or an assistant in a larger school system.

A very important part of working with human resources can be the degree of involvement the music educator has with a parent support group. A properly organized, motivated, and inspired parents' group can relieve a great deal of the organizational pressure a music educator feels, from fund-raising to the assigning and cleaning of concert wear.

Student volunteer workers can be assigned many routine tasks, such as keeping records, maintaining the music library, taking roll, and ushering and dispersing programs at concerts. Qualified student assistants can contribute greatly to the positive, organized environment of the rehearsal room by helping with general housekeeping chores, maintaining bulletin boards, etc. The students can be vital cogs in the promotional machinery for the choral or band program. Almost all junior and senior high school bands and choirs have members who are on the school newspaper staff, for example. They can become liaisons between the performing group and the school and local newspapers.

At least one student in every musical group has a parent who is an avid amateur photographer. Enlist his or her help in taking photos of the group, both posed and candid, in rehearsal and in concert settings. (Note: not *during* a concert.) Young people love to see pictures of themselves, and a rotating photo display is a motivational factor, as well as a public relations vehicle.

Most schools now have reasonably sophisticated video equipment and a staff member trained to use it. Take advantage of this means of capturing your concerts on video for student enjoyment and evaluation. There are also numerous companies that now provide two- and three-camera, professionally edited video productions of school concerts. They generally do this at no charge to the school, with the understanding that they be allowed to sell videotapes of the performance to students and their parents. Before contracting with one of these companies, though, be sure that the price of the concert videos is not excessive—an acceptable price is in the range of $10 to $15 per tape.

The inclusion of parents at after-concert receptions and as chaperones on trips is a common example of making use of available human resources. The bright, enthusiastic, and resourceful music educator will find many more ways to involve others in the school music program.

The community at large is another source for human resources in support of the music program. Community members who play piano are often willing, even eager, to accompany solos and ensembles at contests and recitals. Other individuals in the community may be able to help locate specialists in a certain style of music, or they may wish to assist in a general music class project. Even the smallest community can provide a wealth of human resources. If the objective, for example, is to increase attendance at summer music camps, local service organizations and music clubs can be sources of scholarship funding.

Nonmusician colleagues can be of great assistance to the music educator. For example, the foreign language department can provide expertise in pronouncing the words to choral music, the art department can help with posters, and the drama department can assist in staging a concert or general music class performance.

These are only a few of the many examples of human resources available in the school and community to music educators. The imaginative and secure educator will use many of them and seek out additional ones to assist in the day-to-day organizational functions of the music program.

SIX: RESOURCING
Acquiring and allocating funds.

This function is so important that chapter 5 of this book is devoted entirely to the topic. In fact, the securing of adequate funding for the program is undoubtedly the most important and challenging noninstructional function of any music educator. A teacher who is well organized, provides the taxpayers with a quality product, and develops a thought-provoking and well-researched budget document will often be rewarded with sufficient fiscal support for the program.

In order to write a quality budget document, music educators need to develop an understanding of the total school budget procedure. They should be familiar with potential funding sources, possess the necessary business skills and vocabulary necessary to be successful in securing adequate funding, and demonstrate strong philosophical bases for any requests. They must be able to predict future needs, determine revenue potentials, and stand behind their requests with ample support material.

Music educators can also seek funding for their programs outside the school district. The most common such source is the parent support group, as presented in chapter 12. Other outside sources that can be explored are donations from service and music clubs and rental fees from school-owned instruments and concert wear. Many schools across the country are considering charging a flat fee for participation in music and athletic programs. While this concept is being met with substantial parental resistance, it is not likely to disappear in the foreseeable future.

The final and least desirable option for funding is the music students themselves, through their own fund-raising efforts. Some would argue that students should not be involved in raising money for their own programs. The consensus of music educators on this topic is that if the program is worthwhile and is part of the school curriculum, the school district should support it. This subject will be pursued in chapter 12.

SEVEN: LEADING
Stimulating or motivating personnel to action and toward objectives.

This is one of the most important of the sixteen functions outlined here. Anyone who is in charge of a program, from a 200-teacher school system to a school music class, must develop basic motivational skills in order to be successful. In your own years in school, you can probably recall several teachers and administrators whom you admired and respected and, more than likely, for whom you did your best work. Those teachers and administrators were individuals who possessed a high level of natural or learned motivational skills.

The reason this function is so important to the music educator is that a music education program inextricably involves performance. When individual or collective performance is an integral part of any academic program, the ability of the leader to motivate the individuals involved in the program toward their highest performance level is of the utmost importance.

Personality plays an integral role in motivation. Some of the greatest political and military leaders have possessed strong and charismatic personalities. A shy person will generally find it very difficult to lead and motivate individuals toward goals and objectives.

A discussion of this topic appears in chapter 3; however, it is appropriate at this point to briefly present several techniques that can be used in administering music education programs.

First, motivation of individuals involved in a music program is not possible without a positive approach to discipline. This does not mean you should become overly strict; it means that an environment must be created in which motivational techniques can succeed. The ability to deal in positive rather than negative terms can be the key ingredient to success in motivating students.

In a music education program, there are a number of built-in motivational opportunities available to the instructor. Music contests can motivate students and teachers alike, but they can also be an avenue for abuse. For example, some music teachers use fear of failure rather than musical achievement as the major motivational element when preparing their students for music contests. While this approach can be effective, it is educationally unsound. The level of program motivation that is derived from contest participation must be carefully measured and monitored to maintain its compatibility with the overall objectives of the program.

In addition to concert performances, awards, point systems for those awards or for grading purposes, and wall charts denoting progress toward achieving a particular goal can be used to motivate students. The process of evaluation and grading, while primarily intended to measure student progress and achievement, is often an important motivational tool. Presently a national concern, the evaluation of music students is covered in a thoughtful and organized approach in chapter 9.

The most abstract forms of motivation involve the creation of personal pride within the class or group. The ability of the teacher to take interest in the outside activities of the students, to help the students understand their uniqueness, to appeal to their sense of adventure, to promote group identity, and to create and sustain a positive environment for success are all important functions of the music educator as motivator.

EIGHT: EXECUTING
Monitoring day-to-day operating functions.

The manner in which an administrator handles the daily operations of a program can serve as a predictor of that program's success. Everyone, especially a student, needs some predictability in his of her life. Music educators who cannot settle into some type of daily routine in classroom work will find themselves leading a group of confused and potentially unmanageable students.

In addition to the daily academic preparation for class and rehearsal, the music educator is involved in communication and public relations with peers, parents, administrators, and the community, as well as performing other routine tasks such as hall duty, attendance, progress reports, and meetings. In recent years it has become more common to find music teachers assigned to study hall duty, too. How sad it is to see a bright, energetic, and eager music educator confined to a room, maintaining some semblance of order while students are encouraged to work on assignments for other academic classes. What a waste of pedagogical talent!

Despite the hectic atmosphere of most schools and the myriad activities for which the music educator is responsible, a major key to success lies in the ability to create a functional, routine atmosphere that students can come to rely on and which, in turn, becomes a part of their daily lives. The music educator who is poorly prepared and unpredictable has failed at an important administrative procedure.

NINE: CHANGING

Identifying a change; introducing innovation; managing the change to produce maximum benefits.

The management of change is certainly not a daily and perhaps not even a weekly or monthly function. However, the ability, upon demand, to manage and administer change in a logical and positive manner can serve as a principal indicator of the success or failure of a particular program.

Change for change's sake in a music program is a tremendous waste of energy for students and teachers alike. This type of change usually occurs when there has been a turnover of teaching staff in the program. Often newcomers initiate change to make their own mark on the program. Alterations are often made without any profound thought about their positive or negative implications, the degree of previous success of the program, or what portion of the program is being changed. In fact, this approach often results in confusion and eventual failure.

To be successful, change must follow a patient and thoughtful procedure. It must be introduced carefully, not haphazardly, to prepare the individuals involved. To merit consideration, a proposed change must be articulated in writing. In music education, this means disseminating information regarding the change to school administrators, students, parents, and other individuals potentially affected by it.

During the early stages of change, close monitoring should take place and the results should be communicated to all involved. Constant evaluation of new innovations by the participants is desirable, including other teachers as well as the students directly associated with the process.

In music education, programs often change because of a failure in the management process. When the levels of success are not monitored, recorded, and managed, failure often follows the introduction of new procedures. Far too often innovation is blamed for the failure when, in fact, the mismanagement of that innovation is responsible for the lack of success.

As an example, let's follow a hypothetical program innovation through the three steps presented as part of this function. A middle school instrumental music educator would like to structure a lesson schedule for all two hundred students involved in the program. School administrative policy prohibits students from missing other academic classes on a regular basis for that type of activity.

After a great deal of investigation and research, the teacher decides that a rotating, semiprivate lesson schedule could be the solution. The first step has been accomplished: the teacher has identified a change, a new way to do things. The plan, along with written support materials based on research, is then presented to the building principal. Being a progressive administrator, the principal informs the music educator that if the classroom teachers support the plan, it will have the support of the principal's office as well.

A meeting is scheduled with the classroom teachers affected by the proposed change. The rotating schedule plan is carefully explained and questions are answered. The teachers give their reluctant approval on a nine-week experimental basis.

A letter is then mailed to the parents of students involved in the instrumental music program outlining student participation in the project and asking for parents' support and assistance in reminding their children about the correct day and time of the lessons as they rotate through the schedule.

Finally, a meeting is held with the students involved in the program. Student responsibility for the success of the innovation is carefully and thoroughly discussed. The students are excited about accepting the challenge of their role in the new project.

With the rotating lessons schedule in place and functioning, the music teacher monitors the sentiments of the classroom teachers toward the project, seeking advice on what, if anything, could be done to improve the process. The success and ultimate acceptance of the project depends greatly on the cooperation of the classroom teachers.

Communication with the students and their parents continues at regular intervals during the trial period. Flaws are determined and adjustments made. The principal is kept informed of the project's progress. At the end of the nine-week experimental period, a follow-up meeting with the music educator, affected classroom teachers, and principal results in a positive vote to retain the rotating lesson schedule on a permanent basis. The change was identified, introduced, and managed, resulting in the project's success. (A detailed explanation of the use of a rotating schedule in music education is presented in chapter 7.) This scenario perhaps oversimplifies a difficult procedure, but it should be remembered that it is only an example of how the system works.

When initiating change or innovative procedures, the degree of communication, patience, research, and organization surrounding the project can ensure its success or failure.

TEN: DIAGNOSING AND ANALYZING CONFLICT
Diagnosing conflicts or problems and analyzing possible solutions.

This function is relatively new to the educational administration field, but it can certainly be considered old hat to the music education profession.

Perhaps the best way to begin this discussion is through the examination of a possible problem, one that is startlingly real in music education today: the decrease in participation in the band program between elementary, middle, and high school levels.

Let's say that a band director has diagnosed that there is a dropout rate of forty percent between the students involved with the beginning band program and those entering the high school band in the ninth grade. The diagnosis has been made as to the problem; now analysis of the potential causes must be undertaken.

A variety of causes is uncovered, some of which lead to other conflicts or problems. This band director's list includes several of the causes that he or she determines could be contributing to the unusually high dropout rate:

1. Lack of rehearsal time for the bands in grades five through eight.
2. No private or semiprivate lesson time in the elementary/middle school program.
3. Increased pressure on students to make an early choice on whether or not they plan to attend college. Increased requirements for college entrance pressures students to include more math, science, and foreign language courses in their ninth-grade schedules.
4. High school band meets before the school day begins.
5. High school band participation requirements, particularly marching band.

There could be several other factors involved, but for the purpose of discussion these five causes will suffice.

There are other situations that occur in music education that can require examination and resolution. Poor attitude among those students involved in the high school choir or pep band, for instance, could prompt the music director to formulate a list of potential causes. An elementary school teacher could be facing parental questioning of an evaluation and grading system, demanding further analysis of how grading is taking place. A middle school instructor could face inquiries from parents and school officials over the attempt to create a by-audition-only choir at the sixth-grade level. These are just some examples of situations in music education that require the careful diagnosis and analysis of a problem by the music instructor to determine choices that will eventually lead to the problem's resolution. When one person administers a program, sets much of the curriculum and many of the schedules, secures and allocates funds, and performs other difficult tasks, it is to be expected that the level of conflicts and problems surrounding the program will increase directly in proportion to the amount of responsibility required.

ELEVEN: DECIDING AND RESOLVING
Resolving conflicts through decisive action.

Let's continue with our example of the band director with the dropout problem, which was mentioned in the last section. Preliminary examination of the five diagnoses indicates that lack of rehearsal time and no private or semiprivate lesson time in the elementary/middle school program can be addressed without causing havoc within the system. Increased pressure on students regarding college entrance is part of educational life and must be accepted and dealt with as professionally as possible. The problem caused by band rehearsals held before the school day begins has a solution, but it will take time to implement. The problem of middle school students' lack of interest in enrolling in high school band because of the marching band requirement potentially could be resolved through communication and expanded public relations between the high school director and middle school students.

The wise music educator would do well to concentrate on those problems that are easiest to solve and see what, if anything, results from that effort. For example, the teacher could request from the building principal an extra thirty or forty minutes of rehearsal time during the day, citing dropout statistics. Part of the time could come out of the students' lunch period, the rehearsal could start a few minutes before the regular school day, or the band time could be treated as homeroom. The lack of lesson time could be solved by a rotating lesson schedule, a plan carefully worked out with the classroom teachers for class release time, or some other innovative technique designed to the satisfaction of all parties. In order to introduce middle school students to the concept of performing in a marching band, the high school band director could spend the last two weeks or so of the school year at the middle school during band time leading fun, low-pressure marching activities. Time spent in this manner could pay longterm dividends at the high school level. Again, it should be understood that the choices determined and the solutions recommended are simply examples of what could transpire in a given situation, not necessarily what approach should be followed.

Too many music educators spend time complaining about problems beyond their control instead of recommending solutions. When going to a principal or any other administrator with a problem, always be prepared to offer solutions. If solutions cannot be offered, then perhaps the problem doesn't actually exist. Administrators tend to see teachers who bring up problems without solutions as complainers.

There are many other administrative choices that confront a music educator that, while they don't necessarily result because of a conflict, greatly influence the direction of a particular program. For example, much curriculum decision-making is the responsibility of the music educator, as is a certain degree of the scheduling process. Which athletic events to perform for and whether to participate in music contests, as well the type of evaluative system to use, the number of annual performances, and the style of classroom control, are all decisions that need to be made.

As the reader progresses through this book, the choices should become clearer and the decisions easier to make. Successful music educators learn to accept decisions that are not within their control. This acceptance can be difficult, indeed. If individuals cannot accept that premise, they should be prepared to accept the likelihood that impossible situations will severely inhibit the entire educational process under their supervision.

TWELVE: COORDINATING
Unifying the activities of various components by focusing the function of discrete units onto the objectives.

The music educator is usually responsible for more than one unit. In many small communities, one person is in charge of the entire music program. Even in larger school systems, where the responsibility is divided among several music instructors, each person works with more than one group. The band director may oversee a concert band, a jazz band, and a marching band. The choral director will probably lead two choirs, a swing choir, perhaps a madrigal group, and a music appreciation class. The individual in a one-person music program could be responsible for all of these groups, plus some type of program for the elementary grades. The total responsibility for the successful focusing of the components toward achieving objectives is an overwhelmingly difficult administrative task.

The music educator must coordinate a variety of objectives. There are different objectives for the band and for the choir. The upper-level general music program's objectives need to coincide with those established for the lower elementary grades. The total music program must be focused toward meeting the goals and objectives set down by the school district. Parents' organizations have their own requirements, and there are other objectives established by the Music Educators National Conference and other state and national associations. The most recent national effort to ensure quality and accountability in the arts appeared in 1994 in the form of the National Standards for Arts Education. An in-depth discussion of these important criteria will be offered in chapter 14.

The music educator must provide leadership in coordinating all of the components of the program that fall under his or her supervision. Continuity of objectives throughout the program is the ultimate goal. While the responsibility for this leadership may seem overwhelming, a music educator who accepts the role of an administrator will handle it using common sense and patience. It is difficult to offer one pedagogical approach toward handling this function. Coordination simply *occurs* under the direction of a dedicated and well-organized teacher.

THIRTEEN: COMMUNICATING
Designing information channels to supply relevant information to various points in the system; providing for the information flow (up or down, in or out of the system) essential to the other functions such as unification, motivation, and decision-making.

Corporations realize the value of communication as a basis for building a constituency for their products or services. They call it public relations, and almost every company, large or small, has a specialist or a staff of specialists charged with communicating to the general public a particular image or philosophy.

Figure 1.1. Information flow.

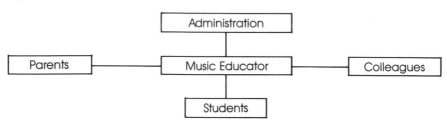

Successful school administrators have also recognized the necessity of open communication channels to their constituencies. A chief administrator in a large urban school district required that his principals systemwide work only four-day weeks. He followed that statement with, "You will spend every Friday in the classrooms of your teachers." That is visionary administration, which leads to a heightened awareness of what is taking place in the classrooms and provides the opportunity for increased communication, top to bottom, throughout the district.

School boards rely heavily on the information provided by school administrators to aid them in the planning and decision-making process. Taxpayers, parents, staff, and students are all interested in and affected by the information provided by administrative communication channels. With this thought in mind, music educators are encouraged to invite administrators to their rehearsals and classes on a regular basis. Music educators must develop the information channels that will allow the broadest possible dissemination of information in the most effective manner. A typical information flow is shown in Figure 1.1. (This integral part of administering a music education program will be developed in detail in chapter 11.)

Anyone who has been involved in music education for any length of time has encountered a person who does a superior job of communicating, of selling the program, even if the program itself is substandard. On the other end of the spectrum is the individual who either lacks the basic communication skills necessary to promote the program or has no interest in "selling" music education. Neither is acceptable as a model for the music education administrator.

Communication with administrators regarding upcoming events, schedule concerns, and funding takes place on an almost daily basis. Parents can best be informed about the program's activities through a parents' organization, as well as monthly newsletters, parent-teacher conferences, and personal contact on the telephone. Colleagues can be kept abreast of necessary information on a day-to-day basis through regularly scheduled teachers' meetings, as well as the daily announcement bulletin. Students should receive their noninstructional information on policy and the music calendar both verbally and in writing. It is also good administrative practice to mail parents a copy of this information.

The music educator can communicate with students, colleagues, parents, and the public through both the school and community news media. The instructor who says "I can't get any publicity" or "I can't get anything in the paper" is failing to implement the most basic communication and public relations skills. Communication in the administration of a music education program assumes incredible significance when it is realized how strongly it influences all the other functions in music education administration.

FOURTEEN: POLITICKING
*Interacting with various internal and external power centers related to
the institution.*

The politics related to the administering of any successful program can run the gamut from insignificant to overwhelmingly important. In music education, its importance largely depends upon the size and scope of the program and the number of teachers involved in the instructional process.

For many music educators, politicking is their least pleasant administrative function. The individual who considers the politics involved in music education administration unpleasant to the point of distraction will find it difficult to adjust to any situation involving compromise.

Politicking for the music educator involves two well-defined levels. The internal level involves the school administration, including the school board, the superintendent, and all princpals. It also includes other instructional staff in the school system, the students, and even secretaries, custodians, and lunchroom or cafeteria staff. The external level includes parents and the general public, as well as other school music programs and state and national associations.

Experienced and successful music educators will tell you that they have used their performing groups to do a little politicking in support of their music programs. Examples include sending an ensemble to an event sponsored by a local service group for soliciting funds for music camp scholarships, meeting the plane of a visiting dignitary, and caroling at the homes of the superintendent and building principal during Christmas break. Many bands, choirs, and orchestras across the country have had a school official, the mayor, or some other influential resident serve as guest conductor or narrator for a concert program. These examples of politicking differ from public relations in the sense that they are occasional incidents as opposed to an in-depth, long-range, and broader communications effort.

This type of activity is certainly permissible and is an acceptable means of gaining support for the entire music program. Several key points, though, need to be made:

1. Music educators must work comfortably with the internal and external influences on the program. They may not always be in agreement but must be able to function with those various influences.

2. The ability to get along with people is an all-important ingredient of this function.

3. Politicking is not necessarily public relations.

4. The ability to see the other side of an issue, as well as the flexibility in dealing with others, can have a positive administrative impact on the program.

5. Compromise is not a sign of weakness; it is often the exact opposite. Music educators must be open to compromise because they share the students involved in their program with several of their colleagues who lead other academic and activity programs.

If a music educator can accept these five premises, the politicking function of administering a quality music education program will be a positive influence on that administrative process.

FIFTEEN: CONTROLLING
Monitoring progress toward objectives; keeping organizational activities locked onto objectives.

Earlier administrative functions dealt with establishing objectives and the means and methods involved in implementing them. However, without subsequent progress monitoring, goals will be difficult to achieve. Far too often, worthwhile and well thought out objectives fail because no monitoring process was used. A means of measuring progress needs to be established.

For the general music classroom teacher, written tests, achievement tests, and close observation are useful tools in monitoring progress. At the high school level, written tests, music achievement tests, and music contests and festival participation may be used to measure specific progress.

Personal teacher "How am I doing?" interviews with administrators and colleagues can be helpful. Often student input can also be of great value. Music educators should consider developing a student evaluation form specific to their own teaching situations. Student opinion need not be the end-all as it pertains to monitoring teacher effectiveness; however, student evaluations can certainly play a major role in this important process.

The monitoring process is not a daily, weekly, or even monthly function of an administrator. It should be used occasionally, even casually, but nevertheless should always be in place.

A word of caution: Do not let performance pressures override the monitoring and achievement of educationally sound goals and objectives. In the music education profession, there is ample opportunity to lose sight of established goals and objectives. The conscientious music educator/administrator is alert to this danger and makes a determined effort to see that it does not happen.

SIXTEEN: APPRAISING
Evaluating final results and reporting them to your constituency.

In music education, appraisal is accomplished in a variety of ways. There is self-examination through a variety of audiovisual equipment. Perhaps because it takes courage to look closely at yourself to determine if objectives are being met, critical self-evaluation is one of the least used means of appraising the final results of objectives.

The appraisal and reporting process can be accomplished through contest or festival participation. It takes a certain amount of fortitude to place performance groups in a contest setting for subjective evaluation. If a music educator chooses this method of appraisal, he or she must also be prepared to share the results of the appraisal with a wide constituency: parents as well as the general public.

Music educators should bring in outside consultants to assist in the appraisal process. For instance, an educator from a nearby college or university could spend a day working with music students at all levels and will then be in a position to report what has already been done and what yet needs to be accomplished. This list can serve as the basis for the next set of objectives.

No one meets all of his or her objectives all of the time. Failure to completely achieve objectives is not in itself a bad thing. Of greater significance is that the attempt was made, the means to meet the objectives were determined, and progress toward achieving the objectives was monitored in some manner. Positive growth for students, the music educator, and the entire music program results from this effort.

Finally, although it does not take courage to appraise success, this part of the process cannot be overlooked. A music educator in an administrative role should be aware of all facets of the complete program and should consistently build on success.

SUGGESTED ACTIVITIES

1. Develop a set of short-term objectives for a situation in your present educational setting, and list the strategies necessary to implement those objectives.

2. Identify something to change in your present educational setting and follow the procedures presented in this chapter to initiate and complete that change.
3. Prepare questions and interview three music educators regarding their approaches to any two administrative functions. Each music educator interviewed should respond to different functions.
4. Identify a problem that you feel exists in the music education profession today and list probable causes and potential solutions.
5. Summarize three articles in periodical literature relating to any administrative function and discuss in class.
6. Secure a copy of the music curriculum from one of your local schools. (a) How current is it? (b) How are program goals and objectives presented? (c) Does the curriculum tend to reflect actual practices existing in the program? Discuss your findings in class.

CHAPTER TWO

THE MUSIC
EDUCATOR AS
A LEADER

INTRODUCTION

The music educator must provide leadership in both the school and the community. Students and the public alike respect and appreciate an educator who is active in community affairs and who can provide leadership outside an academic setting. The five personal qualities of such a leader are enthusiasm, a high energy level, trustworthiness, friendliness, and a confident and able teaching style. There are four different styles of leadership: anarchic, democratic, autocratic, and manipulative. Although each has its proponents, this chapter will show that the democratic leader who involves students in the decision-making process will probably be the most successful. Finally, no matter what the leadership style, all leaders must be proactive, taking the initiative to lead rather than waiting for events to dictate actions.

LEADERSHIP IN THE SCHOOL AND COMMUNITY

Because of the nature of working with performance groups, the music educator often finds himself or herself cast in the role of a leader in school-associated activities. This role should be readily accepted if not actually sought because many of the administrative functions discussed in chapter 1 rely on the acceptance of the music educator as a leader.

A successful music educator possesses a certain sense of vision and can comfortably set and complete objectives. He or she also serves, by example and through practice, as a model of someone who not only can articulate clear and concise goals and objectives, but aid those under his or her direction in doing the same. Being a creative thinker and an initiator of action also helps the music educator in being accepted as a leader by peers.

Community leadership involves participation. To increase visibility, a music educator might become involved in a variety of nonteaching organizations such as service clubs, fraternal organizations, social groups, bowling or golf leagues, or church choirs and related activities. By serving as an officer or board member of at least one organization, the music educator can assume a leadership role. A teacher who associates only with other teachers is in danger of leading a very dull and unenlightened existence. This is not to say that a music educator's colleagues are not interesting, vital, and vibrant individuals, but to really feel the pulse of a community, a teacher needs to make every attempt to broaden his or her spectrum of personal relationships outside the school environment.

Through these community leadership activities, the music educator can generate enthusiasm for music, not only on the part of students but also on the part of adults. If people know the teacher as an individual, they are more likely to support him or her in any future program needs.

PERSONAL QUALITIES OF A LEADER

As music educators, we often fail to realize how many people we have to work with in our daily lives. That realization can be the first step toward becoming a recognized leader. There are strengths and weaknesses to be found in any leader. Although individual music educators may differ in their approach to leadership, several qualities serve as a common thread among those who are successful.

Enthusiasm. The most easily identifiable attribute contributing to the success of a music educator as a leader is the level of enthusiasm brought to the position. The enthusiasm generated must be genuine and have as its foundation educational objectives and sound philosophical judgment, as well as confidence based on educational training. Enthusiasm is the result of an energetic person working on something he or she finds keenly interesting.

Energy. It takes a tremendous amount of energy to lead and administer a music education program. The individual with an energy level sufficient enough to allow him or her to initiate and meet objectives will be accepted as a leader. As with enthusiasm and other personal qualities, the energy level must be contagious; it must rub off on those students and others who work with the music educator.

Integrity and trust. Students and colleagues alike must be able to trust the music educator, knowing that decisions made and policies established will be fairly and consistently administered. They must have confidence in the fact that promises made will be kept. The best reputation a leader in music education can possess relates to displaying ethical conduct. Students in particular have a low tolerance level for broken promises. Music students have to see their teacher as a caring individual, one who consistently follows through on promises and commitments made.

Friendliness. While not necessarily becoming a close friend of the students, a music educator who leads well will develop a friendly approach toward students. This friendliness must be genuine. Again, students are quick to discern any degree of friendliness that is not authentic and sincere.

Teaching ability. All other personal qualities of a leader are worthless unless accompanied by high-level teaching skills. The music educator who is a successful leader is also an outstanding teacher.

You can be a good teacher and lack leadership qualities, but it is impossible to be accepted as a leader without also being a good teacher. If you can develop the level of teaching ability to the point where successful instruction results in fewer orders being issued and greater cooperation taking place, the ultimate balance between leadership and teaching has been achieved.

The five personal leadership qualities presented above usually exist in every individual administering a successful and respected music education program. These administrators may possess other qualities as well, to a varying degree, but enthusiasm for their work, a high energy level, an uncompromising feeling of trust, a professional level of friendliness, and superb teaching skills are the common denominators that create and maintain program excellence.

STYLES OF LEADERSHIP

Four types of leadership styles will be discussed. It is possible that a larger, more detailed list could be presented, but these four types are widely accepted as the styles most common to education. Readers should not be misled into thinking that they can memorize the traits associated with a particular leadership style and simply go out and be that type of leader. It is the intent of this book to guide readers toward understanding their leadership roles and to provide them with sufficient administrative concepts to support the development of their own eclectic leadership styles.

Undoubtedly, as each of the four leadership styles is presented, examples based on past experiences will readily come to mind. Definitions of the four styles of leadership are freely paraphrased from Knezevich (1975).

Anarchic. The anarchic style of leadership grants total freedom to an individual or group of individuals to make decisions without the leader. The leader does not offer direction or participate in the process in any manner. In this type of leadership, the principal role of the leader is to provide pertinent materials, remaining apart from the process and participating only when called on. The leader lacks interest in the decision-making process and rarely offers comments on activities of the members. After a decision has been made and a course of events begins to unfold, the leader makes no attempt to interfere or become involved in any way. In actuality, anarchy is a "leaderless" social situation.

The anarchic style of leadership has no place in education administration, let alone in music education. In a situation of anarchy, the power belongs to the people, and the struggle to bring structure or order to a probable chaotic situation is all but impossible. Education without order is not acceptable in a democratic society.

Democratic. Although the leader participates in the formulation of policies in the democratic style of leadership, group action or decision-making is also involved. In this style, the group, along with the leader, determines what the tasks are and how to organize and accomplish them. Objective in praising or criticizing, the leader does not allow personal feelings to impede the group's process. Allowing those who will eventually be affected by the decision to be involved in making it is called *participatory administration.* This leadership style promotes excellent group productivity. Personalities shaped by democratic participation are more mature, more capable of objectivity, and less aggressive than those products of other leadership styles.

Music performing groups generally have a panel of elected officers as well as several board members who serve the director in a variety of ways. What they do varies, from assuming complete involvement in the decision-making process as it affects the total performing group to acting as a communication link between the director and the group. They may serve as an advisory board to the director or they may just be a token panel with few or no actual responsibilities.

The democratic style of leadership in music education certainly assists students in learning to make decisions. However, many music educators think they use the democratic style of leadership when they don't in fact surrender that amount of control.

Autocratic. The autocratic leader determines policy, makes all decisions, and assigns tasks to members without direction from or consultation with the group. This leader is personal in his or her praise or criticism of members of the group but remains aloof from the group. There are no group-inspired decisions. The leader declares what shall be done and when it shall be done, with no reason offered as to why it should be done. Group members have no choice but to accept these decisions.

Far too often this type of leadership is followed to the letter in school administration. It also has its proponents and followers in music education, particularly for performing groups that have a rigorous competitive schedule. The autocratic style of leadership in music education is not as prevalent today as it was when individuals in charge of music ensembles came from a military background. This style was further perpetuated when educators were trained at the college level by third, fourth, and fifth generations of teachers immersed in the military tradition.

Manipulative. In the manipulative style of leadership, the leader makes his or her desires known, then appoints a committee to consider those desires. In reality, the committee is appointed only to approve the proposal, not to deliberate over it. The committee, without much thought or discussion, automatically endorses the proposal. This system works best when leaders reward those who support them and refrain from rewarding, or actually punish, those who do not support them.

This is one of the dominant styles of governing in a nondemocratic society. The manipulative style of leadership still thrives in some school systems. In music education, this style is infrequently found intact. Music educators sometimes appoint a committee to make a decision, knowing full well what the decision will be, but also knowing that group support for the decision will be stronger if the decision comes from a committee of group members. This practice cannot be considered a negative aspect of leadership, unless carried to excess. A good leader knows when to apply this form of manipulative leadership.

A variation of manipulative leadership occurs when the leaders appoints a committee and lists several options. The committee is restricted to those suggested options and is asked to debate the advantages and disadvantages of each, to select an option, and to report the results to the leaders. This semi-manipulative technique is frequently used by those who picture their leadership style as democratic.

Many teachers, music educators included, use the manipulative style of leadership more than they care to admit. Because students frequently make decisions they feel will please the teachers, teachers must be careful not to abuse this administrative privilege.

Music educators must understand that the development of a leadership style comes with teaching experience. In an actual teaching situation, mistakes—with resulting adjustments—can guide the music educator toward a personal style. The educator will gradually learn to be effective and produce educationally sound results. During this difficult yet extremely important developmental period in a teacher's life, there is little recourse but to model personal leadership style after an admired college or university director or instructor for organizational abilities, vision, and people skills, as well as musical expertise.

PROACTIVITY AND THE MUSIC EDUCATOR

All successful music educators have learned that they must become proactive in their approach to administering (leading) the music education program under their direction. They realize, however subtly, that they must become responsible for their own professional lives as well as the musical lives of their students. Highly proactive teachers recognize that responsibility, and they do not blame circumstances, conditions, or anything else for their behavior. Their behavior is a result of a conscious choice, rather than a product of conditions, such as outside influences that positively or negatively affect the quality of the program under their supervision.

Proactivity involves anticipating, advance planning, and the realistic setting of goals and objectives as discussed in chapter 1. Who among us cannot recall finding ourselves in unfortunate situations in which we have to react to outside stimuli, rather than controlling events—a very uncomfortable, stressful, and exhausting experience. Such things as always trying to catch up, always being behind on meeting advertising and program copy deadlines, and so on are perhaps the most obvious indicators of a reactive "leader."

Music educators need to act rather than be acted upon. Reactive leaders are made, not born, because it is generally felt that humans are, by nature, proactive beings. For that reason, among others, music educators simply cannot realistically blame outside forces such as scheduling problems, budget restrictions, lack of interest in the music program on the part of students, or anything else—except their own reactive approach to leadership—for a programming failure. There are many things in our professional lives that we cannot change, but with understanding of proactivity and dedicated effort, a reactive approach to teaching can be replaced by a proactive one.

LEADERSHIP AND VISION

Music educators who can see the big picture, who can envision long-term responsibilities with their classes or performing groups, and who understand how they personally fit into that picture are the true leaders in our profession. Music educators without a vision for the future and breadth of the music program in their school and their own individual role in that future sadly become managers. They struggle to maintain some type of order in their personal lives and settle for the status quo in their professional lives.

Leaders, in turn, are more interested in instituting change. They do this by challenging the process to some extent, taking some risks, and aiding their student musicians in understanding and sharing the leaders' long-range organizational vision for the music program, or the portion of that program under their direction.

Concepts created by visionary music educators strengthen and support all of the organizational and administrative functions found in chapter 1. This type of leader generally responds more quickly and more effectively in moments of crisis, and as any in-service music educator can relate, there are many, many moments of crisis in all aspects of the music education profession. Finally, visionaries are not necessarily leaders. Anyone, however, who is placed in a leadership position in music education and does not possess vision will necessarily be an ineffective leader.

The chapters that follow will provide a foundation for individual styles; however, the key to success is flexibility. A leader can be likened to a catalytic agent, a unique ingredient that stimulates a desirable interaction between two or more factors. In music education a catalyst translates potential into reality. Set the example. Do what you say you will do. Disagreements very rarely occur among people who possess a common understanding of goals, objectives, and, perhaps more important, purposes.

Suggested Activities

1. Reflect on any teacher you may have encountered during your secondary school education. (a) List five qualities about that teacher you most admired. (b) Relate those qualities to one or more of the four leadership styles presented in this chapter.

2. Make a list of five ways you tend to be proactive and five ways you tend to be reactive. Can an individual be both proactive and reactive in nature? Why or why not? Provide examples.

3. Make a list of five people you deem to be visionaries. Describe why you feel they are people of vision. You do not necessarily need to know all of the individuals personally, but perhaps you know them by reputation or through your own study and research.

THE TEACHER

AND THE STUDENT

CHAPTER THREE

MOTIVATION AND DISCIPLINE

INTRODUCTION

This chapter introduces theories associated with motivation and discipline as they affect music education programs in today's schools. These suggestions should not be considered ultimate answers to any motivational problem or discipline situation. However, when applied under actual teaching conditions, they can greatly assist both experienced and inexperienced music educators in developing the basic expertise that can enable them to be effective forces in the musical lives of young people.

The chapter begins by defining the terms *motivation* and *discipline*. Motivational factors—such as fear and desire, music contests, awards, testing and grading, performance, recordings, group spirit, and compliments—are described as they apply to music education. A brief review is given of B. F. Skinner's behavior modification theories and how they apply to discipline. Three types of disciplinary approaches—authoritarian, permissive, and democratic—are discussed, with the pros and cons outlined for each. Discipline problems common in music education, from gum chewing to poor posture, are the next focus area. Practical suggestions are offered for the classroom and rehearsal instructor on improving student performance. The concept of conflict resolution is introduced as a recent innovation in settling teacher-student problems. The chapter concludes with a primer on how to handle serious discipline problems, along with a brief discussion of the "dressing to learn" movement that has become a hot topic in the '90s.

No attempt will be made to dictate to readers *the* discipline approach to use in specific situations involving misconduct on the part of students. Too many variables are involved in all cases of misbehavior to enable a single mandate to be offered as the best solution. Readers are encouraged, however, to make use of the hypothetical discipline problems listed in the Suggested Activities section at the end of this (and every) chapter and to discuss the best solution to a particular problem as they perceive it.

Perhaps no other element of teaching is of greater concern to future music educators than their ability to control classroom situations. Will their students respond in a positive manner under their leadership? Will those students perform as desired, when desired? Charles R. Hoffer (1983, p. 177) cited a study that asked this question of prospective teachers, "What gives you greatest concern or worry as you plan for your first teaching position?" Nearly 2,500 out of 3,000 students responded, "Discipline."

There are more words in print on the subject of discipline than on any other topic in education. Whether it is called *classroom management, classroom control,* or *behavior management,* the subject remains the same. *Classroom discipline,* an old-fashioned term not often mentioned in certain educational circles, is a key ingredient in the effective organization and administration of any school music program.

Maintaining good classroom discipline is a critical element affecting a music educator's success or failure. Frederick J. Swanson (1973, p. 267) pointed out that of all the college graduates entering the music education profession each year, some will do a superb job, some will *think* they're doing a superb job, and others will, unfortunately, be sad failures. Those in the last category often leave the profession after only a year because their students are "unruly," "discourteous," "uninterested," and "unteachable." In reality, those teachers more than likely had all the necessary musical skills to succeed but lacked expertise in important noninstructional skills: motivation and classroom discipline.

Motivation and discipline in music education are often ignored areas of study in music education classes. Those topics may be vaguely referred to in passing, but no presentation is made of concepts, models, and approaches that can aid a teacher in his or her daily instructional life. Any survey of recent graduates in music education will likely reveal how limited their backgrounds are in this respect. College and university instructors in music education methods must accept the responsibility of classroom leadership in this important aspect of teacher training.

An entire book could be devoted to the subjects of motivation and discipline in music education. What will be offered in this chapter will be a summary of recognized procedures for achieving a positively managed classroom, a classroom that is alive with meaningful activity and filled with students who are alert and eager. Good discipline does not happen overnight, nor can it be haphazard or hit-or-miss in nature. It takes time and experience to develop and maintain and relies heavily on the teacher's ability to learn from and build upon previous mistakes.

Understanding the Terminology

Motivation and *discipline* are two terms with different meanings, but the existence of one in a given situation is nearly impossible without the other. It is difficult to maintain a disciplined classroom unless the students are motivated to perform. It is equally difficult to motivate students toward a specific goal if they are not in a disciplined environment.

Motivation can be defined as the total of all forces that cause a person to expend energy doing one thing rather than another. Arousing student interest, promoting eager involvement, kindling group spirit, and encouraging student action are all forms of motivation. Motivation of students is the responsibility of the teacher.

Discipline can be described as the conduct that results from training. It involves learning to act in accordance with established rules in a manner that is socially agreed upon as appropriate in a given situation. Good discipline is evident in situations in which students exert an optimal amount of energy in trying to learn what a teacher is attempting to teach rather than wasting energy on other, unproductive activities.

In this sense, a teacher may be considered a good disciplinarian when he or she has learned to use the forces of motivation to keep students moving toward their academic goals.

MOTIVATION

There are several natural motivational factors that come into play when working with teenagers. Students involved in elective music performance groups or classes are already motivated to a certain degree or they would not be there. Thus motivation of performance groups is of a different nature than the type of motivation necessary for students involved in required general music or performance classes. Peer pressure to conform, which is such a powerful part of teenage life, can be used in an advantageous manner in motivating students toward elective performance participation and subsequent achievement, but that same pressure to conform can be an obstacle in motivating students in mandatory classes.

Music educators can motivate students by developing an association between music and the type of person that students admire, thus appealing to teenagers' need for a positive self-image. Through their own actions and external influences they can establish role models to serve as motivating forces. External influences could include such things as pictures and stories of famous people who are exceptional musicians but who are equally known for other accomplishments.

Teenagers have a strong need for a sense of belonging. Elective music groups serve this need as well as or better than any other aspect of education. Once again, however, general music classes or other mandatory music offerings do not enjoy this advantage, so teachers must base their classroom motivation on the intrinsic needs of the students.

Motivational factors

External and internal factors can influence a music education program. Research is somewhat sketchy in confirming the degree of motivational success achieved by some of these factors, but common sense dictates that all items will provide some element of motivation for students.

Fear and desire. Some music educators feel that there are only two true motivational elements in education: fear and desire. Fear as a motivating factor is extremely effective. One need only consider the many acts of fear-initiated heroism that have occurred in times of intense stress. Fear of failure strongly affects behavior and perhaps is never stronger than during the preteen and teenage years. However, groups that work in a fearful atmosphere tend to perform in spite of rather than as a result of that fear. When students are motivated by desire—that is, by a genuine interest in achieving a goal—limits are removed and a whole new level of creativity is opened to them. Building a desire to learn holds long-lasting and far-reaching benefits for students, teachers, and entire music education programs.

Music contests. Competitive and noncompetitive music contests contain the motivational elements of both fear and desire, and there is no question as to the motivation created by contest participation as it affects both teacher and student, a subject dealt with to a greater extent in chapter 10. Something appears to be wrong, however, with a system that makes it less difficult to motivate students to be better than students who attend a neighboring school rather than to be the best *they* can be.

Awards. Awards or rewards for the accomplishment of a specific set of objectives is part of American life. Some type of awards system can provide motivational benefits for school music performing groups, as well as music classes. Awards provide an opportunity to recognize students who achieve some degree of excellence in their work and provide extra incentive for students who can be considered underachievers. Very often awards are based on some type of point system, whereby students earn and collect "points" toward an award through rehearsal and concert attendance, as well as extra effort and participation in contests, festivals, all-state events, and so on. Point systems are often used as part of the grading process in performing groups and will be discussed in depth in chapter 9.

Testing and grading. Tests and grades hold some potential for motivating students toward musical success, but because of the lack of evaluative criteria they fall short of achieving the degree of motivation that takes place in other academic areas. After all, no student will be held back a year in school for "failing" band, as might occur if he or she fails to pass a math or English class. Nevertheless, evaluation and accountability in all areas of education have taken on increased significance in recent years. With that in mind, chapter 9 will examine criteria and processes associated with grading performing groups in music education.

Performances. One of the reasons students become members of music organizations is because of the performance opportunities. Young people are natural exhibitionists, and they should be placed in group and solo performances as often as the practical limits of the music program permit. Inviting alumni to participate in a performance upon occasion can be a source of motivation for student participants, as well as a positive public relations effort. Concert programs listing the names of all student participants is another motivational aid. But be sure to include everyone and have all names spelled correctly. Inadvertent omission and/or incorrect spelling of student names can often cause embarrassment and foster feelings of disappointment on the part of affected students and their parents. To avoid such problems, post a list of concert participants in an accessible location prior to program printing and require students to check it for accuracy. This simple step places the burden of responsibility on the students themselves for the accuracy of the concert program personnel listing.

Photographs/recordings. Students like to see and hear themselves in performance, and photographs, recordings, or videotapes of concerts can serve as an incentive for excellence. If a recording is made using quality equipment, cassette tapes or compact discs of a concert can be professionally reproduced rather inexpensively. A cassette or CD recording of their own performance can provide a lasting sense of pride for student participants. That sense of pride translates into motivation for the future.

Group spirit. Group activities appeal to students' need for a sense of belonging. Group spirit and identification can be enhanced by such things as T-shirts, identifying emblems, and jackets. Some type of uniform is necessary for performing groups for the same reason. The importance of developing spirit and identity within a group cannot be overlooked as a valuable motivational aid.

Compliments. Successful teachers can motivate learning through their positive and friendly attitudes, as well as through their personalities. A mark of a good teacher is that he or she knows when to offer a compliment, understanding that compliments motivate only when the person receiving one is aware that it is deserved. Novice music educators are cautioned against using false praise in lieu of constructive appraisal of student efforts.

Tim Lautzenheiser (1985), a noted lecturer on motivation in music education, feels that students cannot be given motivation, but can choose to be motivated. It is up to the teacher to set the example and create an educational environment in which students feel good about themselves. When students feel good about themselves, they perform accordingly.

As a music educator, you will need to look constantly at yourself and determine what motivates you to achieve program excellence. If it is anything less than providing an understanding of and interest in music, perhaps you need to rethink that aspect of your work. Self-evaluation can be a threatening experience for insecure individuals, but it is a necessary ingredient in determining motivation.

DISCIPLINE AND BEHAVIOR MODIFICATION

The behaviorist approach to classroom discipline is derived from the work of B. F. Skinner, whose theories were first published in the 1930s, and involves training children through operant conditioning rather than educating them. Skinner maintained that people relate to pleasant situations and reject unpleasant ones, and that they are likely to repeat a behavior pattern if the consequence of that behavior is pleasant. Behavior can be influenced by what is known as *operant conditioning* and the use of *positive* or *negative reinforcement* in conjunction with specific behavior sequences.

Music educators use operant conditioning much more than they might think. For example, if a musical group automatically becomes quiet when the director steps to the podium, the members have, at some point, been conditioned to do so. When a teacher uses the "counting" method in controlling a classroom situation, the response to counting "one," "two," or "three" is a result of operant conditioning. Students are aware of some type of consequence or group punishment if the teacher reaches "three," and therefore teachers using this method rarely get past "one." The counting system, with accompanying variations, is a popular approach to classroom discipline based on the behavior modification method.

Assertive discipline techniques can also be considered related to behavior modification in that they spell out very clearly for the students what type of behavior is expected and consequences, both positive and negative, that are associated with that behavior. Assertive discipline systems were introduced to education in the mid-1970s and quickly became a mainstay in both music education classrooms and rehearsals, as well as in general education classes, particularly at the elementary and junior high (middle school) levels. The method was first designed to help students develop responsibility and self-esteem, but both assertive discipline opponents and proponents now agree that the overriding goal is to get students to do whatever they are told, without question.

Some teachers tend to like assertive discipline because, as one teacher put it, "It's easy to use. It's all spelled out for you." These same teachers feel that without a packaged system, they would constantly be forced to make choices about how to react to student behavior. Assertive discipline will likely always have its supporters as well as its detractors, and as one author put it, "If this program disappeared from the face of the earth today, another collection of bribes and threats would take its place" (Kohn 1996, p. 58). Many teachers agree that any system based on rewards and punishments is a misguided instrument for controlling students. The principal objective of such a system is simply to get students to comply, an objective that lacks solid support in much of the education profession.

If you decide to investigate the implementation of assertive discipline in classrooms and/or rehearsal settings, be sure to clearly define the details of this approach in writing, and give copies to both students and parents.

Preventive discipline

Avoidance of discipline problems is the key to preventive discipline and is most successful when the students themselves are involved in establishing goals and objectives of classroom behavior. Many educators feel that student involvement in setting these goals goes a long way toward creating a positive learning situation. Students are less likely to break the policies or rules that they have established than they are to violate procedures established for them by an "outside" source— namely, the teacher. Further discussion on preventive discipline techniques appears later in this chapter.

THREE COMMON APPROACHES TO DISCIPLINE

The following discipline approaches generally parallel the descriptions of leadership styles offered in chapter 2.

1. AUTHORITARIAN

An authoritarian teacher compiles strict classroom rules and regulations that are enforced by severe punishment. An authoritarian offers no explanation of the reasons behind the strict restraints. This approach produces conformity but leads to resentment, which in turn creates an unhealthy learning situation.

2. PERMISSIVE

A permissive teacher makes little attempt to set limits on students' behavior. An air of egocentricity and self-assertiveness prevails on the part of the teacher. Because students do not know what to do and behavior limits are not established, they often start to feel insecure. Chaos is the rule rather than the exception.

3. DEMOCRATIC

The democratic approach to discipline is generally considered the best method for teachers. In such an approach, students receive explanations of how they should act. Good behavior is rewarded with praise and inappropriate behavior is punished. The democratic approach creates a positive learning atmosphere based more on "do's" than on "don'ts."

COMPONENTS OF GOOD DISCIPLINE

Goals and objectives

Inspiring or improving classroom behavior involves some of the same teaching aspects as those found in teaching the subject matter, the most important of which is the establishment of goals and objectives. If behavioral goals and objectives are decided upon with the students' cooperation, progress is likely to be measured and evaluated through group effort. Students must realize that the reason they need to behave is so that they can learn. After good classroom control is established, teaching can become a pleasant vocation. Once young people feel comfortable and relaxed in a classroom setting, communication can take place. Interaction between teacher and students, and among students themselves, begins to occur, and an extremely rewarding experience for all participants is the end result.

Developing social skills

The manner in which people treat each other is another important ingredient in creating a positive classroom climate. Students must learn social skills along with the subject matter, or no learning will take place at all. They don't necessarily need to personally like everyone in a class or ensemble, but they do need to develop a respect for each other as individuals and to work toward classroom relationships built on that respect. Most young people yearn for recognition from their peers, but their peers are a very critical group, at times almost to the point of being cruel. It is up to music teachers at all instructional levels to ask their students to perform activities they can do well so that they are able to achieve some type of group recognition. Music class offers an opportunity not normally found in other classes to improve social skills because of the close rapport that is generally present between the students and the teacher and because the subject matter appeals to the feelings of those students. The establishment of some form of social goals and objectives in music class is certainly appropriate.

The role of physical stature

A teacher's physical size has little to do with success in motivating students and developing a disciplined classroom atmosphere. Everyone can recall at least one educator who was small in stature but who ran a tight ship in the classroom. Even the largest youngster in class could be handled by a firm comment or warning glance. At the same time, that teacher created an atmosphere of congeniality in the classroom; students felt comfortable in class and looked forward to attending. How did this teacher achieve that level of control and respect? The next section in this chapter should provide some clues.

One can also recall the big, husky teacher whose classrooms were in a state of constant chaos; very little learning took place. How could students who were normally well behaved in the class taught by the teacher in the first example suddenly become disrespectful and boisterous to the point of distraction in the classes taught by the teacher in the second example? The answer is that the first teacher created a firm but caring classroom atmosphere, where behavior parameters were clearly defined and understood and where daily lessons were presented in a logical, well-prepared, and exciting manner.

PRIMARY AREAS OF CONCERN IN MUSIC EDUCATION DISCIPLINE

There are numerous problems that can surface during a school year, but the ones that a prospective music educator must deal with from the very first day he or she walks into the classroom are extraneous talking, poor attendance, and students who, for one reason or another, are unable to participate in performance group rehearsals on a short-term basis. Minor behavior problems, such as chewing gum in class and poor posture, will also demand attention.

Talking. Novice teachers are wasting their time and effort teaching or giving instructions while extraneous talking is occurring in the classroom. Complete silence at all times is an unreasonable expectation, but students must understand that they will not talk when the teacher is teaching or providing rehearsal instructions. In a rehearsal situation, a group director is most likely to encounter talking when he or she stops the group to correct an error or offer performance advice and when working with one section of the ensemble while the remainder of the group sits idle. By discussing this problem on the first day of class and explaining why a certain type of behavior is required, the students are much more likely to eventually conform than if infractions are handled on an individual basis.

Several years ago, this writer observed two sixth-grade band rehearsals in two separate middle schools, with two different directors, during the same day. This situation was made even more unique by the fact that the two directors were father and son. The younger music educator was in his first year of teaching, while the father had over twenty years of teaching experience. Both instructors were highly enthusiastic in their presentations and both possessed positive motivational skills, evidenced by the fact that enrollment in each band program was extremely high when compared with total sixth-grade enrollment.

The young instructor continually gave rehearsal instructions and discussed scheduling and other matters with the band without the students ever becoming completely quiet. This practice caused unnecessary repetition of instruction, which cost valuable rehearsal time. By contrast, the father was just concluding an extended rehearsal period and the students were tired and somewhat fidgety; however, when instructions were given, the students remained quiet and attentive. At the close of the rehearsal, the experienced director simply said, "I have something I need to tell you before you leave." There was some talking and moving about, but the teacher waited for several seconds, saying nothing. The minor noise level quickly dropped to complete silence, and the teacher then made the final announcements to a tired but attentive sixth-grade band.

The difference between the two rehearsal atmospheres was dramatic. The younger music educator undoubtedly would eventually come to realize that it is just as easy and more efficient to function in an environment where his students are quiet and attentive than it is to continue working in the present atmosphere. Unfortunately, this transition could take a period of years.

Music instruction—whether in the general music classroom or in a rehearsal room—need not take place over student conversation. Patient music educators can be successful in achieving this goal by refusing to accept unnecessary conversation.

Students who can't participate. Sore throats, cold sores, bad colds, and dental problems are just some of the reasons music students will legitimately offer to request that they be excused from one or several rehearsal periods. In dealing with these problems, music educators should require that students make their requests prior to the beginning of rehearsal. Excused students should sit in their regular chairs during the rehearsal and follow the activities taking place in it. These students should not be allowed to study (after all, they can't practice the tuba in biology class) or perform library or other work in the music room, and they should not be excused from the room. Students who are allowed to study during a rehearsal or who are permitted to leave the music room because of minor ailments may begin to abuse this priviledge, using their "afflictions" to avoid class or rehearsal work. Again, the teacher should clearly state this policy early in the year, and students who fail to follow the rules must be dealt with in a consistent manner as situations arise.

Rehearsal and performance attendance. Rehearsal and class attendance normally is not a problem for music groups and is governed largely by the administrative policies of the school. Attendance at any extra rehearsals, and more specifically, performances, is another matter. If students are notified far in advance of the event, there is absolutely no reason for an unexcused absence from a performance. Students who miss a performance without permission are sending a signal to the music educator concerning their feelings toward the group, and, with very few exceptions, they probably should be asked to resign from the organization. To allow students with an unexcused absence from a performance to remain part of the group creates morale problems within the organization and reduces the importance of a quality music performance in the minds of all participants. It is important that a policy regarding absenteeism be established early on in the school year. The punishments should be developed with administrative approval, and a written version of the attendance policy should be distributed to parents and students. A complete calendar of all dates throughout the year should be compiled and attached to the policy, including all home performances, concerts, and shows, as well as contests and festivals and all-state auditions and performances. If both the students and their parents are aware of and understand the attendance policy, the responsibility for students' behavior will rest directly on the students themselves. Students will become more responsible for their own actions, which is exactly the way it should be.

Some teachers place a calendar in each music folio, with all performance obligations marked in suitable squares for each date. As changes arise, each student makes the appropriate adjustment in his or her personal calendar. This organizational device does not take much effort on the part of the music educator to construct and provides a degree of involvement in the scheduling process for student participants.

Gum chewing. Some schools have a general policy against chewing gum in the school building; those schools that do not have such a policy place the music educator in a position of policing action that has no place in the music education classroom. Students should not be allowed to chew gum in any rehearsal setting, or for that matter in general music classes where singing takes place, as well as the handling of special equipment and instructional aids. A wastebasket placed conveniently by the door should serve as a repository for all gum. Once the policy prohibiting gum chewing in the classroom is established, the teacher should not provide violators with extra attention by passing a wastebasket around the class and asking students to place their gum in it; the receptacle by the door should be sufficient. Students with repeated infractions can be scheduled for an after-school conference. This seemingly insignificant part of classroom discipline in music is actually an important step in establishing teacher credibility. By being clear about this rule, the teacher demonstrates his or her seriousness about creating a classroom atmosphere conducive to quality education.

Posture. Good posture, whether in the general music classroom or in rehearsal, is another requisite for good behavior and is necessary to create an optimal physical situation for music performance. Students who maintain good posture in class are more alert and attentive and behave better than those whose posture is poor. Music educators cannot let students slouch in their chairs or sit cross-legged during rehearsals. As in other aspects of discipline, if students are prepared in advance for the requirement, they are more likely to respond positively. Anything less than complete compliance results in game playing between teacher and students; the teacher often is placed in a no-win situation by relaxing the policy, which signals the beginning of a potential breakdown of control in that class.

PRACTICAL SUGGESTIONS FOR DISCIPLINE IN THE MUSIC EDUCATION CLASSROOM

It is easy to understand why so many new music educators begin their teaching careers feeling apprehensive about their ability to control a classroom. As undergraduates, they lived in a controlled and generally comfortable environment, where many decisions were made for them by their college or university and by their academic advisors. In three short months following graduation, they were suddenly expected to move from the role of students to teachers of students. The transition from the *motivated* to the *motivator* is a difficult period in the life of many teachers. The next several pages offer practical suggestions that can facilitate that transition.

Appearance. The visual impression a new teacher makes on students will influence their behavior before a note of music is taught or before those students can become aware of the teacher's depth of musical knowledge. The teacher must look, act, and talk like a professional. This transformation must take place rapidly, and it should begin with the student-teaching experience.

The casual look of the college and university student must be replaced with the professional look of a music educator proud to be a member of the teaching profession. This will involve, in many cases, an adjustment in wardrobe. For example, earrings often worn by male undergraduate students should be discarded as a part of the "been there, done that" attitude of the professional image of music educators. Interestingly, the teacher most highly respected by students and peers alike in any school system is usually the person who presents a neat and well-groomed appearance.

It can be argued by some undergraduate students that how individuals feel about and treat others, their level of professional knowledge, and their genuine concern for the educational welfare of their future students transcend personal appearance. While that may be true, certain standards for personal appearance have been established in the minds of students and their parents through the years, and a casual approach to grooming and overall appearance sends the wrong initial message to students and colleagues alike. That message can inhibit a young educator's efforts to establish a professional relationship with students, which is necessary for learning to take place. In your own classroom, take advantage of the opportunity to present a positive and professional appearance to students through your personal grooming and manner of dress. Students will notice and appreciate this concern.

Teacher/student actions. Students are quick to pick up on how teachers act. They can respect a teacher who is friendly but not determined to be their friend. Many novice music educators have failed because they attempted to establish the type of friendship with their students that they themselves enjoyed with one of their favorite college instructors. Students have to feel that the teacher is on their side, that he or she really wants them to succeed in their musical efforts. They can then honestly respond to leadership they respect.

Professional relations. You should discourage students from referring to you by your first name. This practice reduces the level of professionalism and air of dignity that must exist between you as the teacher and your students. A professional atmosphere promotes positive and respectful responses from students and helps maintain a productive classroom. The earlier in your career that you develop dignified approaches to your work, the more effective and successful you will be.

The teacher's voice. The strength and loudness of a music teacher's voice are also important considerations in motivating students and can be developed with practice over a period of time. Of even greater importance, however, is what the teacher says and how it is said. An immediate requirement for many new teachers is to replace the slang, half-sentences, and catchy phrases that once might have been part of daily conversations with their peers with clear and concise instructions, delivered in professional terms to their students. This can be another difficult but extremely important adjustment for prospective music educators to make. Novice teachers cannot allow slang phrases or unacceptable language to become a part of the manner in which they provide instructions to their students. Even lesser swear words such as *damn* or *hell* have no place in music rehearsal rooms and are looked upon with disfavor by parents and school officials alike.

Preparation. Nothing can build an individual's confidence more when approaching a particular project than being well prepared for the task. Teachers who prepare diligently for every class are able to anticipate and prevent potential behavior problems, prepare answers in advance for difficult questions, and, in general, provide a setting in which optimal learning can take place.

Teachers who are well prepared for their classes or rehearsals are able to keep things moving and to pace activities at a level that limits opportunities for misbehavior. Maintaining an appropriate rehearsal or classroom pace is perhaps one of the most consistent difficulties for new music educators. Beginning teachers need to plan every detail of a class period, including anticipating questions, and they should write out in advance the definitions or explanations of terms they plan to offer during each class, leaving nothing to chance.

In general music classrooms, the pace of moving from one activity to another needs to be planned by a beginning teacher. Experienced teachers usually move smoothly and effortlessly from one activity to another during a class period. The ability to pace classroom or rehearsal activities can take years of experience. The novice teacher must think through the process, plan carefully, and write out those plans to expedite good classroom pace.

An experienced middle-school music educator observed by this writer spent a considerable amount of time prior to the start of the school day tuning guitars for a beginning guitar class consisting of thirty eighth-grade boys. This eliminated the potentially chaotic tuning process during the early stages of the class and, at the same time, provided the opportunity for the students to hear and appreciate what in-tune instruments sounded like. As the class progressed through the term—after a positive classroom environment had been established and a fundamental expertise level had been reached by the students—the tuning process was efficiently and successfully addressed with the class. Through planning and preparation this teacher was able to facilitate learning and maintain an orderly classroom.

Students are uncanny in their ability to recognize unprepared teachers or teachers who lack confidence in their abilities. The saying "Those who hesitate are lost" is never more true than when discussing the need for preparation for music education classes and rehearsals. Students can be unforgiving if they sense their time is being wasted. Remember your own high school and college classes and recall how frustrated you felt when a teacher was not prepared.

Veteran teachers with years of experience can, upon occasion, teach classes or rehearse performing groups with little or no advance preparation. Those teachers generally have a broad background from which they can draw that provides students with a quality educational experience. Inexperienced teachers do not possess this background and need to carefully think through every classroom procedure. All educators learn sooner or later that teaching by whim is an invitation to disaster. Exacting preparation can go a long way toward creating the image of authority and confidence so necessary for successful teaching efforts.

There are three primary ingredients in establishing confidence in a music educator's approach to instruction: knowledge, preparation, and experience. Beginning teachers lack experience, so they must necessarily rely on knowledge and preparation, both of which go a long way toward establishing confidence in the classroom. Confidence, however, must not be confused with arrogance. There are, unfortunately, a few music teachers who approach their first teaching positions with an arrogant attitude, at least outwardly, regardless of their preparation level. Students will not accept this approach on the part of any teacher, let alone a young and inexperienced music educator. If those same teachers are unable to replace arrogance with confidence based on their training and daily preparation, they are likely to soon leave the profession, citing unruly and disinterested students as the cause for their departure.

Eye contact. An inability to maintain eye contact with people can be considered a sign of insecurity. Eye contact with students in music classes is a key to preventive discipline and is also a prime ingredient in projecting an image of confidence. Even the best students are likely to misbehave or be unresponsive if the teacher continually fails to look at them. A teacher can be saying the correct or proper things to students, but true communication does not take place without eye contact.

Instrumental instructors have been known to look constantly at the method book while their elementary students are rehearsing even the simplest music. Choral and general music instructors often use the piano as a sanctuary shielding them from their students. This behavior can inspire classroom inattention and disruption.

Many new teachers fail to maintain any degree of eye contact with their students, even after they have become more confident in their abilities, simply because it has become a habit. The importance of maintaining good eye contact with music students cannot be overemphasized. If it is not a natural part of the way in which you present yourself, you will need to develop that skill to be successful in motivating students and in maintaining a disciplined classroom environment. This development can begin at the undergraduate level and can be practiced in everyday situations, starting with your next conversation.

An additional benefit of having good eye contact with students is that it allows the instructor to learn their names more expediently. Students appreciate the fact that a teacher cares enough about them to quickly learn their names. Name tags may be used for younger students. Consulting a preceding year's school annual can be another source of assistance in learning students' names. A music teacher generally has many more students under his or her direction than other classroom teachers; therefore, some type of organized effort must be made to memorize names. Maintaining good eye contact and knowing students' names are just two more of the ingredients that contribute to the air of dignity and confidence necessary for successful music instruction.

Sense of humor. The finest music educators are blessed with a good sense of humor, and they use it judiciously in their classes to create a relaxed atmosphere. This does not mean, however, that they spend their time telling jokes and trying to entertain students. Rather, they use humor to make learning fun. A sense of humor prevents walls from developing between the teacher and students and makes the instructor more approachable from the students' point of view. A good sense of humor is a necessary ingredient in successful teaching, and competent and confident music instructors feel comfortable with allowing levity now and then into their classroom or rehearsal situations.

Admitting mistakes. What prevents knowledgeable adults from admitting an occasional mistake in front of a class of elementary, junior high, or high school students? The only logical answer is that these teachers are insecure in their abilities and feel that acknowledgment of their errors is a sign of weakness. Individuals with inflated egos often have the most difficulty in admitting mistakes. The fact is that almost all students are completely aware of when an instructor makes even the most simple mistake, and quite frankly, so is the instructor. Ignoring the mistake is bad enough, but attempting to cover the error or explain it away can result in feelings of resentment on the part of students. Confident music educators are quick to admit their mistakes and often use the occasion to exhibit an element of humor, such as, "I'm sorry. I made a mistake four or five years ago, too. I hope it isn't getting to be habit forming." Students are likely to appreciate this revelation of fallibility.

An egotistical person has difficulty admitting mistakes. There is no place for such an individual in a music education classroom. Students simply will not respect, respond to, or work with a person who allows ego to be the dominating classroom influence. Everyone makes mistakes. Students admire teachers who acknowledge errors and have little time for those who don't.

Motivation and praise. Most students respond in a positive manner to praise. Praise makes them feel good, and when they feel good they work harder, perform better, and learn more. Be generous in praising your students when praise is warranted. Students are completely aware when compliments are deserved. Praise where praise is not earned, or false praise, is worse than no praise at all and is generally not appreciated by the recipients. Too many music educators spend time telling their performing groups how wonderful they sound or what a fine job they've done when the participating students know that is not the case. It would be much more appropriate if the progress made was praised and work yet to be done was also noted. For example, following a contest or festival performance when a choir receives a Division II rating, some teachers might tell their students they did a really fine job but the adjudicator failed to fully appreciate their efforts. It would be much better for all involved if that same teacher provided a valid evaluation of the performance, complimenting work done well and also noting the elements of the performance that still need more effort as indicated on the adjudication form.

Offering heavy praise for less than outstanding accomplishments is simply not a good instructional and motivational practice. However, it is extremely important to be positive about what students have achieved. Try to spend more time "catching" students doing something right and praising them for it rather than constantly looking for mistakes and offering criticism. Results are bound to be better when you build a program based on positive rather than negative responses.

Discipline and the reprimand. When reprimanding students for some unacceptable behavior or action, extreme care must be exercised not to resort to sarcasm or to personalize the reprimand. As the teacher, you must remember to criticize the action, not the person. For example, there is a difference between "That was not a very smart thing to do" and "Only people who are not very smart would do something like that."

Realistically, it is often difficult to like a student who is a source of class disruption, but it is an unacceptable practice to personally attack him or her in order to gain a better response from that student. It simply doesn't work. When reprimanding a student, your comments must be direct and clear. The student must understand exactly what was done wrong, why such behavior is unacceptable, and how that behavior negatively affects the class or group. Only the briefest criticism or reprimand should take place in front of the student's peers. Extensive discussions regarding behavior should take place in private between yourself and the offending student. You have absolutely nothing to gain and much to lose by becoming involved in a lengthy reprimand or discussion of offensive behavior before a student's peers. If nothing else, such action can provoke a response from the wrongdoer, thus setting the stage for a confrontation. There are no winners in public confrontations. Avoid making threats when reprimanding a student or group of students. There is always the distinct possibility a student will accept the threat as a challenge and force you into the uncomfortable position of following through on a comment that was likely made in the heat of the moment with little or no advance thought.

Finally, you should never be reluctant to reprimand a student because you fear that the student or other class members may not like you as a result. Just the opposite is true. Offending students actually expect to be reprimanded and/or punished. Those teachers who fail to respond quickly and efficiently to misbehavior because they fear a loss of personal popularity are not living up to a basic educational responsibility that they have to their students.

Consistency. Students quickly come to realize whether or not a particular teacher is consistent in terms of praise and punishment. Both preteen and teenage students need to know where they stand with a teacher. Inconsistency in administering praise and disciplinary action can only create insecurity on the part of the students. With few exceptions, every time a student gets out of line, an appropriate reprimand should follow, and every student should receive the same punishment. Good behavior also should be recognized and rewarded in proportion to the importance of the behavior to the individual or the group.

A high grade on a music test received by a normally good student might receive a nod of approval or pat on the back, while a struggling student who earns a good grade on the same exam might deserve and receive a bit more lavish praise from the teacher. Students have a deep awareness of and appreciation for music educators who are fair and consistent in their dealings with all students. They tend to see teacher consistency as a strength that they admire and on which they can rely.

One-on-one conferences with students. When a student commits some infraction or otherwise misbehaves during a class or rehearsal, and the behavior can't be handled by a look of disapproval or a quick comment, consider handling the matter in a teacher-student conference separate from class time. To chastise a student in front of peers often satisfies the offender's need for recognition that may have caused the offensive behavior in the first place. A misbehaving student often subconsciously feels that negative recognition is better than no recognition at all. Perhaps your most difficult task will be to avoid reinforcing an offensive act or, in other words, ignoring a student at the proper time.

If you ignore unacceptable behavior during the class period, you can ask the offender to remain after school. At the after-school conference, be friendly but firm in order to distinguish between the person and the act. Displays of anger, ridicule, and sarcasm are generally ineffective, although they are occasionally a part of the misbehaving student's home life. Encourage the student to explain the problem. Don't force him or her into a defensive situation but instead attempt to arrive at a solution through mutual understanding. This approach may sound somewhat idealistic, but all you need do is reflect back on your teenage years to recall an instance of parental or teacher beratement and the frustration caused by the stern lecture approach. Experienced music educators have found that pupils often propose satisfactory solutions to difficult situations if given the opportunity. A receptive attitude on the part of the teacher is often disarming to belligerent or misbehaving students. It is not at all uncommon for students who have been approached in this way to talk their way through difficult situations, arrive at appropriate solutions to their problems, and subsequently become leaders in and contributing members of a particular class.

An aid in solving all but the most serious behavior problems, the personal teacher-student conference is an extremely valuable motivation and discipline tool. Explore it as an option, and you may be pleasantly surprised by the results.

Positive classroom environment. The classroom environment has both mental and physical components. The mental aspect of the classroom environment has already been addressed; here we will review the physical environment and how it contributes to successful motivation and discipline.

Students respond positively to established routines. If the class takes place in a regular music room, chairs, music stands, and other equipment should be in place before or as the students enter the room. If an instrumental music teacher travels from one school to another, perhaps using the school lunchroom for a rehearsal room, students can be responsible for the daily setup and replacement of chairs and stands in that room. Whether the class is general music or performance oriented, an established daily routine is important and provides an element of security for participating students. *If they sit on the floor, it's good*

✗ Music classes, if at all possible, should be conducted in a neat, well-organized, and pleasant environment. A messy, disorganized, drab classroom can indicate to students that little is expected of them. A general music classroom where equipment and sheet music are scattered around the room will probably inspire chaotic classes and rehearsals. Freestanding or built-in storage racks and cabinets, display cases, bulletin boards, good audio/visual equipment, and adequate lighting and ventilation all contribute to a positive classroom environment where exciting and lasting music instruction can take place.

A class or rehearsal room need not approach an antiseptic state, but a comfortable and pleasant place in which equipment and other physical needs of the students have been anticipated by the music teacher tends to improve student motivation and decrease discipline problems.

CONFLICT RESOLUTION

Schools at all levels across the country are beginning to put in place a process to resolve conflicts between students and, at times, faculty. In its most simple form conflict resolution requires participants to

1. Describe the problem in very specific terms, avoiding general comments.
2. Think of solutions by writing down every idea for solving the problem, even those that appear to be unrealistic or silly.
3. Weigh all of the ideas and include consequences and advantages of each.
4. Choose a plan by picking the best one through consensus, then carry it out. Participants need to set dates for future conferences to determine whether or not the plan is working.

Conflict resolution usually involves negotiation or mediation as a means of problem-solving. The negotiation process exists when two groups or parties decide to work out a problem between themselves. Mediation exists when a third party, ✗ not directly involved in the conflict, assists those involved in the conflict in determining a solution. A mediator's job is to ask questions, listen to both sides, determine what each side wants out of the situation, make sure only one person at a time talks, and help the two parties agree on a way to settle the problem, all while making both parties feel they have won, not lost, their point. Whether negotiation or mediation is involved in conflict resolution, the four steps outlined above should be followed.

Peer mediation can be a successful and stimulating way to resolve conflicts among students. Find out about student mediation in your school. If a program does not exist, ask a counselor to consider starting one. Such a program can help develop social skills in music education classes and performing groups.

OUT-OF-CONTROL CLASSROOMS

If you find yourself faced with a classroom or rehearsal situation that, over a period of time, has gotten out of control, you may be tempted to set out to restore complete order immediately. Or you may want to give up or just maintain the status quo until the next semester, this time vowing to start with a specific set of rules and regulations. Neither of these potential solutions to the problem is likely to produce satisfactory results.

A better approach might be to schedule individual meetings with the apparent leaders in the class and involve them in establishing policies governing only one of several aspects of misbehavior. Make every attempt to get students to understand, on an individual basis, why a certain type of behavior is not acceptable, and let them offer solutions to the problem. Draw out responses from individuals by asking leading questions, such as "How would you handle this problem if you were the teacher?" Offer solutions and ask students to determine what they feel is the best one. This is a difficult situation, and the process must be well planned in advance and possible objections anticipated, or failure to change behavior is likely.

Say, for example, you have determined to work on unnecessary and unsolicited talking in class. One rule has now been established: "No talking without raising your hand." For several days this rule is strictly enforced. During this time, not much teaching and learning will take place, but it is likely that little worthwhile instruction was occurring in the chaotic state anyway. Punishment of violators must be uniform and consistent. Other discipline problems must not distract from the primary goal of curbing extraneous talking. One problem at a time!

What should the punishment be for talking without raising one's hand? The answer will vary from teacher to teacher, but an example might be: One violation—a reminder; second violation—fifteen minutes after school; subsequent violations— additional fifteen minutes after school, and so on. In the final analysis, whatever will work best for a particular teacher is the criterion for such punishment. Bear in mind that other aspects of negative behavior are likely to improve as "talking without raising your hand" improves.

You may want to consider establishing some type of class reward for the first day no comment has to be made regarding extraneous talking. A reward in this instance could range anywhere from treats brought to class to a recording day in which students can bring a song of their choice to play for the rest of the class. A word of caution here: It is wise to screen the lyrics or establish guidelines for submitted songs on recording day to avoid any embarrassing situations. Parents tend to react negatively to music with questionable lyrics, whether or not it is played accidentally or by intent.

Rehearsal Discipline

Many journal articles and book chapters have been written on the subject of rehearsal techniques for performing groups. Unfortunately, the most efficient conducting and rehearsal techniques are of little or no value when put into practice in an undisciplined rehearsal atmosphere. A good deal of the material on classroom discipline already presented in this chapter can be applied directly to performance group rehearsals. However, these rehearsals raise special problems due to the number of students normally involved in large ensembles. For example, each student has a potential source of "noise" on hand during the rehearsal of instrumental ensembles. Rehearsal techniques and discipline are extremely individual matters for music educators. Two different directors using the same approach to rehearsal problems may get opposite results. With that thought in mind, several suggestions common to all music rehearsals are offered.

Pacing rehearsals

Teachers need to become accustomed to conducting fast-paced rehearsals. This is one of the major areas of deficiencies present in the work of new music educators. When a director stops a rehearsal, clear and concise, straight-to-the point instructions for improvement must be provided, and little should be said that is unnecessary. Name the section, the error, and the prescription for improvement. Long dialogues during rehearsal stops are of little value and are appreciated even less by the performers. Talking on the part of students during rehearsal stops is unacceptable behavior; however, if the music educator is asking the students to be quiet, he or she is well advised to have something important and relevant to say.

Preparation

Preparation as a preventive measure affecting classroom discipline has perhaps its greatest application in the rehearsal room. All ensemble directors, at all levels of performance, need to prepare carefully for rehearsals. This is never more true than in the case of young teachers holding their first positions. Every last detail needs to be predicted, planned, and prepared. Questions need to be anticipated and instructions to the group need to be outlined. Until nervousness and uneasiness in front of a group subsides, nothing can be left to chance.

All music educators who work with performing groups owe it to their students and themselves to be well prepared for rehearsals. Students quickly detect an unprepared director and respond accordingly. Music directors expect their students to practice and learn their parts. They cannot expect anything less from themselves.

Rehearsal room

If possible, chairs and music stands should be in place before rehearsal. (When both choral and instrumental groups share the same rehearsal space, all music stands should be removed from the seating area for choir rehearsals.) All equipment necessary to the rehearsal should be readily available as well. Music should be in folders and stored in cabinets with easy access for students when entering and leaving the room. Before the students enter the room, the rehearsal schedule for the day and necessary announcements should be on the blackboard. A confused and disorderly rehearsal room atmosphere has a tremendous negative impact on young ensemble members. As mentioned earlier, students want and appreciate order in their lives.

Rehearsal rules

Rules and regulations associated with music rehearsals should be few, simple, and direct. Posture, gum chewing, talking when the director is on the podium, attendance at rehearsals and performances, grading policy, and practice expectations are several points that need to be considered. These considerations, along with others the director deems important, are best put in writing and presented to the students. Special rules governing trips and other out-of-school activities should be discussed with the school principal and included in the general rehearsal policies.

Eye contact during rehearsals

Many experienced and inexperienced musicians simply ignore the conductor. The only way this can happen, though, is if the conductor allows it. Why should the performers watch the director if he or she never looks at them during a rehearsal or performance? Novice music educators need to move their eyes away from the security of the score and *look* at their young musicians. There isn't a reader of this book who can't recall at least one instance of a band director with his or her head buried in the score of the "Star Spangled Banner." How ridiculous! To earn and maintain control of a performing group, the director must sustain some degree of eye contact with ensemble members. Those educators who make it a practice to occasionally look at the members of their ensembles are likely to find some of them looking back.

SERIOUS DISCIPLINE PROBLEMS

It would be naive to think that all discipline problems that can ever occur in a music classroom can be handled by putting into practice the suggestions presented on the preceding pages. Every day in the United States classroom teachers are threatened, assaulted, and verbally abused in some way. The likelihood that these occurrences could take place in a music classroom is not very great because, for the most part, students participating in these classes elect to be there. Schools that have a high incidence of violence generally have their own policies governing teacher response in threatening situations.

A music educator should never attempt to take a weapon away from a student, nor should he or she physically attempt to break up a fight in or out of the classroom. In both cases ask in a loud and authoritative voice that the weapon be dropped or that students stop fighting. A responsible student should be sent as quickly as possible to the principal's office for assistance from school officials. In-classroom telephones are being installed in many schools across the country and, along with the school intercom system, can be used to summon assistance in threatening situations. It is not in any classroom teacher's domain to get involved any more than verbally in potentially violent situations. The risks are too great and the benefits too small. *Direct, forceful commands*

Sending students to the principal's office

Some music educators go through their entire careers having rarely sent students to the principal's office for disciplinary purposes. Others initiate an almost never-ending parade from their classroom to the office. There is no doubt that school administrators admire and appreciate classroom teachers who can handle discipline problems, but they are also willing to provide assistance to any teacher who experiences disruptive or otherwise unacceptable behavior by one or more students. School principals are also usually ready to help the teacher who has severe discipline problems find a different and more successful approach to classroom management.

In general, music educators should not be reluctant to send misbehaving students to the principal's office, but they should do whatever they can to prevent it from becoming a regular practice. If the procedures presented in this chapter are observed, music educators are likely to be able to handle personally all but the most extreme disciplinary cases.

Professional in-school assistance

A student who is a serious discipline problem in a music class is very likely causing problems in other classes as well. Music educators experiencing difficulty with a particular student should consult other teachers to determine if there is a behavior pattern and if a combined approach toward a solution to a student's problem might be in order.

Another source of great comfort and reassurance for all classroom teachers can be the professional staff members who serve in support of their instructional efforts. School counselors, health staff, principals, and assistant principals are all available to provide assistance should a particularly difficult or serious disciplinary situation arise. These individuals have the necessary training and are in a position in the administrative structure of the school that allows them to deal effectively with serious problems.

Be careful about becoming too deeply involved in counseling or advising troubled students. Many times disturbed students face a difficult home life or may be suffering from medical or mental conditions that need to be addressed. While it may be flattering when a student seeks your advice, that student should instead be referred to members of the instructional support staff. The school district employs well-trained professionals for that purpose, and no one will ever think less of you for calling on a professional colleague for assistance in difficult situations.

Detention

Most schools have some means of retaining misbehaving students after school hours for both relatively minor and more serious offenses. Quite often teachers can handle detained students in their own music room, or they can be sent to a central classroom for detention.

Be cautious about requiring students to do special tasks while in detention. For example, asking a misbehaving student to write a report on Bach as punishment is destructive to the goals of the English teachers, who are attempting to interest students in the joy and benefits of writing, not to mention your own ultimate goal: to excite students about music. Perhaps the greatest punishment for students in detention is to require them to do *nothing* during that time: no studying, no writing, no talking. With nothing else to occupy their time, wayward students at least have the opportunity to reflect on the appropriateness of the actions that brought them to detention in the first place.

Dressing to Learn

Many schools, both rural and urban, have initiated school uniform policies in one form or another. In such schools, students no longer argue over whose sneakers are more expensive or more cool, and they no longer have to worry about what other kids will say about their clothing on a given school day.

In January 1996, even President Clinton got involved in the school uniform discussion during his State of the Union Address when he said, "If it means that the schoolrooms will be more orderly, more disciplined, and that our young people will learn to evaluate themselves more by what they are on the inside instead of what things they're wearing on the outside, then our public schools should be able to require their students to wear school uniforms."

A veteran music educator recently visited a number of schools in Baltimore County, Maryland. During a visit to an urban middle school in a racially mixed area of the county, one of the first things he noticed was how quiet and orderly the hallways were during the transition between classes. That same sense of order and attentiveness prevailed in classroom and rehearsal environments. Then he noticed the students were all wearing T-shirts and sweatshirts in a variety of colors, all with the name of the school imprinted on them, casual slacks and skirts (no jeans), and black or brown footwear (no athletic shoes). *Uniforms!* The school did not appear to have a strict uniform dress code, but nonetheless one was definitely in effect. The music educator reported that teachers and students alike were highly supportive of the dress code and that the visit to that middle school was genuinely enjoyable and enlightening.

In 1994, Long Beach, California, became the first school district to institute a mandatory uniform policy. One parent noted, "The kids all basically wear the same thing so you're forced to look at the children for what they are—not what they have on."

Music groups have been uniformed for decades. Music educators and contest adjudicators are aware of the difference the wearing of uniforms can make in the attitudes of young musicians in performance settings. Why would students in general classrooms be any exception?

It appears that some form of uniform dress code could be part of the classroom environment in the years ahead. Another note: Some school districts have begun mandating appearance codes for faculty members. Music educators, for the most part, are way ahead of the game on this one.

Ten Discipline Principles

As a means of summarizing successful motivation and discipline guidelines for music educators, the following principles are offered:

1. Be sure that music students understand the reasons why certain behavior is expected and what that behavior is. Involve them in determining behavior guidelines.

2. An aggressive attitude on the part of the teacher tends to develop students who adopt only an outward sense of conformity. Expect the best and look for and build upon good behavior traits. Be generous with praise.

3. Rebellious or difficult students are generally troubled students. Seek help in determining the underlying causes.

4. Young people need to be needed. Students who don't feel needed are likely to seek recognition and self-esteem through undesirable behavior.

5. Young people who are interested in an activity are rarely behavior problems.

6. Keep class activities moving. Confusion and behavior problems often appear in music classes when the group is going from one activity to another.

7. De-emphasize the importance of minor behavior problems. No one, not even the teacher, behaves perfectly all the time.

8. When involved in a difficult discipline situation with students, let them present their point of view.

9. Be firm, be fair, and mean what you say. Students expect and need to rely on these qualities in their teachers.

10. Be consistent. Variability on the part of the teacher breeds instability in students. Learn from your mistakes in dealing with student motivation and discipline, then build on your successes. The result can be one of the most enjoyable and satisfying career choices you could make.

SUGGESTED ACTIVITIES

1. Compile a list of the reasons why music classes should theoretically be less susceptible to student behavior problems. Lead a class discussion on the subject.

2. Interview a junior high and a senior high school student regarding their favorite teachers in their particular school. Compile a list of qualities that make each teacher special.

3. Prepare a five-minute report based on periodical literature concerning some element of motivating positive student behavior. Present the report to the class and have class members rate your eye contact.

4. Interview a local music educator and determine his or her most recent serious discipline problem and how it was resolved. Lead a class discussion on the topic.

5. Lead a discussion on the importance of uniforms for music groups as motivational aids. Support the discussion with two published sources.

6. Visit a local school music class or rehearsal and list (a) what you determine to be minor discipline problems and hypothesize how they could be prevented,

(b) apparent proactive steps taken by the teacher to prevent undesirable class-room behavior, (c) what the teacher does during class to promote a positive environment for learning, and (d) the type of behavior that is reinforced and how it is reinforced.

7. Determine how you would respond to each of the discipline situations below and what, if anything, could be done to prevent the problem from occurring in the first place.

   a. A choral member is slouching in her chair at the beginning of rehearsal. The teacher, in a quiet, offhand manner says, "Mary, please sit up." Mary complies but calls the teacher an unprintable name, just loud enough for the teacher and several students to hear. What would you do?

   b. The teacher catches two senior students drinking on the bus while on the trip home from the state music contest. What would you do?

   c. A student asks to be excused from a concert performance to go sailing with his father. The teacher denies the request. The student goes sailing anyway. What would you do?

   d. The teacher asks a misbehaving student to stay after school for punishment and the student fails to appear. What would you do if the student failed to appear a second time? What would you do?

   e. A teacher observes a student reading a book at every break during a band rehearsal. What would you do?

8. Lead a class discussion on what administrative functions presented in chapter 1 come into play in dealing with motivation and discipline. How? Why?

CHAPTER FOUR

So You Got the Job!
Now What?

Introduction

It's a well-documented fact that teachers new to their positions enjoy varying degrees of success. While personal success is often determined by a teacher's experience level, more often than not, the manner in which the new position is approached is the major determining factor in the level of success that a particular teacher enjoys.

It is not unusual for an experienced music educator as well as a first-year teacher to leave the profession following a particularly difficult and frustrating year in a new teaching position. This chapter offers some preventive measures and suggestions, as well as remedies, for common problems in the classroom. Among the positive techniques suggested are establishing high personal visibility, visiting with other teachers, quickly identifying student leaders, meeting separately with each student and learning each student's name as soon as possible, meeting with the school administrator to review goals, and maintaining an organized classroom and professional personal appearance. To be avoided are exchanging negative comments about past music teachers or curricula, taking on more responsibilities than you can handle, and being unwilling to seek help when necessary. The best teacher is one who is proactive, meeting challenges by anticipating problems, communicating results, and organizing the classroom and curriculum.

Throughout this chapter, when the phrase "first-year teacher" or "first-year music educator" is used, readers should understand that both experienced music educators in new positions and first-year teachers new to the profession are being addressed.

There is no in-service music educator in this country who has not heard a student say, "Well, Mr. Jones didn't do it that way" or "That's not the way Miss Juarez told us to breathe," or some similar comment. These types of comments are especially heard by teachers beginning a new position. A first-year teacher is particularly vulnerable to these comments, because it is generally known by students and parents that they are dealing with an inexperienced music educator. "Does this first-year person *really* know anything about teaching music?" they may be thinking. Teachers with years of experience are in a better position to deal with such implied criticism because of their background, but first-year teachers may feel intimidated.

A new music teacher is more likely to face skeptical students than are other teachers because all the music students (except beginning instrumentalists) have had instructional contact with the previous instructor. Senior members of a choral or instrumental ensemble, for instance, will readily compare a new teacher to their old, more familiar instructor. If the comparison is negative, the change of directors will be seen as an opportune time by some students to drop out of the ensemble program.

Some music students may also question the manner in which the new teacher rehearses an ensemble or handles group or private lessons. Again, differences in teaching style may be criticized by students who are used to working with another teacher. An interesting study might be to determine the percentage of reduced ensemble enrollment between the close of music classes in May and the opening of school in the fall quarter when a new music teacher is involved. The study would become even more interesting if a major trip was taken by the surveyed ensemble at some time during the past academic year (such as a performance in a football bowl parade, a music festival in a distant locale, or a concert appearance).

As a new music educator, it is only natural to be apprehensive about what lies ahead when approaching your first job. You've gone through the interview process and have carefully checked out such factors as the program's budget, facilities, contest/festival appearances and results, school size, program size, teacher responsibilities, equipment, schedule, administrative philosophy, and so on. With few exceptions, all of these points were covered in your college courses, and you have used them in deciding on accepting the position.

You can offer numerous reasons as to why you accepted the position, including the location of the school, the size of the program, the starting salary, and a recommendation from a professor. But you have left out two important factors: your future students and soon-to-be fellow faculty members. What are their feelings about the former music teacher and the music program? How are they likely to view you? These are considerations that will affect your future classroom success.

A final note: a change in teachers offers some students a perfect reason to drop out of the program. They will cite every reason to withdraw except the most honest one: they have grown tired of their involvement in the program, and the experience is no longer (in their eyes) beneficial or fulfilling. Remember, their withdrawal has absolutely nothing to do with you as the new music teacher.

POSITIVE STEPS FOR FIRST-YEAR MUSIC EDUCATORS

Increase your personal visibility

When starting your new position, you should seriously try to become visible throughout the school and community. This can be achieved in a variety of ways.

Examples include accepting hall-duty assignments and volunteering to serve as a chaperone for school dances. These and similar activities also provide the opportunity to get acquainted with students who are not in music classes. How you as the new teacher are viewed by the general student body can influence the way your own students react to you.

Community organizations, particularly churches and synagogues, often look to new music educators as potential choir directors. Never mind that the teachers may have absolutely no choral experience; they are seen as "musicians," and musicians can direct choirs. At the very least, membership in a local choir served by a teacher's school district is strongly encouraged.

Service clubs and fraternal organizations are always looking for new members to assist in their benevolent efforts; they need ideas and suggestions for club programs, someone to lead group singing at meetings, and so on. You may want to consider joining one or more organizations to help increase your visibility in the community.

Visit with classroom teachers

Schedule a personal meeting with all classroom teachers whose students are participants in your program. Their support is badly needed early in the year. They, in turn, must see you as someone who understands their needs as well. As the new kid on the block, you can expect to be viewed with a degree of skepticism and apprehension by some more experienced classroom teachers. Much of that concern can be erased by a warm, friendly, and understanding approach on your part.

Identify student leaders

Determine student musical leaders along with ensemble officers, if any are in place. Early one-on-one meetings or small group meetings with the officers or leaders is essential. It is important that you are seen as nonthreatening during these meetings. Such informational meetings present an opportunity for student leaders to become better acquainted with you and, at the same time, become aware that your primary goals involve making student musical experiences educational, enjoyable, and productive for all involved.

Hold one-on-one meetings with students

Very early in the first semester of the new year, arrange a "get acquainted" meeting with every instrumentalist or choir member. A number of music students will probably not be scheduled for regular lessons during the year; therefore, these sessions can be an opportunity for you to introduce yourself. Schedule meetings during students' free time or after school, or work closely with classroom teachers for a one-time disruption of their daily schedule. To ensure success in your first year, one-on-one meetings with all student musicians is vital. If you are in a school district that mandates parent-teacher conferences, try to schedule meetings with all the parents of student musicians. To do so will be very demanding from a scheduling standpoint, but it is a surefire opportunity to develop communication channels that could benefit the music program for years to come.

Learn names

Make every effort to quickly learn names of both your students and colleagues. One-on-one meetings, as described above, can be of tremendous value in the tedious process of learning student names. For additional help in this process, refer to last year's school yearbook or class pictures. Everyone appreciates being greeted by name, especially when the acquaintanceship is relatively new. Because of the number of classes you may have, you will need to learn more names than any other teacher in the school district. However, the extra effort that is required is well worth it.

Meet with school administrators

As a new teacher, you should reaffirm administrative expectations of the music program by meeting with the principal during the first month of school to share with him or her program goals and objectives that have been developed for the year. If your ideas are not reasonably in line with administrative expectations, some type of adjustment will have to be made, most likely in the form of a compromise. As a result of the job interview process, you should already have some idea of what your immediate administrative supervisor expects from the music program; however, a meeting can reaffirm for the supervisor that you are serious about your work and, at the same time, can provide a solid foundation for the administrative evaluation that will take place later in the school year.

Many school administrators readily acknowledge that they understand less about the music program and what it takes to make it work than they know about other academic programs under their supervision. A teacher's ability to communicate and articulate program needs and objectives can be a valuable asset to any administrator seriously concerned about the quality of the total education received by all the students under his or her direct supervision.

Be professional

Be professional in meeting all expectations of students involved in any portion of the music education program. As suggested in chapter 3, be fair, be firm, and above all, be consistent in your dealings with students. Young people are quick to reject any type of authority and direction that they deem unfair, regardless of whether that perception is accurate.

Involve students

Involve students in the objective and goal setting process early in the school year. Work with officers or other leaders from classes and/or ensembles, and encourage them to present the findings from goal and objective meetings to the rest of the students. It is very important for students to feel they have played a part in the decision-making process. It is also important to remember that this may be the first time in their lives that they have been asked to be involved in decisions that will directly affect them and their musical education.

Organize instruction

Be organized in your instructional approach, both in the physical setup of your rehearsal area and during the rehearsal and classroom periods themselves. Students of all ages become extremely proficient at determining when their time is being wasted and tend to respond to poorly organized teachers in a negative manner. An organized approach to your work not only is an aid to classroom/rehearsal management, but plays an important role in the total success of your instructional efforts as perceived by your students.

Maintain an appropriate appearance

As stated in chapter 3, music teachers need to dress and act in a professional manner. This is particularly true for new teachers. Students appreciate this effort on the part of their music instructors, and they do notice.

Developing a professional appearance can be a difficult transition. Acting professionally may even seem harder. Be friendly and open with your students, but again, do not attempt to become their *friend*. Teenagers have friends their own age. What they need from you is a nonthreatening yet firm, friendly yet respectful, professional relationship.

ACTIONS AND COMMENTS TO AVOID

The positive suggestions made in the preceding section are important to keep in mind. Of equal importance are the possible errors in judgment made by new teachers in dealing with their students, both personally and in classroom and rehearsal settings.

Avoid negative comments

Refrain from speaking negatively about your predecessor, both to your students and to your coworkers. Even indirect comments have a way of getting back to students. They quite frankly do not want to hear "bad" words about a former teacher, regardless of how they may have felt about him or her. If some students, other teachers, or parents speak negatively about your predecessor, do not comment on or support their statements, even in an innocent, inadvertent manner. To do so can be seen as an indication of weakness or insecurity on your part. To elect not to become involved in such conversations, in fact, to find something positive to say about your predecessor, can be seen as a sign of strength and confidence.

Don't try to do too much at once

As a new music educator, you may think you need to teach everything you know in the first or second lesson or class meeting. You may feel that you must appear all-knowing in early dealings with your students. You may tend to overdiagnose faults and overprescribe remedies. This approach can lead to frustration, if not rebellion, on the part of all but the most talented and dedicated students. Relax, and tackle one situation at a time.

A positive approach pays dividends

New music teachers are often too quick to point out all of the performance faults exhibited by students in the first or second lesson. They may be all too quick to adapt this authority role because they hope to be seen by their students as individuals possessing high skill and knowledge levels. This, too, can create feelings of frustration and resentment on the part of students. No one likes to hear about all the things he or she is doing wrong. This type of negative approach places students in a position of defending what they presently do, as well as defending their previous instructor.

Instead, try a more positive approach. Seek out and praise the things a student is doing, selecting a rather minor flaw and suggesting steps for improvement. A more gradual process toward problem-solving can leave the student with positive feelings about his or her own performance level. At the same time, a student can leave a lesson without feeling frustrated. The saying "Rome wasn't built in a day" may never be more applicable than in your early contacts with students.

Don't criticize previous music literature

Be sure not to make an issue out of the quality of the literature that was previously programmed for your performing groups. New teachers often damage their relationships with their students and the developmental process when they attempt to "exorcise" students of "bad" music and bring about their musical salvation.

A more successful approach could be to review the literature previously performed, refraining from making anything more than very minor suggestions to aid the performance. After several "get-acquainted" rehearsals, present new material of a similar quality and level, and work hard on making it as accurate and musical as possible. All of the important performance elements (intonation, articulation, phrasing, rhythmic accuracy and precision, expression, etc.) can be improved upon and achieved through quality rehearsal efforts on music of any style or perceived quality. The pedagogical approach to "take them where they are, and guide them to where you want them to be" is perhaps never more appropriate than when a new director is presenting literature to a performing group early in their relationship.

Music educators new to a position must avoid public criticism of the music their students have performed in the past. The potential exists for students to personalize this criticism and subsequently respond accordingly. Students could see a teacher as criticizing them for what they just did during rehearsal, not what they did (or did not do) under someone else's direction during the past school year. Competent, confident, and knowledgeable music educators always establish a strong teacher-student relationship based on positive feelings. Again, a negative approach to previously programmed musical selections provides a perfect inspiration for defensive attitudes on the part of music students.

Don't be afraid to ask for help

Never be reluctant to ask an administrator for help. Keep in mind, however, as discussed in chapter 1, that when going to an administrator with what can be perceived as a problem associated with a new job, you should always be prepared to offer a solution, or variety of solutions, to the problem. Without offering a solution, you could be seen merely as a "complainer." If a solution cannot be offered, perhaps a problem does not really exist. Ideally, you want to be viewed as a person of vision. Offering solutions to existing problems aids that view.

Don't make comparisons

Be careful not to make comparisons to your former students, ensemble successes, or former school or administrators when attempting to make a musical or professional point with current students, parents, or administrators. Nothing worthwhile can be gained from making comparisons between past and present teaching experiences when dealing with any of the individuals involved in a new teaching situation.

Regardless of the situation or the cause surrounding the departure of a former music educator from a particular school, one thing is certain: a wide spectrum of student emotions will be associated with that departure. Such emotions can range from relief to betrayal, from anger to joy, from concern to anxiety, and more.

A particularly difficult environment for a new music educator is one in which the former teacher moves to a different position in the same school district. A "ghost" remains in the rehearsal room, an image of an individual who is still visible within the community as well. The difficulties to be overcome by a new teacher are related in direct proportion to the manner in which the former music educator handled (and continues to handle) his or her departure. For example, if the departing educator provides an informative and upbeat rationale for the career change, accompanied by statements of support for the incoming teacher, the possibilities of a smooth transition are dramatically increased.

The worst-case scenario is when some type of conflict is associated with the departure of any music teacher, ranging from serious disagreements with the administration, to charges of some type of misconduct, to poor contest ratings, to staff and program reductions. In such cases, there are those parental and student factions that support the departure and those that regret it, with the latter being the most vocal. It is difficult, but possible, for a new music teacher to achieve early success with performing groups in the midst of that type of adversity.

It will take an experienced music educator, one who is secure in his or her abilities and teaching skills, to bring some sense of order to a confused and emotionally charged group of student musicians.

PROACTIVITY TO THE RESCUE

Anticipation. All of the steps discussed in this chapter rely on a proactive approach to be effective. Another proactive step you can take is anticipating questions or statements from new students relating to previous instructional methods. If you anticipate student questions and comments and develop appropriate and professional responses, the likelihood of being caught off guard will be dramatically reduced. Responses that are ad libbed in haste when your professional credibility is threatened are generally much too defensive to be effective and taken seriously by questioning students.

Advance communication. Time permitting, a letter introducing yourself to all of the future choral and/or instrumental musicians at the middle or high school levels can contribute to a smooth instructional transition. The letter should be upbeat in nature and include comments concerning your educational and professional background, along with some short-term objectives and long-term goals for the music program. Sometime before the first day of school, you may also want to schedule get-acquainted meetings with student leaders or group officers, as well as the officers of the music booster organization, if one is in place.

The common thread that runs through any written or verbal communication with new music students and their parents is your commitment to work extremely hard to provide an enjoyable musical experience for all students.

Organization. The need to be organized, to prepare a structured instructional environment, is mentioned repeatedly in this book. That necessity is never more important than during the first meetings with your new students. To strive for perfection in rehearsal preparation and environment, leaving nothing to chance when working with new students, is likely the ultimate proactive step that can be taken by any teacher in a new teaching position.

Readers are urged to involve themselves totally in the positive and proactive approach to their work. Career satisfaction, success, and enjoyment will be the result.

Suggested Activities

1. As a class, determine five comments related to the former music instructor that students under the direction of a new teacher might make.
   a. Based on the material in this chapter, decide what would be the most appropriate response to each of the five comments.
   b. Are there any proactive steps that you feel could have been taken by the new music teacher to avoid some of the comments?
2. To what extent do you feel that multi-aged student participants in performing groups help or hinder a music teacher new to a position? Lead a class discussion on the subject.
3. What items of information do you think should be included in an introductory letter sent to music students by their new teacher prior to the official opening of the school year? Lead a class discussion regarding the importance of each item.

WITHIN THE SCHOOL

ENVIRONMENT

CHAPTER FIVE

EFFECTIVE
MUSIC BUDGET
PROCEDURES

INTRODUCTION

The financial support of music education programs across the United States has been in a state of gradual but identifiable change since the early 1970s. There are few schools in this country that have not been touched by the trend to reduce music budgets, staff, or both. Rising school costs, combined with declining school enrollment figures, have caused school administrators to seek ways to stretch limited tax dollars. Music programs, in many cases, have unjustifiably suffered severely from the budget-cutting process.

With declining tax dollar support for music education across the country, concerned parents and music educators have turned to outside fund-raising to support the type of program the school and community have come to expect. This need for alternative funding has placed an additional burden on the music education staff and often on the students participating in the program.

Seeking adequate funding to support a quality music education program can be a complex, demanding, and at times nearly overwhelming obligation for the music educator. This is particularly true at the secondary level, where performance groups are involved. Depending on the structure of the program and how it is viewed by the local school administration, the budgeting process is often the most demanding administrative task facing a music educator. For this reason, music educators need to develop business skills and learn budget procedures, as well as the pertinent vocabulary, and must gain a basic understanding of the total school budget structure. Only then can they estimate the amount of funding potentially available to the music program.

This chapter begins by giving an overview of the revenue sources available for a music education program. A brief rationale for the budget process is offered, followed by an overview of four types of music budgets: departmental, autonomous, split, and the "no budget" approach. These will be applied to both multi-unit and smaller school districts. A section on establishing the budget process discusses the pros and cons of single and multi-year budget plans. Finally, a comprehensive guide is given to organizing a budget plan, along with a complete sample budget for a grades five through twelve music program.

REVENUE SOURCES

For the purpose of simplification, potential revenue sources for the music education program are divided into five categories:

1. Taxes and state aid to education
2. Special funds collected by the music department
3. Fund-raising
4. Gifts
5. Grants

Taxes

All music educators, regardless of their years of service, should have a basic understanding of how their individual schools, and thus their music programs, are financed. Where does the money come from that they request on an annual basis in support of their instructional efforts? While there are no hard-and-fast rules regarding school finance throughout the United States, several things remain constant when determining financial support for public education.

Generally speaking, school districts are supported from tax monies collected from citizens and commercial entities residing within the boundaries of a particular school district. In some states, the amount of tax money allocated to each school district is determined by a city or county council or commission and, for the most part, is based on the budget figures submitted by the local school board. Regardless of the state, there is some degree of aid available to school districts to be used to support public education.

Schools in some states may find themselves tied to some type of "formula funding" enacted by the state legislature and administered by a state agency that limits each district to a maximum dollar figure that can be spent per pupil, per year in that school district. All schools in the state are placed under that maximum financial mandate. If the funding formula calls for a $4,000 per student per year ceiling, for example, and $2,400 per pupil was available for public education through local and county sources, then $1,600 per student would be forthcoming to the district from the state's general fund for that particular year.

The primary advantage to this method of financing public education is the stability built into the process from year to year: the $4,000 per pupil figure will be available next year, regardless of whether there is a reduction in tax revenue at the local level. Formula funding is usually linked with a cost-of-living index; therefore, the $4,000 figure could increase in subsequent years, based on cost-of-living figures in a state. The downside to funding education in this manner as seen by some so-called rich school districts is that state financial support for districts with lower tax bases is significantly higher than for the wealthier districts. The rich districts therefore feel that formula funding discriminates against school districts that have the capability, through their tax base, to raise more funds than some of their neighbors.

In addition to state and local monies that support public education, there are often county apportionments, utility grants or rebates, federal funds that support school districts through a hot lunch (and often breakfast) program, special education, math, science, and drug-free grant programs, as well as Title 1 programs supporting remedial reading and math.

Music education budgets generally are drawn from two special funds in each district: the *general fund* for supplies and instructional materials and the *capital outlay fund* for equipment purchases necessary for the successful day-to-day operation of any music department.

The school funding process is complicated and varies from state to state. Music educators should have a basic understanding of the potential school district sources of funding for their own budget requests and should make every effort to seek out that information at the local level. Any school administrator would be mildly surprised and genuinely appreciative of the effort put forth by a music educator to become better informed about school finance and the place of the music budget as part of the overall school budget process.

Special funds collected by the music department

This source of funding has great potential for contributing financial support to a music education program. For one reason or another, it also is a source that is largely ignored by music educators nationwide.

Admission fees for concerts are almost nonexistent at the public school level. For that matter, it is not all that common in higher education. A nominal fee associated with concerts is readily accepted by the public. The fact of the matter is, concertgoers expect it. The traditional "no admission fee" statement accompanying publicity for school concerts does nothing to attract additional audience members.

Charging admission for concerts also aids in publicizing the event. Advance ticket sales can be boosted through student participation in the effort. A $2 or $3 charge for adults attending each concert can bring a significant amount of money into the music budget. A reduced fee or perhaps no admission charge for students could be considered. Reduced ticket prices for senior citizens, or perhaps a "senior citizens free" policy, would be appropriate as well. Advertising the concerts at senior centers will increase the number of retirement-age people attending concerts.

Any music educator willing to change the "admission free" to an "admission fee" policy will be pleasantly surprised by the results. Charging a small fee for school concerts is simply a good administrative management procedure.

Rental fees for school-owned instruments and concert wear is another source of funding for the music education program. Many schools charge no use fee for instruments or uniforms owned by the school district. Those that do often charge less than the cost to maintain the equipment.

Most schools have a significant investment in musical instruments, as well as in uniforms, robes, and other concert wear, which are an important part of any performing group's inventory. Again, parents and students alike will not object to paying a reasonable fee for the use of school-owned equipment necessary to the music education program. An appropriate rental or use fee can be difficult to determine, but a general rule of thumb is twice the amount of the annual maintenance figure divided by the number of students using the equipment. For example, forty students might be using school instruments and the annual repair, overhead, and maintenance bill is $1,200. Doubling the dollar figure and dividing by 40 results in a $60 instrument fee per student, per year. The same principle applies to concert wear maintenance and cleaning. The excess funds beyond the actual maintenance expenditures can be placed in an equipment replacement fund. The rental or use fee may be higher than described, but it should never be lower.

Another legitimate benefit of charging some type of fee for the use of school-owned instruments and concert wear is that students tend to take better care of an item if they are paying for its use. Music educators have traditionally refrained from initiating rental or use fees because they feared a decrease in student participation would result. This is simply not the case.

Should the situation arise in which a student's family cannot afford the most nominal use fee, some type of agreement can be worked out between the student and group director for monthly payments of the fee or a possible work/service arrangement for the student in the department. No student should be denied access to a musical instrument or ensemble participation because of an inability to pay a rental or use fee.

If you plan to implement an admission or rental/use fee policy, review the goal and objective procedures presented in chapter 1 regarding approach, information dissemination, and follow-up.

The activity fund/activity tickets

Most schools have a established system whereby all students are encouraged to purchase for a nominal fee an activity ticket that allows the purchaser "free" admission to a majority of school-sponsored events that occur during the course of the school year, ranging from concerts to athletic events. Because of royalty obligations, school theater productions generally do not appear on the list of school-sponsored activities. The activity fee can amount to many thousands of dollars, and this income is more than likely part of a school's general fund.

Because the music department is a prolific contributor to the success of many of these activities, a music educator should consult with the school's principal to determine if any of the funds can be allotted to the department.

Fund-raising

In the mid-1980s total funds (taxes, funds raised, grants, etc.) supporting a typical music program were increasing approximately 3 percent per year. This increase was occurring despite the fact that tax monies supporting music programs were decreasing 1.3 percent per year. Funds raised by music students and their parents became a significant factor in supporting public school music education.

In the 1970s about 48 percent of a school's music budget came from fund-raising. By the mid-1990s that figure had increased to 70 percent, a dramatic increase. By 1997 available money (from all sources) to support school music budgets increased by a total of 22 percent. Of this total increase, 13 percent was received from tax monies and 26 percent was a result of heightened fund-raising activities.

Clearly, music programs have benefited from moderately increased financial support from individual school districts. It is somewhat disturbing, however, that the majority of funds supporting music education programs in the U.S. come as a result of fund-raising efforts on the part of music students and their parents.

Bands and choirs at the junior high school level are beginning to be involved in travel in unprecedented ways. A music parent proudly described to this writer the thousands of miles her children had traveled as members of their junior high school band. This trend is of concern to music educators across the country, especially secondary choral, orchestra, and band directors, who fear that extensive travel and performance opportunities prior to high school can cause burnout and reduce student participation in music ensembles at the secondary level. Travel also requires a significant amount of funding, which results in substantial financial demands on the total music education budget.

The number of students involved in music performance schoolwide continues to increase at a moderate rate each year, which in itself causes a need for increased funding in music education. This rising participation level and increased travel on the part of performance groups are perhaps the two greatest reasons for increased fund-raising by music students and their parents in today's schools. In recent years, booster organizations have become more active in the support of musical performance groups. Currently 96 percent of the high schools in this country are involved, in one way or another, in fund-raising; 91 percent of those high schools have booster organizations, whose primary goal is to raise funds to support music programs.

Fortunate is the music educator who is employed in a school system which supports the following administrative policy: if a program is worthy of being a part of that school, then it is worthy of being funded by that school. Of course, this administrative attitude is the exception rather than the rule, and music educators must accept fund-raising as a realistic part of their budget process if program activities are to be sustained at current levels. The subject of fund-raising and parents' organizations is so important and so much a part of music education in today's schools that chapter 12 is devoted to this subject.

Gifts

Local businesses, corporate and private foundations, as well as wealthy individuals can all be a source of additional funding for music education. Donations from performances for private organizations, parades, or similar functions cannot be ignored as a potential revenue source. Local service and music clubs are also potential sources. Outright donations often result from some special fund-raising effort in support of a particular event, cause, or trip. Music scholarships or music camp stipends often come from service and music clubs within a community. Numerous music educators have been surprised by the financial support available for their programs that is simply there for the asking.

THE BUDGET PROCESS

Imagine the chaos that would result in even the smallest school district if an organized approach to determining annual budget needs did not exist. The system, as cumbersome as it often appears to be, is the only logical manner in which a school district can handle public monies with a high degree of responsibility and accountability. The requesting of bids on items to be purchased, the voucher system, and the need to file purchase orders prior to buying equipment and supplies can often appear to be a needless exercise. These procedures, however, provide the type of fiscal documentation of expenditures of public monies that the taxpayers expect and deserve.

The budget process allows the school district and the associated government agencies to project school program needs into the future. Based on past expenditures for particular programs, school administrators can predict program needs, not only for the next budget year, but for the next several years. A music educator can positively influence this part of the budget process by submitting a multi-year budget request, a procedure that will be discussed later in this chapter.

Estimated revenue

The budget process also requires the estimation of anticipated revenue from the sources that financially support a school district. Local and state government agencies must be actively involved in the projection of tax revenue available for dispersal to public education.

Projected expenditures

School administrators must compile detailed and accurate estimates of all anticipated expenditures. A good administrator will request input in this portion of the process from even the smallest program in the school district and will insist that a budget proposal be submitted for music education.

Funds to be raised

Should the anticipated expenditures considerably exceed the anticipated revenue for a school district, school administrators must raise additional funds through increased tax support and government grants or reduce the amount of expenditures for the district. This need to limit expenditures has adversely affected music education in recent years and has resulted in increased fund-raising efforts by music educators and parents who support the program.

By preparing and submitting an annual budget request, the music educator assists in the overall operation of the school. Planned spending for any program is an important demonstration of the competence of an educational administrator.

TYPES OF MUSIC BUDGETS

There is no single budget type or plan for music education programs. Four of the more common approaches to budgeting for the needs of a successful music program are presented here.

Departmental budget

This plan is generally found in large school systems and is compiled by a music supervisor or music coordinator. Budget support for all music activities within the entire system, from preschool to senior high, is included in the departmental budget request. The final proposal is submitted by the music supervisor to the superintendent of schools or the business manager of the school district. The plan allows the music supervisor to ensure unity throughout the district for the entire music ogram, but care must be taken to coordinate budgetary planning with other de-rtment heads and building principals.

utonomous budget

This type of budgeting for music programs also is generally used in cities with .rge school districts where a music supervisor or coordinator oversees individual rograms. However, in the autonomous budget approach, each school or unit .vithin the district is granted funding according to the activity level of the music program in that particular school. The music educator compiles a budget document and submits it to the building principal. The principal includes the music budget in the total budget request, then submits the schoolwide budget package to the superintendent or business manager.

The danger of the autonomous budget style is that it fragments the total music program and creates a balance problem throughout the entire district. The music supervisor has little or no control over the budget process, which reduces his or her effectiveness in administering the entire program.

Highly visible and active school music programs are likely to receive greater budget support. Yet the total activity of a music program cannot be used as the only measure of that program's success: the quality of the program's activity must be considered. It can be argued that the more active programs are justified in receiving greater budgetary support than their less active counterparts in the same district, but the primary problem with the autonomous budget procedure is the degree of administrative control taken out of the hands of the music supervisor.

Split budget

The split budget approach allows for separate budget requests from all music units within a given school. The band, choir, orchestra, and general music sections all have to submit individual budget requests. This approach to securing funds for a music program most often is used in smaller school districts where no single individual is charged with the responsibility of program coordination. There is often a lack of real communication between group directors, and the potential for dissension and animosity is great.

The split budget may make up part of either the departmental or autonomous budget plans but is not in itself a positive approach toward securing funds for music education. Music educators have felt for years that "no school should have a vocal music program, an instrumental music program, and a general music program. All should have a *music* program, which includes all possible avenues of activity and experience" (Snyder 1965, p. 197).

"No budget" budget

The "no budget" approach to funding music education exists when the school administrator allows the music educator to present expenditure requests "as the need arises," then takes positive or negative action on each request. This practice occurs most frequently in small school districts where school officials pay lip service to wanting a quality music education program and where they are dealing with an inexperienced music educator. It literally requires the music educator to beg for financial support for the program. Knowledgeable music educators and school administrators alike realize that a no budget approach toward program funding is a totally unacceptable and unsuccessful administrative procedure.

Although the first three approaches to budgeting are flawed to some degree, the no budget approach holds absolutely no future for building a strong music program. If you should find yourself in a school music program with no specific budget, you may decide to accept the status quo for one year. During that year, seek administrative approval for a budget proposal for the following year. If the approval is not forthcoming, you can then decide to either accept the situation, realizing there is little chance for improvement, or seek a position in another school system.

MULTI-UNIT SCHOOL DISTRICT BUDGET PROCEDURES

In a school district with several junior and senior high schools, as well as numerous elementary schools, a combination of the first three types of budget approaches would be the most appropriate. For example, a departmental budget generated by a music supervisor and based on requests by music departments throughout the district would be a logical first step. The various units in each school would compile their own individual budget requests, then submit them as one budget document, representative of the needs of the entire music department of that school. The music supervisor would organize all the department requests into a single document and in the end would distribute funds to the various schools within the district based on the amount of money allocated districtwide to music education.

There is no single system that can be presented as the ultimate approach to the budget process for music education in large school systems; there are too many variables involved. One factor should remain constant, however, and that is the high level of involvement on the part of the music supervisor in the procurement and allocation of funds for music education in the entire district. This involvement is necessary to maintain the continuity of the music education curriculum throughout the school system.

SMALL SCHOOL DISTRICT BUDGET PROCEDURES

For the purposes of this discussion, a small school district comprises one high school. A small district can have only one music educator or several teachers, each with an area of speciality. The approach to budgeting used in this system combines most of the elements of the split budget with some of the elements of the autonomous budget plan. When no music supervisor or coordinator is involved, the teachers responsible for the band, choir, orchestra, and general music classes must develop their own budgets. The primary ingredient for success in this approach is that the requests must be submitted to the administration as a total package for the department as a whole. This process requires a degree of leadership on the part of one music educator in bringing the various requests together in a single package. Separate budget proposals from the choir, band, and so on can only provide an opportunity for hard feelings and dissension to occur.

The music educator who is solely responsible for the music program in a small school will submit a budget that combines general, vocal, and instrumental needs in a single request package. In this situation, the music educator is also responsible for the continuity and balance of the program.

ESTABLISHING A BUDGET PLAN

There are three situations in which a budget plan needs to be developed: (1) a music educator is in a first-year position and no budget plan for the music program exists; (2) an experienced music educator accepts a new teaching position and is dissatisfied with the existing budget; (3) a music educator, established in the position, decides to seek an expanded base of funding through a different approach to budget development. All three situations can be approached in somewhat the same manner. But, in the first case especially, the music educator needs to recognize the need for establishing a budget plan. The *why* question must be answered.

An effective budget plan aids the administration in determining the total fiscal needs for the school district and in planning for the future. When the music department's financial needs appear as part of the overall school budget, the credibility and importance of the program are bolstered. A budget plan allows the music educator to formulate highly organized plans for controlled growth and development. Because the curriculum usually involves equipment of one kind or another, new equipment must be budgeted for, and maintenance expenses must be anticipated. For example, it is not uncommon for elementary or middle school general music programs to have computers in their classrooms, but limited funds with which to acquire necessary software.

Most important, the budget plan provides the music educator with an opportunity to justify the program. Without a line in the total school budget, it is difficult to justify the existence of music education on even the best of philosophical grounds. When the music educator is allowed to submit an annual budget proposal, the opportunity is also available to justify to the school district administration and the members of the school board increased support for the program. A logical, professional approach toward an effective plan for procuring and dispersing funds is simply a good procedure for all involved to follow. Far too often those music educators blessed with supportive administrations that allow them to submit annual budget requests look upon the occasion as an obligation, a task to be completed, rather than what it actually is: an opportunity to justify, build, and develop the music education programs in their schools.

DECIDING ON A BUDGET APPROACH

There are two primary approaches to the submission of a budget request: the annual budget proposal and the multi-year plan (usually three to five years), which is generally reserved for major equipment expenditures. Both methods are very effective when the proper organizational groundwork has been completed in conjunction with the proposal.

The *annual budget* represents a yearlong effort on the part of a music educator. The request consists of a list of categories, or *line items,* with additional subcategories. Accurate records of expenditures and future needs should be kept on a weekly, if not daily, basis. Retail costs of any projected purchases must be included, along with approximate bid prices, and any piece of equipment to be used as a trade-in on new equipment should also be noted. Some time should also be spent investigating new products, which come on the market with increasing frequency.

The *multi-year budget* is useful in outlining suggested major expenditures, particularly when the cost of the equipment needs to be distributed over more than one fiscal year. For example, suppose a high school music program has only two timpani, both in poor condition, no chimes, no xylophone or vibraphone, and no choral risers, and the music room piano is a 1925 upright model with a cracked soundboard. Needless to say, that program is in trouble. If a music educator were to ask the school superintendent for $20,000 to replace the old equipment and to purchase additional equipment, the response most likely would be negative. However, if the educator submitted a budget that extended the equipment costs over a three-year period at approximately $6,500 per year, or over a five-year period at $4,000 per year, the request would be more manageable in the eyes of the administration. The music educator has furnished the superintendent and school board with alternative solutions to a serious music department deficiency.

When submitting any multi-year plan, it is always wise to indicate what effect inflation will have on the cost of the same equipment in three or five years. For example, a piano purchased today could cost about $4,000; in three years, that figure could be $4,500, and in five years, $5,200. Any reliable music dealer would be pleased to assist a music educator in developing a multi-year budget proposal, complete with approximate bid prices and three- and five-year inflation projections.

It is possible that when the proposal is presented to the school board for discussion, some board members will note that the district can save over $5,000 by purchasing all the equipment immediately rather than dividing the cost over a three- or five-year period. The school board might even approve the immediate purchase of the equipment. All affected music educators should attend the board meeting to answer questions and to provide support for the request.

ORGANIZING THE BUDGET REQUEST

The level of acceptance of any budget request is directly related to the manner in which it is organized and submitted. In interviews with music educators in preparation for this book, the author asked for a copy of their most recent budget proposals. What resulted were far too many handwritten, generally sloppy, and poorly structured budget proposals. To a person, the same music educators complained about inadequate budget support, the lack of adequate equipment, and a general lack of administrative interest in the music education program. These instructors are missing a tremendous annual opportunity to justify their programs and at the same time generate support, both moral and financial, for music education in their school systems. What follows is a step-by-step plan for developing a successful budget request for music education programs.

The cover letter

The budget should include a concise cover letter that provides an explanation for the request. Because the cover letter is the first item in the budget proposal, it must be carefully structured to encourage the reader to consider thoughtfully the information that follows. General support information should not be presented at this point, but should be included in the "Support Materials" section, which appears later in the request. It can certainly be mentioned in the cover letter that this material exists, and perhaps even a brief summary of the material would be in order. At any rate, this portion of the budget proposal definitely depends on the personality of the music educator, his or her relationship with the school administration, the history of past budget requests, and the size of the request. Bear in mind that the cover letter is an important aspect of a professional budget proposal.

Budget summary

Following the cover letter is a summary of the budget. To be effective, the budget request should be divided into at least eleven line-item categories. In the summary, administrators and administrative boards will be more interested in the total budget figure than in the various elements that go into it. For example, it would be better to list the total music library cost of $2,300 than to note that the marching band needs music totaling $800, the concert band, music totaling $600, and the choir, music totaling $900. This breakdown can be listed on another page as subcategories of the budget.

The eleven line-item categories are as follows:

1. New equipment
2. Replacement equipment
3. Music library
4. Travel
5. Awards
6. Printing and publicity
7. Repair and maintenance
8. Contest and festival fees
9. Contractual services
10. Concert wear maintenance
11. Contingency

Dollar amounts accompanying each line item, anticipated nondistrict income (if any), and a total budget figure at the bottom of the page are all that is included as part of the budget summary. This page should be widely spaced and uncluttered, with the information readily available to the reader.

BUDGET DESCRIPTION BY LINE ITEM

The next section of the budget request includes a list of the eleven line items and accompanying subcategories, complete with a list of separate needs within each subcategory.

New equipment

In this category, any equipment new to the program is listed. For example, if an additional piano or a new bassoon is requested, and neither one is actually replacing an old or obsolete instrument, the item would be listed in the budget proposal under "New Equipment." The rationale for the purchase of new equipment can be presented in the "Support Information" section of the budget request, which appears as the final section of the proposal.

Replacement equipment

If a piece of equipment is traded, sold, or retired from use and new equipment is requested as its replacement, the request appears here. Documentation for the need for equipment replacement is very important and should appear in the "Support Information" section. This might include the approximate trade-in value of the old instrument and the new equipment's approximate life expectancy, as well as its importance and relevance to the music education program.

Music library

All library materials—books, tapes, recordings, films, computer software, music, and other related items—are requested here. Anything that can be even vaguely associated with the music library is listed as part of this line item. Special nonmusical supplies, such as file folders, tape, and labels, are usually available from the main office of the school and need not be included here. The music educator can also consult the school librarian to see if school library funds can be used to purchase materials other than printed music to support the music library. School librarians often have access to government funds, part of which they are willing to release for music-related library materials; however, the music educator, more often than not, must take the initiative to secure these funds.

Travel

Included in this line item are anticipated travel expenditures associated in any way with the music education program. This category includes both student and educator travel expenses incurred during the year and should cover transportation, meals, and lodging. School districts have a standard per diem rate established for staff travel that regulates maximum reimbursement for travel expenses. The music educator should review this policy prior to budgeting for student and personal travel. Student travel expenses, for example, can include contest and festival travel, all-state auditions and participation travel, special out-of-town concerts, and similar events. Travel expenses for the music educator to attend state and regional professional association meetings are most definitely the responsibility of the school district and should be included here. A special note: Be sure to carefully observe deadlines for submitting personal and group travel requests for administrative approval.

Awards

The inclusion of an awards line item in the music education budget is in no way to be considered an endorsement for awards programs in music education.

Awards, however, are an integral part of many band, choir, and orchestra programs. If a music educator has a system for providing awards to students, the cost of providing those awards must be included in the budget proposal. It is not uncommon for a music instructor to have some type of annual fund-raising project for the express purpose of supporting the purchase of student awards. If this is the case, awards should still appear in the budget proposal and funds raised should appear elsewhere in the request as income.

Printing and publicity

Far too many school concerts are presented each year accompanied by poorly produced, photocopied programs for the audience. The audience and students deserve better, and the music education program has an obligation to provide a neat and informative printed program for concertgoers and performers alike. The music educator has the responsibility to project a positive image of the program, and a printed concert program is part of that image. Most music educators have access to a computer, desktop publishing software, and a laser or ink-jet printer that can expedite the layout and eventual in-house printing of programs. If appropriate equipment is not available for in-house printing of programs, a music educator should secure bids for a typical four-page program for each concert from a local printer and include associated costs as part of the budget proposal.

Promotional mailings, newspaper and radio ads, and film for student photos, along with any other publicity-related expense are included in this line item.

Repair and maintenance

The repair and maintenance line item of a budget request can often be underestimated, particularly when extensive repair and overhaul of wind, percussion, and stringed instruments is involved. When budgeting for this type of work, the music educator should have reasonably solid bid figures from a repair shop to submit as part of the budget proposal. Repair costs and equipment overhaul rates have increased significantly in recent years, but a quality, top-line instrument that is properly overhauled can provide many years of service at a fraction of the cost of a new piece of equipment.

Also difficult to predict is the number of expensive emergency repairs to school-owned instruments. Perhaps the best guide is to determine the dollar figure spent on this type of maintenance in previous years and add a percentage to cover inflation to that amount.

In addition to all planned and unplanned instrument repair and overhaul, tuning of pianos, repair of equipment other than musical instruments, and all repair supplies needed by the band and orchestra directors should be included in this line item. Be certain to estimate adequately the number of tunings needed by school pianos and obtain a performance bid from a local piano technician as part of the budget proposal.

Contest and festival fees

Performance is a natural result and benefit of participation in a music education program. Contest and festival opportunities abound for all levels of solo and ensemble participants and for marching and concert bands, choirs, and orchestras, as well as the more select groups that are associated with a respective large ensemble. You need only pick up a monthly music journal to see the variety of festival opportunities available throughout the year for school music organizations. These festivals are in addition to the local and regional events scheduled annually by individual schools and professional music organizations. Generally, participation fees are charged for these events.

If the contest or festival has the support of the local music education staff and the school administration, the entrance fee required for participation in the event should be paid by the school district and not the students involved. The students are representing the school as part of a music program supported by the school and simply cannot be asked to pay any fee associated with that representation. Music educators need to plan contest and festival appearances very carefully. Advance costs for these events are reasonably easy to determine and should pose no particular difficulty when it comes to estimating expenditures. In addition, all fees associated with all-state and any other honor group participation should be included as part of the contest and festival fee request. Any travel expenditures for students or staff that will result from contest or festival participation can be included as part of the travel line item.

Contractual services

Fees for soloists, clinicians, adjudicators, and any other outside type of service for the music education program should be included here. Any compensation for work associated with the music program should also be included in this line item: outside-the-school accompanists, recording costs, and equipment transportation are several examples. With the increased sophistication of marching band drill and music, many band programs spend upwards of $5,000 for their annual competitive show and musical arrangements. Even directors in small high schools are contracting with specialists to write their drill for them each year. Any costs associated with writing, arranging, or teaching any element of a marching band show should appear under this item unless paid for by the local booster organization.

Most successful school music programs employ guest artists and outside clinicians in some manner on an annual basis. The constructive criticism and positive reinforcement that evolves from student and teacher association with professional artists and music educators is a most viable and legitimate expense for any music education program. Dedicated music educators are eager to expose their students to musical concepts and opinions other than their own and are fully aware of the long-range benefits those outside ideas bring to the music program. Outside involvement of artists and clinicians in school concert performances should be seen as a legitimate strength of a music education program.

Concert wear maintenance

The proper cleaning and storage of uniforms, choir robes, and other concert wear can add years of use to the lives of these garments and contribute significantly to their appearance during that lifetime. Annual dry cleaning of concert wear is an absolute minimum, and, in the case of band uniforms, which are used frequently during the fall marching season, two cleanings per year are certainly in order. Bid figures per unit to be cleaned, solicited from dry-cleaning operators serving the local area, can be used to calculate this line-item amount. To reduce costs, a trend in recent years has been to require users of instrumental and choral concert wear to return the garments to the school freshly dry-cleaned at their own expense.

Also included in this category can be such adjunct items as good wooden hangers and proper storage racks. Preventive maintenance items, such as rain gear for marching band uniforms, should appear as part of the new equipment request.

Contingency

Every realistic budget request includes a line item for emergencies that may arise that require some type of expenditure. Rather than appealing to the board of education through the school administration for supplementary funding, a music educator in an administrative role should have access to contingency funding as part of the total music budget. Countless unplanned situations can arise during a school year that require some financial support. The marching band, for example, could get caught in a rainstorm during the first parade of the year and the uniforms need to be cleaned immediately; two of the new choir members could be either very large or very small, and additional concert wear is needed; perhaps the orchestra receives an invitation to perform at a regional conference, and supplementary travel funds are required. One thing is certain, however: emergency situations involving a certain amount of expense will occur. The most expedient and professional manner in which these situations can be handled is to have a contingency fund as part of the annual music education budget request. By the way, this is the only budget line item that need not be exhausted each year. An annual carryover of funds in the contingency line item is appropriate, school policy permitting.

Bear in mind that these eleven categories represent a basic minimum into which a music budget request may be divided. As the need arises, line items or divisions can be added to support a particular program concept or philosophy.

SUPPORT INFORMATION

Following the budget summary and description, justification for the budget request is included in this section. This includes specific reference to particular line items, as well as comprehensive support information.

A general statement of justification for the request can open this section, followed perhaps by cost-per-pupil figures. A comparison of music budgets in area schools of similar size can also be included. For example, most schools belong to an athletic conference for varsity sports programs. If a music educator can gather music budget information from all the schools in the athletic conference, he or she can make a case for increased financial support. One way to present this information is to average all conference music budgets and also specifically point out which schools have the highest music budgets in the conference. If averaging the conference music budgets does not provide a distinct benefit to the proposal in terms of support information, then abandon the averaging concept and use as examples the conference schools with higher music budgets. School administrators are by nature somewhat competitive and necessarily proud of their schools, and very often budget comparisons lend credence to a music budget proposal if it can be demonstrated that other area schools are giving their music programs better support.

School administrators and their boards of education rarely realize the number of school and community appearances made by the music performing groups in their own schools. Add to in-school performances all contest and festival performances, musical productions, and appearances at civic and social functions and the resulting figure generally becomes very impressive. Include a complete list of all appearances and performances in this section of the annual budget request to demonstrate to the school administration the full extent of the music program's activities.

Cost-per-pupil figures in support of a budget request are often extremely effective. To determine this, take the total budget request (do not include teacher salary figures) and divide that figure by the number of students involved in all performing groups and classes that will be affected by the music budget. The resulting amount is what it costs the school district per pupil for the music education program in that school for one year. The resulting total will be surprisingly small when compared with other programs within the school because of the large number of students touched by the music program.

Following the general statement, a justification for each line-item expense should be given. For example, if a new oboe and bassoon are requested, the music educator might include under the head "New Equipment" comments by adjudicators at past music contests indicating a need for double reeds in the band. In addition, he or she might assign a life expectancy to each new piece of equipment, with the cost of the equipment divided by that life expectancy. The resulting dollar amount is the annual cost to the school district for the life of the equipment. Such figures generally are very low. For example, a bassoon with a purchase price of $3,000 and a life expectancy of thirty years (in a district that maintains its instruments) results in a cost-per-year figure of $100 to purchase the instrument. Because new equipment is often the most difficult expense to justify, as much support information as possible should be included.

Replacement equipment is easier to justify because the school district already owns a similar piece of equipment. The support information should include the approximate age of the equipment, its present condition, why it shouldn't or can't be repaired, and the future cost-per-year to the school district. Music stores with quality, full-service instrument repair departments are more than happy to assist in developing this information. Given adequate support information, administrators and school boards are frequently receptive to equipment replacement requests.

The music library line-item support information can include a statement citing increased costs of music purchase and rental over the past ten years. A performance group director need only identify a set of music purchased ten years earlier and a set of recently purchased music and compare cost figures to point out how drastically inflation has affected such purchases. The number of students served by the music purchased is another valid piece of support information. In addition, you might point out that technology has drastically increased the number of items available and necessary to a music education program.

Travel for the purpose of student participation in contests, festivals, honor groups, auditions, and performances at athletic events is readily supported by school administrators. Personal travel by the music educator to professional conferences is another matter. To make a compelling case for this expense, a music educator needs to identify other music instructors in the district who receive per diem assistance for the purpose of attending professional conferences. He or she might also seek information about the district's degree of financial support provided for athletic coaches who attend clinics and state-level events, to support the personal portion of the budget request. It is the responsibility of the school district to financially assist music educators in staying up-to-date with the myriad of innovative instructional practices and technical advances in music education by encouraging and supporting attendance at state, regional, and national conferences and clinics.

The support information for printing and publicity is primarily associated with performing groups and subsequent concert performances. This category does not require a great deal of financial support. It can be pointed out that music stores commonly offer to subsidize the printing of concert programs. While some music educators feel that program printing is a school-associated responsibility, commercial financial assistance in the printing of concert programs is a budget-saving idea worthy of consideration.

The age, present condition, and anticipated life expectancy of equipment to be overhauled should be included as support information for the repair and maintenance line item. The cost of new equipment can be compared with the expense of overhauling equipment presently owned by the school district. Routine repair and maintenance of music equipment is simply a responsibility that comes with owning the equipment. This portion of the line item can be supported by costs incurred in previous years. Administrators understand that the useful life expectancy of a piece of equipment can be extended through a regular maintenance program and are apt to enthusiastically support this portion of the budget request.

Contest and festival fees are relatively easy to justify based on expenditures in past years. Increased entry fees and additional participation in contests or festivals are more than likely the two principal causes of a funding increase and would require further substantiation.

Comparison with area school music programs might be useful in providing support information for contractual services. This line item need not be an extravagant annual request but should allow exposure of music students to concepts and ideas from clinicians and music educators outside the system. The point can be made that inviting professionals not affiliated with the school district to provide lectures, concerts, and clinics on a regular basis creates an atmosphere conducive to ongoing program evaluation. This benefit, in addition to furnishing the opportunity to remain professional and up-to-date, is an administrative tool that cannot be overlooked. As noted earlier, any costs associated with writing drill and music for the marching band and choreography for the show choir should appear under this line item.

The same philosophy that justified repair of instruments explains the need for concert wear maintenance. That is, uniforms, robes, and other garments used in musical performances need to be routinely dry cleaned, stored, and maintained to provide optimum return to the school district on a very large investment. Several hundred dollars of annual maintenance cost to protect an investment of many thousands of dollars is a concept that should be readily acceptable to school administrators.

As previously indicated, all realistic budget requests include a contingency, or emergency, line item. It is impossible to anticipate and plan for every situation that requires funding during the year. All music educators can recall numerous situations during their careers that called for some type of emergency expenditure. A contingency fund included as part of the music budget is the most expedient and administratively effective manner in which to handle unanticipated circumstances requiring financial resolution. Any monies remaining unspent in the contingency line item should be carried over into the budget for the following year and shown as income, thereby reducing the contingency request from the figure represented in the previous budget period.

These methods of gathering and supplying support information for a budget request are offered only as guidelines. Support information will certainly vary and will be presented in a different style when this budget model is applied to a specific school situation.

PREPARATION AND PRESENTATION OF THE BUDGET PROPOSAL

A final concern in preparing the budget document is the format of the separate sections of the proposal. The major format guideline is to leave a great deal of white space when typing each page. The budget request will read more easily and have a much better chance of being considered by the appropriate individuals if the format is clean, uncrowded, and uncluttered. Include more pages in the proposal, but make each page easily readable and accessible.

After the document is submitted to the appropriate administrative budget agent, the music educator should plan on being called upon to defend the proposal to the school administration. If properly prepared, the budget proposal will nearly speak for itself, but the music educator can humanize the proposal by personally explaining any portions of the request that relate directly to students or student ensembles. The music educator should also plan to appear at a board of education meeting when the budget request is to be discussed. However, he or she should attend strictly as an interested observer and a source of additional information, if needed.

At first glance, this approach to compiling a music budget request may appear both tedious and time-consuming. Yet very few worthwhile accomplishments result from minimum effort. The reader is also reminded that once the initial work is completed, a budget format can be prepared in future years by simply changing figures, descriptions, and some support information.

If a professional, businesslike approach is used to demonstrate a need for funding to support a music education program, the chances of the proposal being carefully considered at the school administrative level are vastly improved.

ADMINISTRATION OF THE BUDGET

Following the approval of the budget request, a systematic means of administering the budget must be implemented. A small ledger can be purchased and a section devoted to each line-item category. Computer software designed to track income and expenditures is also available. If that is not an option, almost every school has at least one individual on the instructional staff who could design a program tailored to the specific budgetary and record-keeping needs of the music educator.

At all times, the music educator needs to have an approximate idea of the funds remaining in each line item. School office personnel can also be a great help in updating balances. All schools now have computerized bookkeeping systems that produce periodic printouts, an important aid in the accounting process.

Every attempt should be made to avoid overspending on any line item. A certain amount of overdrawing on occasion can be expected, but habitual overspending will be looked upon as poor or sloppy management and negate positive benefits to be derived from the budget process.

Finally, a reminder file needs to be established for budget purposes. Upon checking school policy, the music educator might learn that it is not necessary to budget for student travel, that school bus costs are anticipated in a school transportation fund. School policy theoretically could also prohibit the carryover, from one year to another, of contingency funds. There could be a variety of school-associated provisions that would influence the "anticipated income" and the "anticipated expenses" structure, in the sample budget. However, it is the format, with its division of the proposal into three logical and comprehensible sections, that provides strength to this particular budget procedure.

The music educator should place planning dates on the calendar indicating when to begin the annual budget preparation process. In doing so, the chaos and panic that results when the school administrator announces that "all budget requests are due in the office in two days" can be avoided. More important, a budget proposal prepared in haste, without much thought given it, is likely to be treated in a like manner. Music educators receive daily mailings about new equipment, concepts, materials, programs, and publications. Those that warrant further consideration can be placed in the reminder file and studied during the budget process for the following year. Ideas for equipment and materials evolve throughout the year. Unless these ideas are noted and revived at budget time, there is a very good chance they will not be remembered until it is too late to include them in the budget request. A reminder file is simply another administrative tool to help keep a very busy music educator organized and efficient.

Budget preparation and administration is an obligation that can't be taken lightly. However, if you learn to accept the budget as a professional challenge, you may actually begin to enjoy the process. To be successful in your chosen career, you must take responsibility for providing resources for the program at the maximum level the school and community can afford. This effort can be an extremely rewarding and satisfying aspect of music education administration.

The Role of Booster Clubs

It has become common for booster organizations to be involved in some manner in the budget process. These organizations' roles in raising funds to support music education will be presented at length in chapter 12.

Sample Budget Request

A sample budget proposal dealing with the needs of a hypothetical music program is shown in Figures 5.1–5.4. It is an example of a proposal that might be submitted by one music educator charged with the responsibility of administering a program in a small school system, grades five through twelve. The sample is included to demonstrate a budget request format and to provide a model for its actual use. The dollar values assigned the various pieces of equipment, as well as other budget items, are given for demonstration only, not as a recommendation for actual costs.

The format presented here works equally well for large music programs with many staff members; it also applies readily to separate choral, orchestra, or band budget requests. Simple adjustment in line items is all that might be required. The process and format remain the same.

Figure 5.1. Sample budget cover letter

Mr. I. M. Smart, Superintendent
Bea Flat Public Schools

Dear Mr. Smart:

Enclosed please find the 1998—99 music department budget proposal. Please note that the request represents only a 3% increase over the 1997—98 budget proposal of just under $18,000.00. It also must be mentioned that of the $18,545.00 total figure, only $9,600.00 is requested in Bea Flat School District funds.

Section One of this proposal is the summary of anticipated needs and income. Section Two includes a more detailed breakdown of each budget line item, and Section Three provides support material and additional information pertaining to the budget request.

Information included in Section Three indicates low per-pupil costs for music education in the Bea Flat schools, and the level of requested school district funds remains below the average for music programs in other Southwest Conference schools. Included information also indicates that the activity level for appearances by students associated with the music education program remain high.

Finally, please note that the number of students enrolling in the music education program continues to increase. It is respectfully requested that budget support be forthcoming to sustain program quality and to maintain a systematic pattern of growth. This budget proposal reflects an honest, yet conservative representation of funding needs for music education in the Bea Flat Public Schools for the 1998—99 academic year. There is no "fat" included in the request and it is hoped it will be considered in that light.

Sincerely,

John C. Kleff
Music Instructor

Figure 5.2. Sample budget summary

```
                        Section One

                  1998-99 Budget Summary
                    Music Department,
                  Bea Flat Public Schools



ANTICIPATED INCOME

Source                                      Amount

Student Activity Fund                    $1,800.00

Music Boosters                            2,500.00

Student Fund Raising                      1,245.00

1997-98 Contingency                         390.00

Concert Admission                         1,500.00

Rental/Use Fees                             860.00

Arts Council Grant                          650.00

Bea Flat School District                  9,600.00

TOTAL                                   $18,545.00


ANTICIPATED EXPENSES

Line Item                                   Amount

New Equipment                            $3,960.00

Replacement Equipment                     6,400.00

Music Library                             1,340.00

Travel                                    1,160.00

Awards                                      285.00

Printing and Publicity                      380.00

Repair and Maintenance                    1,390.00

Contest/Festival Fees                       460.00

Contractual Services                      1,650.00

Concert Wear Maintenance                  1,020.00

Contingency                                 500.00

TOTAL                                   $18,545.00
```

Figure 5.3. Sample budget description

Section Two

1998-99 Budget Description
Music Department,
Bea Flat Public Schools

NEW EQUIPMENT

Item	Retail	App. Bid	Subtotal	
Concert Chimes	$3,800.00	$ 2,200.00	$2,200.00	
40 Choral Folders	5.00	4.00	160.00	
Used Baritone Saxophone	1,900.00	1,600.00	1,600.00	
TOTAL			$3,960.00	$3,960.00

REPLACEMENT EQUIPMENT

Item	Retail	Less Trade	Subtotal	
French Horn	$1,400.00	$400.00	$1,000.00	
Oboe	1,350.00	550.00	800.00	
One Set Choral Risers	2,600.00	-----	2,600.00	
Concert Tuba	2,400.00	400.00	2,000.00	
TOTAL			$6,400.00	$6,400.00

MUSIC LIBRARY

Ensemble	Retail	School Price	Subtotal
Marching Band	$ 320.00	$ 280.00	$280.00
Concert Band	450.00	450.00	450.00
Choir	360.00	360.00	360.00
Small Ensemble	250.00	250.00	250.00
TOTAL			$1,340.00

Figure 5.3. Continued

TRAVEL

Student	Trans- portation	Meals/ Lodging	Subtotal	
Music Contest	$400.00	$----	$400.00	
All-State Auditions	80.00	----	80.00	
Tri-State Festival	340.00	100.00	440.00	
Instructor				
State Conference	120.00	60.00	180.00	
All-State Concert	60.00	----	60.00	
TOTAL			$1,160.00	$1,160.00

AWARDS	Subtotal	
Choral	$165.00	
Band	120.00	
TOTAL	$285.00	$285.00

PRINTING AND PUBLICITY	Subtotal	
Four Concert Programs @ $50.00	$200.00	
Four Newspaper Ads @ $45.00	180.00	
TOTAL	$380.00	380.00

REPAIR AND MAINTENANCE	Subtotal	
Six Piano Tunings @ $40.00	$240.00	
Baritone Horn Overhaul	350.00	
Stereo System Repair	220.00	
General Instrument Repair	500.00	
Supplies	80.00	
TOTAL	$1,390.00	$1,390.00

Figure 5.3. Continued

CONTEST/FESTIVAL FEES	Subtotal	
Music Contest	$190.00	
Tri-State Festival	150.00	
All-State Auditions	120.00	
TOTAL	$460.00	$460.00

CONTRACTURAL SERVICES	Subtotal	
Clinician's Fees	$700.00	
Guest Soloists	150.00	
Marching Band Drill	800.00	
TOTAL	$1,650.00	$1,650.00

CONCERT WEAR MAINTENANCE	Subtotal	
Band Uniforms (two cleanings)	$800.00	
Choral Robes	220.00	
TOTAL	$1,020.00	$1,020.00

CONTINGENCY	Subtotal	
Unanticipated Expenses	$500.00	$ 500.00

TOTAL ANTICIPATED EXPENSES		$18,545.00

Figure 5.4. Sample support information

Section Three

1998-99 Music Budget
Support Information
Music Department,
Bea Flat Public Schools

General Information

The music education program in the Bea Flat Public
School District provides classroom and music ensemble
experience for what is expected to be 320 students in
1998—99, grades 5 through 12. Based on this budget
request, a cost-per-pupil ratio of $30.00 in district
funds results. Both the cost-per-pupil figure and the
total request in district funds are well below average
when compared with other schools in the Southwest
Conference. The average conference school district budget
for music is just over $12,000.00, and the cost-per-pupil
figure for students in music education is approximately
$43.00. Treble East, the conference school closest in
enrollment to Bea Flat, supported music education in the
1997—98 academic year with a budget of district funds
totaling $14,000.00.

Students participating in music activities in the Bea
Flat Public School District in 1997—98 made 74 appearances
at school and local functions, as well as at regional and
state events. This 6 percent increase in the number of
appearances made in the previous year can be regarded as
the maximum number of appearances that should be made by
students involved in the Bea Flat music education program.
In addition, the total number of students involved in
music education will increase by slightly more than 6 percent from 1997—98 and over 30 percent in a 3-year period.

Figure 5.4. Continued

Specific Information

NEW EQUIPMENT

Concert Chimes. Much of the concert band music available has a chimes part included. The instrument will also be used in the percussion ensemble. Life expectancy of the instrument is 40 years.

Choral Folders. The choir has never had folders specifically designed for choral music, but instead has resorted to the use of manila envelopes. The new folders offer much better protection for music while it is in use.

Baritone Saxophone. A baritone saxophone is needed to complete the saxophone choir in the band and is an absolute necessity for the newly organized jazz ensemble. This saxophone is a reconditioned instrument and should provide 10 years of service at a considerable savings from the $4,000.00 cost of a new instrument.

REPLACEMENT EQUIPMENT

French Horn. Three of the school-owned French horns are over 30 years old and are literally beyond repair. Plans are to purchase one new horn each year for the next three years. Anticipated life expectancy of the new instrument is approximately 30 years.

Oboe. The school oboe has not been used for a number of years and is badly in need of a complete overhaul. It also has a crack in the upper section that needs to be repaired.

Figure 5.4. Continued

Rather than spend $400.00 to repair a very old instrument, it is proposed that a "student line" replacement instrument be purchased. Life expectancy of the instrument is 15 years.

Choral Risers. The choral risers presently in use were made for the choir by the 1964 industrial arts class and are very heavy and not at all portable. They also take up a great deal of storage area. The new risers will be portable and fold in a much smaller "package" for easier storage.

Concert Tuba. Tuba players in the concert band must play their parts on fiberglass sousaphones. This is not an acceptable concert instrument (see attached adjudication ballot from last year's music contest). An old brass sousaphone no longer in use by the music department will be traded in for the new concert tuba.

MUSIC LIBRARY

Marching Band. Commercially arranged music for marching band costs $45.00 to $65.00 per arrangement, and four tunes are needed for a marching show.

Concert Band. The cost of new music for junior high and senior high school concert bands has risen to between $50.00 and $100.00 for each composition. To cut costs in this line item, much of the concert band music for 1998–99 will be borrowed from other schools.

Choir. Similar increases in costs have affected the purchase of choral music. Single copies of choral music average $1.00 to $1.75 per copy. The choirs will perform nearly 30 pieces

Figure 5.4. Continued

of music annually and will borrow music and rely on present library holdings to hold the line on costs next year.

Choir. Small Ensemble. The basis for success in many music programs is the level of activity in small choral and instrumental ensembles. The music department must continue to build music library holdings for small ensembles.

TRAVEL

Student. Music contest and All-State-related travel remains the same as previous years. The Tri-State Band and Choral Festival has been added to our 1998–99 schedule. The festival is a one-day event, and expenses include transportation and a sack lunch for the return trip.

Teacher. This year Mr. Kleff is requesting travel and per diem expenses to attend the state in-service music education conference. The conference is an important source of new music education concepts to keep music teachers up-to-date. Several concerts, clinic sessions, and seminars will be attended. A copy of the 1997 conference brochure is attached.

AWARDS

Traditionally awards have been made annually to high school students based on total points accumulated in association with ensemble activity. The $285.00 figure is only an

Figure 5.4. Continued

Section Three

Page 5

estimate based on awards presented during the previous year. The students themselves annually conduct a small fund-raising campaign to support the awards system, and that amount appears in Section One under "Income" [Fig. 5.2].

PRINTING AND PUBLICITY

Two band and two choral concerts next year will require commercially printed programs. Acme Printing, Inc., has submitted the lowest bid for the work. It is felt that printed programs provide an air of professionalism to the music concerts and also provide a nice souvenir for students and parents alike. Several senior citizens have called and indicated they would have attended some music events in the past, but they were unaware of when they were scheduled. A newspaper ad preceding each concert should provide ample notice to the community of each upcoming event.

REPAIR AND MAINTENANCE

The music room piano needs to be tuned at least twice a year, and the three practice room pianos require a minimum of one annual tuning. The baritone horn overhaul will extend the useful life of that instrument by at least 10 years. The overhaul includes a new case for the instrument. All components of the school stereo system need cleaning

Figure 5.4. Continued

and adjusting. The left channel on the amplifier does not work, and the compact disc player "skips" at times. Other instrument repair estimates are based on actual expenses from preceding years and, considering the age and condition of most school instruments, are quite conservative.

An increase in the rental/use fee that is charged for student use of school instruments and concert wear will have to be considered in another year. The amount in that account is presently falling somewhat short of providing funds to maintain equipment.

CONTEST AND FESTIVAL FEES

Music contest and all-state audition fees remain constant from year to year. The Tri-State Festival is a new expense for 1998–99. It provides noncompetitive performance experience for students in both band and choir, with adjudication by highly respected judges. It is felt that the Tri-State Festival will be a valuable educational experience for music students in the Bea Flat public schools.

CONTRACTUAL SERVICES

Clinician Fees. Next year university staff will be retained to spend an entire day in residence providing evaluation and constructive criticism for solo, small ensemble, and large

Figure 5.4. Continued

music groups. This type of individual attention by several specialists will be of great personal and collective benefit to the Bea Flat music students.

Guest Soloist. An out-of-town guest soloist will perform with the choir in the concert just prior to Easter. The soloist will also conduct a clinic session for choral students on the afternoon of the performance.

The clinician and guest soloist expenses are included in an Arts Council Grant proposal. Should the grant be only partially awarded, the remaining expenses could be paid from contingency funds.

CONCERT WEAR MAINTENANCE

Because of the amount of use during the marching season, the band uniforms must be cleaned in November and again at the end of the school year. The choir robes will be used six times during the year and must be dry cleaned at the close of school. This type of care should extend the life of the garments by several years, and the cost is partially defrayed through a use fee, which appears as part of "Income" in Section One.

CONTINGENCY

An allowance is requested to cover any unanticipated expenses up to $500.00.

SUGGESTED ACTIVITIES

1. Secure a copy of a recent music budget request from a local public school or the public school you attended. Analyze each proposal and determine the following:
    a. Is the budget type autonomous, departmental, or split?
    b. Is the information in each document easily available? Does it read well?
    c. What are the sources of funding for each budget proposal?
2. Develop a list of questions and interview a local music educator regarding his or her
    a. greatest source of frustration involving the budget process.
    b. position on school equipment rental/use fees.
    c. thoughts regarding a concert admission fee policy.
3. Interview a school administrator and determine his or her views as to the future direction of school district funding for music education.
4. Read and summarize one periodical article dealing with the school music budget process.
5. Visit a local music store, interview its owner/manager, and summarize pricing trends in equipment associated with music education. Compare these figures with those of ten years ago, and project costs ten years from now. Use specific equipment as examples.

CHAPTER SIX

HOUSING AND EQUIPMENT

INTRODUCTION

Through the years, music educators have been making do with facilities and equipment far less adequate, on a comparative basis, than those provided for sports, drama, home economics, or science. They continue to teach instrumental lessons in broom closets, rehearse ensembles in school lunchrooms, push carts with general music teaching aids from classroom to classroom, and perform concerts in dimly lit gymnasiums with horrendous acoustics. Fortunate indeed are those music educators who teach in quality, well-equipped facilities.

The housing and equipment plans that will be presented in this chapter offer a goal for every music teacher to achieve. However, a music education program must prove itself to be a valuable part of the total curriculum before new facilities and equipment can be justified. Once the importance of the music program is recognized and new facilities are planned, music educators must seek outside professional assistance through personal contact, seminars, and printed material so that they can give informed advice to the project designer. One suggested strategy is to arrange a visit by school administrators and board members to a nearby school with outstanding music education facilities before any construction plans are finalized. School board members, a number of whom are likely to have children involved in the music program, often respond to a comparison with a neighboring school that supports its music program with high-quality equipment and well-designed facilities. Careful planning by qualified experts can avoid the "pay now or pay later" syndrome by eliminating the need to make costly remedial improvements in new construction.

Cabinet space, audiovisual equipment, and other instructional aids should be factored into the cost of any construction project. If not, you could find yourself in a new facility with old and inadequate seating, storage, and instructional materials. Remember that you can never have enough storage in a music facility.

Room acoustics and sound control are two of the most important aspects of any remodeling or new construction. An acoustics specialist should be involved in the planning and design of any project from the outset. Continuous exposure to high noise levels can be a very exhausting experience and can bring about permanent hearing loss. The cost of hiring an acoustics consultant to minimize fatigue and health problems in a rehearsal setting can be considered negligible when compared with the long-term gain through increased instructor efficiency and longevity.

This chapter provides a checklist dealing with construction specifications and equipment. It should also prevent music instructors from realizing after the fact that a new room has a poor traffic flow pattern, restrictive sound transfer problems, inadequate storage, or any of a number of encumbrances that could have been prevented if they had been recognized early on in the design process.

GETTING STARTED

At some point in their teaching careers, most music educators will be called on to offer suggestions and comments on a new construction or remodeling project that will affect their music facilities. When this opportunity occurs, teachers should be prepared to provide qualified and knowledgeable input to school administrators, construction contractors, and even project architects. This consultation should take place early in the planning and designing stages of the facility, with follow-up examinations and conferences occurring during the construction process. The music educator is the individual who will be using the facility and therefore should have the most valuable and practical advice to offer. Everyone associated with the construction or remodeling of any music complex has an obligation to consider very seriously all suggestions and recommendations offered by the professional music staff.

Far too often music educators almost blindly accept recommendations regarding facility specifications made by administrative personnel and their engineering consultants. This oversight could be the result of excitement and anticipation related to new or improved facilities, as well as a desire not to rock the boat. As is the case when music educators are faced with the prospect of change that will affect their professional lives, the credo remains, "Get involved!"

Music instructors themselves are often unaware that they have a role to play in the building process, and they are uninformed about where to go for the information that can make them positive contributors. Three brief cases illustrate what can happen when music specialists are not involved in construction projects.

Case number one involves the construction of a band/choral room in a small, rural high school in the Midwest. The room was constructed using the existing outside wall of the gymnasium as an inside wall of the new room, and the ceiling height was just under ten feet. This height is too low for good acoustics, and the proximity of a noisy gymnasium made the space less than ideal for music practice. To make matters worse, all instruments were stored in cabinets at the rear of the room, creating a tremendous traffic flow problem at the opening and close of each band rehearsal period.

Case number two concerns a beautifully constructed high school music complex, complete with an auditorium located in close proximity to the band and choral rehearsal rooms. One small problem surfaced, however, when the seven-foot grand piano from the old choral room was moved to the new building and it was discovered that it wouldn't fit through the door. The piano had to be dismantled and moved through the door on its side.

Case number three involves a totally new fine arts center constructed by a major university. In the design, the instrumental and choral rooms shared a common wall. After the first day that the two rooms were in simultaneous use, the major contractor was called back to add an additional wall between them. The area of dead space between the walls reduced but did not eliminate the transmission of sound between the rooms. This flaw occurred in a building that cost taxpayers many millions of dollars.

Similar scenarios are repeated each year across the country. Informed music educators have an obligation to become involved in construction projects that affect their programs; school officials and others charged with the fiscal responsibility of those projects should involve music educators as a source of information and in an advisory capacity. The key word here, of course, is "informed."

To become better informed when you learn that your school district is considering some type of music construction project, secure a copy of the Music Educators National Conference (MENC) publication by Harold P. Geerdes entitled *Music Facilities: Building, Equipping, and Renovating*. Published in 1987, this extremely valuable book contains much of the information necessary to ensure that a well-planned and acoustically sound facility will be built—a facility that gets the maximum benefit from funds available and uses the space allotted for the project most efficiently. In fact, you will want to include this book in your own personal collection or as part of your office library of how-to books of valuable reference materials. Printings of this book after 1995 include relevant sections from the Opportunity-to-Learn Music Education Standards.

After reading the MENC manual, meet with school officials and encourage them, as part of the construction contract, to acquire the services of a specialist skilled in the construction of music rooms to assist in development plans and provide on-site consultation before and during the construction process. While employing a specialist can be an additional up-front expense, in the long term he or she can save the school district and the taxpayers substantial remedial expenses, such as the construction of an additional wall between rehearsal rooms, as was necessary in case number three. The national office of MENC can provide names of individuals qualified to serve as professional music building consultants.

Chapter 14 covers the development of a music education philosophy. Whatever your philosophy may be, it should be a major determining factor in implementing space and equipment requests that relate to the new construction of music facilities.

Planning for music room construction involves a keen awareness of many factors such as room acoustics, facility layout, size, ceiling height, isolation of sound, noise control, lighting, and ventilation. The goal of any construction project involving tax dollars is generally to meet high performance standards with a limited construction budget. What follows is an attempt to aid music educators in their efforts to meet those high performance standards.

SPACE AND FLOOR DESIGN REQUIREMENTS

Rehearsal rooms

Space requirements for music rooms generally vary according to the educational level of the school facility; however, a general figure of twenty square feet of floor space for each instrumentalist and fifteen square feet of floor space for each choral student can be used as minimum requirements for instrumental and choral music rehearsal rooms. This space is in addition to all space taken by cabinets, pianos, podiums, and so on. Some publications recommend higher square footage requirements for music rooms, but none list lower figures. Be sure to plan for future growth. Buildings outlast students, teachers, and even theories of education.

Ceiling height should be an area of great concern when planning rehearsal rooms. The general consensus suggests a minimum height of twelve feet for rehearsal room ceilings, but fourteen to sixteen feet is more the norm. A recent school of thought recommends that rooms requiring a high sound-power level have a ceiling height of twenty-four feet, with a subceiling of acoustical panels to drop the ceiling to the twelve-to-sixteen-foot level. The dropped ceiling is suspended from the twenty-four-foot ceiling and not attached to the walls. This arrangement allows the room to comfortably accommodate a large volume of sound while eliminating high levels of noise. What is most desirable is a high sound-power level as opposed to a high noise level. Too many instrumental rehearsal rooms have too high a noise level; over a period of time music educators teaching in such rooms may suffer some degree of hearing loss. This aspect of facilities design will be discussed in greater detail in the acoustics section of this chapter.

Floor design

Acoustics specialists who deal with rehearsal room construction generally agree that such rooms should be somewhat rectangular in shape with no parallel walls. This is a floor plan consideration. An equally important decision must be made regarding the physical design of the floor in rehearsal rooms. Three basic options are available to music facility designers: (1) flat floor, (2) built-in risers, and (3) excavated risers.

Most choral and instrumental rehearsal rooms constructed in the 1950s and 1960s had risers built into the floor plan. More recently, however, music rooms with flat floors have begun to appeal to music educators and administrators alike because of the obvious flexibility of the rooms. It is now quite common to see instrumental rehearsal rooms with flat floors and portable risers.

The practicality of portable risers is quite evident. For example, most instrumental ensembles that rehearse on risers perform concerts without the benefit of risers. It is somewhat of a mystery why band and orchestra directors ask their ensemble members to perform in a seating configuration different from the one in which they rehearse. If a music room is constructed with a flat floor and portable risers are installed, those risers can be moved out of the rehearsal room into a performance area, allowing students to perform in an arrangement identical to that used in rehearsal. Figure 6.1 shows an example of an instrumental rehearsal room with portable risers.

On the other hand, an increasing number of college and professional performing organizations have abandoned the use of risers in both rehearsal and performance

Figure 6.1. Rehearsal room with portable risers

Figure 6.2. Permanent risers constructed from existing floor line

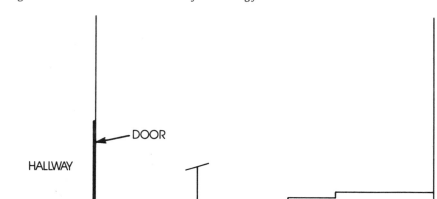

settings. In this way, they can maintain their seating arrangement as they move from the rehearsal room to a single-level performance area.

Choral rehearsal rooms continue to contain some type of built-in risers. This practice is easily justified in that choral groups, almost without question, always perform on standing risers. This author would carry the design of choral rehearsal rooms one step further to include enough floor space for portable risers to be set up on a semipermanent basis; this way, a choir could move from their seated choral risers to standing risers that would more accurately simulate performance conditions.

Permanent risers can be built at the time of construction in either of two ways. The first option is to build the risers up from the existing floor line, which is the

Figure 6.3. Permanent risers excavated from existing floor line

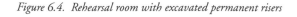

Figure 6.4. Rehearsal room with excavated permanent risers

level at which students enter the room and the instructor conducts rehearsals. This floor plan requires that the percussion instruments be moved up and down the risers before and after each performance. The piano, however, can be easily moved around the room and even moved from the room with a limited amount of effort. Ceiling height is a major consideration when planning this type of built-in riser. For proper sound control, the ceiling should be a minimum of eight feet above the heads of those students seated on the top riser. Figure 6.2 is a cutaway drawing representing built-in risers designed from existing floor level.

The second option available to music room designers is one in which risers are "excavated" from the level of the existing hallway and the level at which students enter the room. In other words, the director and those students who sit in the first row descend three or four steps to the "main floor" level of the room. Percussion instruments are on the top level of the rehearsal area but remain at door and hallway level, which makes it easy to transport them to and from the performance area. Figure 6.3 is a cutaway drawing of risers excavated from the level at which students enter the room.

Figure 6.4 is a photo of an instrumental music rehearsal room with excavated permanent risers. Architects often find it advantageous to use the excavation method to construct permanent risers, because it provides additional ceiling room without disrupting the outside roof line of the project.

Specifications for built-in risers vary from choral to instrumental rehearsal rooms. Risers in both instrumental and choral rooms should be six to eight inches in height. Choral risers should be a minimum of thirty inches and more ideally thirty-six inches in depth, and risers designed for instrumental groups vary from forty-eight to sixty inches deep. The top riser in both choral and instrumental rehearsal rooms should range from a minimum of seventy-two to 120 inches in depth to allow for easier movement and additional equipment needs.

Before determining whether to include risers in the design of new rehearsal rooms, try to visit schools both with and without permanent risers. Administrators and designers should consider your opinion when making final design decisions. Whether or not permanent risers are installed, a set of portable risers and storage for those risers should be included as part of the cost of building and equipping the facility.

PLANNING A MUSIC DEPARTMENT

Sound containment, traffic flow, location of rooms, access to performance area, practice rooms, auxiliary music rooms, and storage space are but a few of the considerations facing anyone involved in laying out a music facility. The following guidelines are offered to assist music educators and building designers in this effort.

Sound containment and isolation. Rehearsal rooms should be located in a part of the school where the rehearsal sounds will not interfere with other classes. Rehearsal rooms should not be placed contiguous to one another. Use corridors, offices, and storage rooms as sound isolators whenever possible.

Some type of dead space between hallway doors and outside rehearsal room doors should be planned. Figure 6.5 is a simple drawing of a sample sound lock. An entry plan including some type of sound lock will reduce significantly the amount of rehearsal sound that reaches the corridor outside a rehearsal room.

All walls, not just the major supporting walls, should extend to the roof deck. If this practice is not observed, sound can travel from room to room through the false ceilings. All joints and wall penetration by pipes, wires, and ductwork require special sealant consideration. Electrical outlets should not be placed back to back from one room to another, and all doors should possess acoustically treated seals that inhibit sound transfer.

Practice rooms. One of the most serious and consistent errors in music facility design is the location of practice rooms. Practice rooms should simply not be placed in a location that requires students to pass through a rehearsal room to gain access to them. This common design limits their use, because students are unlikely to use

Figure 6.5. Sound-lock example

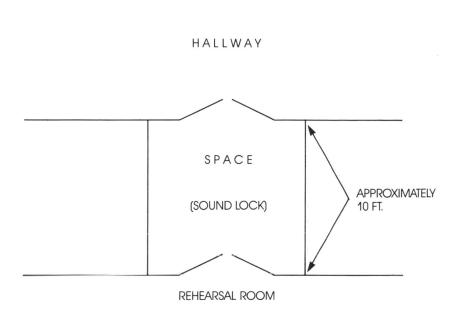

HALLWAY

SPACE

(SOUND LOCK)

APPROXIMATELY
10 FT.

REHEARSAL ROOM

them when a large ensemble rehearsal is taking place. If they do choose to use the practice rooms, they will probably distract—and be distracted by—the group in the rehearsal room. Also, any time the rehearsal room is locked, student access to the practice rooms is restricted. Another major concern in practice room location is access to student instrument storage. For these reasons, it may be best to place practice rooms on a corridor outside the rehearsal room or between rehearsal rooms with a short hallway providing access from the main corridor.

In short, the two principal considerations in the location of music practice rooms is that they not be located inside the rehearsal room, but rather situated for easy student access, and that student instrument storage or lockers be accessible from the practice room area.

How many practice rooms should be included in a construction project? To determine this, you must look at the number of students who will be making use of these facilities. At the very least, there should be at least one practice room for every forty music students, but preferably one room for every twenty students. Your estimate should be based on *projected* enrollment in the music program, not the enrollment figures at the time of construction.

Figure 6.6. A corridor of manufactured practice rooms

The size of the practice rooms should vary. Sixty square feet is sufficient for a single practice room, and 140 square feet is adequate for small ensembles with a pianist. Each room should have at least two electrical outlets and a mirror. A window should be in each acoustically treated practice room door. Some newly constructed facilities include intercom systems between the practice area and directors' offices to better monitor student practice.

Figure 6.6 shows a view of manufactured practice rooms. While these may be more expensive than contractor-constructed rooms, they guarantee the highest degree of sound insulation and can make a phased-in purchase plan practical. These units also add a degree of flexibility, because unit relocation is always possible. A newer version of manufactured practice rooms has a computerized option available that allows the room to be tuned to simulate the amount of reverberation in rehearsal rooms or concert halls, all at the push of a button.

The music library. If possible, the music collection should be located in a room separate from the rehearsal rooms rather than placed on shelves or filing cabinets against a rehearsal room wall. An orchestra, a choir, and a band can all utilize a single library room within a music complex, so it is important to have the library adjacent to the rehearsal rooms. Far too often the music library is a construction afterthought, and shelves or file cabinets are placed in a practice room to house the department's music library holdings. This design prohibits the use of proper sorting, cataloging, and filing and makes a newly constructed facility inadequate before a single note is sounded within its walls.

Space should be included in the library room for cabinets or shelving for all music, a sorting rack, worktables, a desk, and a supply cabinet. A minimum of 300 square feet should be allowed for a music library that will house combined choral/instrumental music holdings.

Uniform/concert wear storage. A separate room for storing uniforms and concert wear should be included in the design of a new music facility. The room should be cedar-lined for moth protection, have a door that opens to an outside corridor, and be large enough to comfortably house garments based on future enrollment figures. It is a rare case, though, when uniforms and other concert wear—which may cost tens of thousands of dollars—are allowed adequate storage space.

Some schools require that uniforms and concert wear be left at school. This practice requires students to change clothes before and after each performance. If this is the policy in your school, you need to make sure that dressing facilities are available for both sexes. It is ludicrous to think that the garments receive less wear and tear and are more secure if left at school when students are forced to change in small, general restroom areas. In such settings garments are draped over sinks and/or placed on the floor because there are no hangers. All uniforms and formal concert wear should be placed in the hands of students during the school year unless adequate dressing rooms are provided.

Another, but less attractive, storage option for uniforms and concert wear is built-in storage cabinets along one wall of the rehearsal room. This type of storage is less secure than an independent room, and, with the numerous uniform pieces that are generally part of today's marching band uniforms, a large amount of cabinet space is required. Such storage could usurp valuable rehearsal floor space.

Instrument storage. The minimum space requirement for an instrument storage room is 600 square feet. This space should be located near the entrance to the instrumental rehearsal room and should have two sets of doors that provide good traffic flow to and from the rehearsal room. Ideally, the space should be used to store instruments currently being used by students, whether they are personal or school-owned.

There are several storage options available. Freestanding wooden or metal storage cabinets are one option. Built-in, open "pigeon-hole" storage units are perhaps the most economical to construct, but could prove to be expensive over the long term because of security problems. One good option is a commercially produced locker/cabinet with a grille front made of steel. This model allows air to circulate and provides visual access to a locked storage space. Check out catalogs from music storage suppliers to determine style and cost before meeting with school officials and/or the building designer or architect.

All school-owned instruments not checked out to students, as well as seasonal equipment, such as marching percussion, sousaphones, marching brass, and swing choir props, can be housed in a separate instrument storage room. A suggested location for this room is in the back of the instrumental rehearsal room, near the area where concert percussion instruments are stationed.

Instrument repair room. To some music facility designers, an instrument repair room is an unnecessary frill. But students cannot be expected to keep their instruments clean and in good repair if the basic space to do so is not provided. A small room, adjacent to the band director's office, with emergency repair equipment, a workbench with a vise, and a large steel sink to clean and flush brass instruments is a minimum requisite. A room designated for the proper care and repair of student- and school-owned instruments is simply a sound investment by the school district.

Office space. Separate office space for orchestra, band, and choral instructors is highly desirable. The offices should be contiguous to the directors' respective rehearsal areas. Music office space and equipment vary depending on the size of the school and the music program. The office space need not be overly large, unless it will also serve as a teaching studio, music library, and instrument repair room. A pleasant office for music educators charged with the responsibility of administering any portion of a program should be a priority in the design of any facility.

An example of how not to provide proper office space in the construction of new facilities occurred in one Midwestern city. Two identical high schools, each designed for over 2,000 students, were constructed five years apart, with pleasant rehearsal, class, and practice rooms allotted for the music department. The entire music instructional staff, however, including one choral director and a half-time assistant, one band director and a three-quarter-time assistant, and one orchestra director were given one office with one telephone, two computers, and only three desks, in an area totaling less than 300 square feet of floor space. Additionally, all of the music library holdings for the instrumental and choral programs were housed in the same office. Such an area is likely to be disorderly and inefficient in terms of personal space and privacy necessary for the successful administration of any music program. To make the situation even more intolerable, access to the office area was only possible through one of the three rehearsal rooms, which had classes and rehearsals scheduled during all but one class period of the day. To construct such poorly planned facilities once was unfortunate. To duplicate that same lack of planning without music staff input was an unforgivable waste of taxpayer dollars.

SPACE CONSIDERATIONS

The facility requirements previously mentioned represent what should be considered a minimum standard for any new construction. What follows are suggestions for school district planners who wish to provide their students with optimum music education opportunities, particularly at the secondary level.

Ensure recording and television capabilities

Modern rehearsal rooms should be able to support in-house recording and closed-circuit and cable television hookups. At the time of construction, builders can install conduit and appropriate cables leading to a separate control room or a room adjacent to the rehearsal room, such as a music library/control room. The services of an audio engineer are mandatory in determining the proper locations of microphone outlets in each rehearsal room. It goes without saying that conduit and wiring should also be included in new facilities to facilitate the networking of computers between offices, the music library, and instrument storage areas.

Instruction with piano

The most modern music complexes provide a room designed for class instruction in piano, complete with a minimum of eight student electronic keyboards and a teacher instruction and control station. An example is shown in Figure 6.7. Numerous electrical outlets must be carefully planned as part of a class piano room. Full-size keyboard synthesizers are now priced moderately enough to make class keyboard instruction worthy of serious consideration.

Set up auxiliary classrooms

Music classrooms designed for teaching music theory and/or appreciation, as well as separate guitar classrooms, have been included in contemporary music facilities at elementary, junior high, and secondary levels. These rooms need not be overly large and may have ceilings of normal classroom height. A music listening

Figure 6.7. The class piano room at Corona del Sol High School, Tempe, Arizona

room can also be considered for larger schools. It is this author's belief, however, that music listening stations and appropriate recordings should be housed in the school library or resource center, where use of the equipment can be supervised on a full-time basis.

Training with technology

A growing number of schools are promoting the use of computers in support of course work related to music education. Computer software has become readily available for use at all levels for basic music theory and composition, as well as ear training and private lessons assistance. A computer lab, complete with MIDI keyboards, will be an integral part of the complete music education program in the twenty-first century. Again, providing an adequate number of well-located electrical outlets is an important consideration.

Separate orchestra rehearsal room

Funds permitting, a separate orchestra rehearsal room should be included in the design of a music complex. Recent studies indicate that orchestra rooms require less reverberation time than band rooms. The floor damage from cello pegs, the need for greater riser width, and the installation of oversized-instrument storage cabinets are just several of the special considerations that should be made when separate rehearsal areas are planned for orchestras.

OTHER CONSTRUCTION CONSIDERATIONS

Acoustics. Most music rehearsal rooms should have a reverberation time of between 1.5 and 2.0 seconds. Choral rooms should generally be more "live" than instrumental rooms. Multipurpose music rehearsal rooms should possess acoustical tuning capabilities to deaden or liven the room, depending on the type and size of the ensemble presently rehearsing. This can be accomplished in the most economically efficient manner by hanging floor-to-ceiling pull-type drapes on one or more walls.

It has become quite popular to carpet rehearsal rooms, particularly band rooms. You need only ask yourself one question when determining whether to carpet a rehearsal area: "We don't perform on carpet, so why rehearse on carpet?" There are numerous alternative means of acoustically treating a rehearsal area other than installing permanent, inflexible acoustic material in the form of carpet. Granted, carpet is pleasing to the eye and provides a "warm" atmosphere; however, the lack of acoustical flexibility makes it a questionable design option in new construction of music rehearsal rooms.

Many music educators, particularly band directors, have been diagnosed as suffering from job-related hearing loss of a permanent nature. In many cases, these band directors had been rehearsing their ensembles for years in rooms that were architecturally aesthetic but acoustically flawed (for example, rooms featuring sound-absorbent material covered by enamel paint).

Any instrumental rehearsal room should be planned to the specifications of a professional acoustician to provide a rehearsal setting in which a high sound-power level is possible without a loud noise level. Continuous exposure to a noise level of 85 dB (decibels, the unit for measuring loudness) can cause permanent hearing loss. Many large bands produce 85 dB at a piano dynamic level. Imagine the decibel level produced by a large marching band! The sound-power capability of an instrumental rehearsal should be of utmost concern to music educators, school administrators, engineers, architects, and contractors. You may want to share the article "The Not-So-Silent Menace," by Ed Solomon (1986), which is about hearing loss, with whoever is ultimately responsible for designing or approving new music rehearsal areas.

Lighting. A combination of artificial and natural light is most desirable for music rooms. Either an easterly or westerly exposure is considered to be the most advantageous source of natural light. Fluorescent lighting appears to be the most satisfactory for rehearsal rooms. Type A ballasts should be specified for music room lighting fixtures because they are considerably less noisy than the less-expensive Type B ballasts.

Outside entrance doors. A rehearsal room should have a direct exit door in order to move instruments directly to and from the room for outside rehearsals and for the easy loading and unloading of equipment. A small loading dock with vehicle access is also helpful. An outside entrance door makes entry for evening rehearsals and concerts more convenient.

Heating and ventilation. Air-exchange capabilities in music facilities are often inadequate, and the equipment responsible for heating and circulating room air is frequently too noisy. Air ducts supplying and returning air from rehearsal and practice rooms should be lined with fireproof, sound-absorbing material and contain baffles to prevent unwanted transmission of sound. The desirable range for humidity in a music room is between twenty and sixty percent; humidity control should be a specific requirement in building plans.

GENERAL MUSIC CONSIDERATIONS

General music education needs differ from performance requirements in that general music classes can be and often are taught in regular classrooms. By and large the ceiling height and acoustical treatment are not as critical for the general music classroom, but room size is an important consideration. Ten square feet of floor space for each student in the room can be considered a minimum. Ample storage space for the multitude of books, recorders, ukuleles, guitars, autoharps, Orff instruments, and similar critically important teaching aids should be of prime concern in designing an area specifically for general music classes.

Relatively soundproof areas for individualized instruction and computer use are certainly not a luxury in the contemporary general music classroom. A good stereo playback system, complete with turntable, compact disc player, double cassette deck, high-quality speakers, and remote control, should be an equipment goal of every elementary and junior high general music educator. Such a unit can perhaps be purchased with student activity fund assistance if the music educator is willing to allow the equipment to be used for an occasional school function.

CD-ROM technology has made it possible to utilize computer equipment as an integral part of the way general music classes are taught by creating technological teaching stations with equipment that can project images from a computer screen onto a large movie projection screen large enough and bright enough to be viewed by an entire general music class.

A small room adjacent to the music room can serve as a storage area for project props, musical instrument projects, and instructional materials and supplies that are used on an infrequent basis. Special cabinet space should be available for audio- and videocassette tapes, slides, filmstrips, and a recording library. Because of the movement that often takes place in general music classes, a carpet is often appropriate.

A good quality piano with cover, a lined chalkboard, a permanent projection screen, filmstrip, slide, and overhead projectors, as well as an in-residence videotape machine and monitor complete the housing and equipment needs of today's general music classroom.

Your author admits to a degree of idealism when describing general music equipment plans, but he has seen music classrooms similarly equipped. The variety of musical experiences available to young music students in these situations is indeed impressive.

MODEL MUSIC FACILITIES

Three floor plans of music facilities follow. Figures 6.8. and 6.9 are offered not as outstanding examples of architectural design but as examples of floor space allocations based on information included in this chapter. Figure 6.10 is included as a model of contemporary music facilities at the secondary level; this design is presently in use at Corona del Sol Senior High School in Tempe, Arizona. The only major shortcoming of the Corona del Sol complex is the size of the choral rehearsal room, which covers about 1,000 square feet.

SUGGESTED ACTIVITIES

1. Design a music complex that can house a 100-piece band, an eighty-voice choir, and a sixty-piece orchestra. Incorporate space and design requirements included in this chapter. Include dimensions and square footage for each room. Use graph paper and employ a scale of 1 inch per 10 feet. Include cutaway views.
2. Design a music complex with one rehearsal room, a music library, practice rooms, an office, an instrument storage room, and a uniform/concert wear storage area to house an eighty-piece band and a sixty-voice choir. Incorporate space and design requirements included in this chapter. Use graph paper and employ a scale of 1 inch per 10 feet. Include cutaway views.
3. Invite a university physics professor to class to discuss sound-power level and noise level, as well as implications of reverberation time as it relates to acoustics. Prepare a list of discussion questions in advance.
4. Interview a local music educator and report to the class on what facility and equipment strengths and weaknesses that individual sees in his or her present teaching situation.

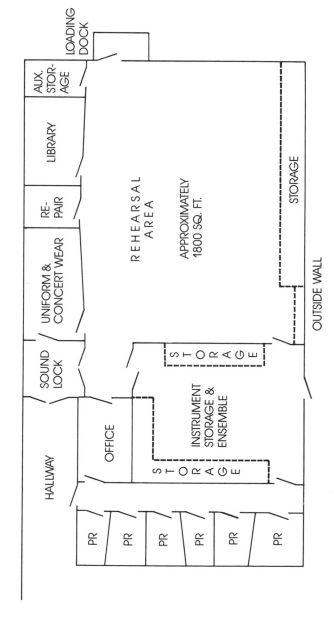

Figure 6.8. A one- or two-teacher music facility with a single rehearsal room

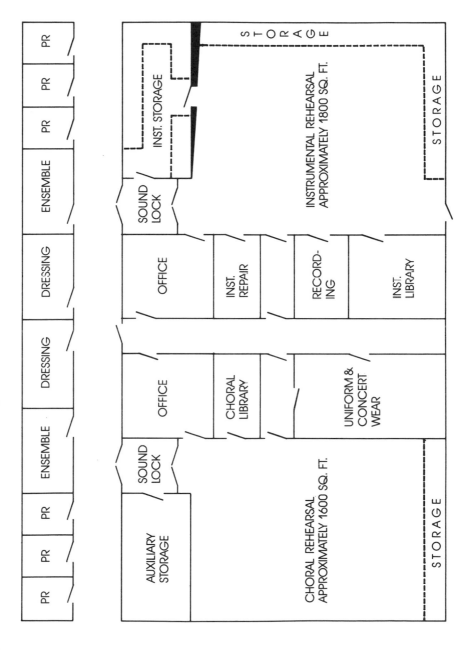

Figure 6.9. A two-room, two-teacher music education complex

Figure 6.10. Floor plan of music complex at Corona del Sol Senior High School, Tempe, Arizona

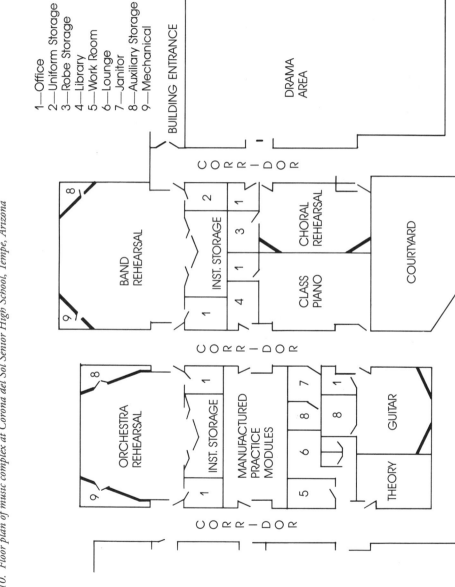

1—Office
2—Uniform Storage
3—Robe Storage
4—Library
5—Work Room
6—Lounge
7—Janitor
8—Auxiliary Storage
9—Mechanical

CHAPTER SEVEN

SCHEDULING

INTRODUCTION

Music educators need to be aware of the problems and procedures involved in class scheduling, given the number of courses being offered in schools today. They must also understand the different types of schedules and the effects scheduling practices can have on their music programs.

This chapter begins with an overview of scheduling issues. The basic terminology is defined to better facilitate an understanding of these issues. The heart of the chapter is a description of various scheduling models and how they affect a music program. First, the traditional or conventional schedule and its many variants are described. Next, more flexible models are introduced, including modular plans. What has become known as "block scheduling" has been sending unsettling ripples of anxiety throughout the entire music education profession since the early 1990s. Various forms of block scheduling are described in this chapter, along with their positive and negative effects on music programs. Procedures to be followed, as well as a sample block schedule favorable to music performance programs, are also offered.

Extending the school day has been suggested as one way to meet the increased demands of student schedules, which often are loaded with a wealth of AP (Advanced Placement) and elective courses besides the required classes. A sample model for an extended day is offered, along with some of the benefits of this type of plan.

Finally, the rotating-lesson schedule is offered as an ideal vehicle for increasing a music educator's access to students for private or small-group instruction. A properly proposed and implemented rotating lesson schedule can benefit the teacher, the students, and the entire music program. Instituting this type of schedule may be the best way to resolve schedule conflicts and improve music instruction.

The chapter ends with a discussion of other calendar issues that go beyond daily and weekly scheduling. Music educators need to apply organizational skills to their personal schedules, as well as to the annual school calendar of events.

SCHEDULE INFLUENCES

It is not unusual for new teachers to be unaware of the influence that scheduling can have on their schools' music education programs, or even how the scheduling process works. Besides being aware of the different types of school schedules and their resulting effects on music programs, music educators must be prepared to discuss scheduling options with administrators and be willing to make recommendations in support of those programs. Scheduling has always been and will continue to be a critical factor in the maintenance of a successful music program.

Scheduling of classes on all levels in schools has become increasingly difficult over the years, as national priorities have changed regarding the types of courses that should be offered. Beginning in the late 1950s increased school enrollments created unusual demands on school administrators, which resulted in creative and innovative scheduling techniques.

Traditional or conventional school schedules have been unable to accommodate the rapid increase in curriculum offerings in today's schools. Computers have made possible opportunities for schedule flexibility, and numerous schedule models have been initiated on an experimental basis. Flexible, modular schedules, first introduced in the 1960s, were instrumental in solving a wide variety of scheduling problems and to this day appear to be the most favorable model for music education.

Other influences on academic class scheduling over the years have included an increased emphasis on core courses for college preparation (what are known as AP or advanced placement courses), a need for school administrators to pay greater attention to staff desires, and an extension of work-related school experiences or vocational programs. The most obvious influence, however, has been the rapid proliferation of courses. Particularly at the high school level, students today have a vast array of academic and activity-oriented offerings from which to choose. That academic variety, along with the emphasis on college tracking, has forced music educators to defend the curricular importance of their programs and to devise creative ways to ensure that those programs are included in the curriculum.

The school schedule manifests the educational philosophy of the community, the school, and its administrative staff. If a school administrator is convinced of the importance of music education, music will remain part of the daily schedule. If an administrator views music education as a frill or as an extracurricular school activity, music offerings are likely to be placed before or after the school day or scheduled at a time during the day that limits student participation. There is no school administrator who will fail to find an advantageous spot on an academic schedule for a program in which he or she strongly believes.

If the philosophy of a school is traditional, the schedule of that school will likely be conventional. Conversely, if a school's philosophy is nontraditional, its class schedule is apt to be flexible or blocked in some manner. In either case, the quality of the schedule—and the type of educational experiences provided for students—will be a direct reflection of the competence and experience of the building principal, as well as the total school administration. The construction of the school schedule is considered by many educators to be the supreme test of administrative and managerial skills (Dempsey and Traverso 1983). By the same token, what a music educator does with the amount of time provided in the schedule is indicative of the administrative and organizational abilities possessed by that teacher. Too many teachers use lack of time as an excuse for inadequate music instruction. Much can be accomplished by a dedicated, creative, and well-organized music educator in as little as one class period per week.

UNDERSTANDING THE TERMINOLOGY

There is some disagreement among educators about the definition of a variety of terms associated with scheduling. For purposes of clarity and consistency, an explanation of several frequently used terms follows.

Schedule

Scheduling may be defined as the organization of time, facilities, and personnel to meet the needs of the students for whom a school is responsible. Quite simply, the schedule is a school's blueprint for present and future action, reflecting directly the educational philosophy that is promoted there. Richard A. Dempsey and Henry P. Traverso define a school's schedule as "a program and time design bringing students, teachers, curriculum, materials and space into a systematic arrangement for the purpose of creating an optimal learning climate" (1983, p. 13). The school schedule establishes the means through which instructional goals can be achieved and is a strong indicator of a principal's familiarity with the capabilities of the school's staff. A wise administrator does not schedule beyond the educational and instructional competency limits of available staff.

Conventional/traditional schedule

These two terms are used interchangeably in referring to a scheduling style. In this chapter, a conventional or traditional schedule is one that presents classes in the same order on a daily or weekly basis. Class periods are generally of a standard length, and each class meets for the same amount of time, regardless of the subject matter.

Flexible schedule

The term *flexible schedule* has become widely used to suggest a departure from conventional scheduling. Over the years, any change, no matter how small, from the conventional or traditional method of scheduling classes has been considered flexible. The result has been a degree of chaos in understanding what is actually happening in a particular school.

In the truest sense, the term "flexible schedule" is based on the view that each day's class order in a schedule need not be like every other day of the week. As originally established, flexible scheduling called for classes of varying sizes within and between courses, provided for the meeting of instructional groups at varying frequencies and for varying lengths, promoted team teaching in any content area, and required countless professional decisions by teachers about students, course content, and teaching methods (Manlove and Beggs 1966).

Modular scheduling

In modular scheduling, the school day is divided into ten- to twenty-five-minute modules or "mods," and an administratively prescribed number of mods are assigned to all classes and activities within the school. Class length is thus determined by what is being taught. Students are not always in formal class arrangements or study halls and an opportunity is provided for students to involve themselves in independent study, i.e., work at your own pace. The modular schedule generally repeats itself every five or six days, rather than following the more structured daily pattern of the conventional schedule.

Properly constructed and implemented, a modular schedule must be considered a flexible schedule; however, a flexible schedule need not necessarily be modular in construction. Readers are cautioned to make this distinction. Far too often, unknowledgeable educators fail to distinguish between flexible and modular scheduling.

Block scheduling

In its purest form, block scheduling involves four class periods per day. Class length averages ninety minutes per class. Students may enroll in up to four classes in a given semester, and at the end of that semester receive one credit per class taken, which is equal to the credit they would normally receive for a yearlong class. In the second semester, students again enroll in four more classes and receive one full academic credit for each semester of class work. There are several variations of block scheduling, all of which will be presented and discussed later in this chapter.

Individualized instruction

Music educators have been involved in individualized instruction for many years through their work with students in private and group lessons, as well as with small and large performance ensembles. The concept behind this type of flexible scheduling is that individual students—with their unique capabilities, interests, and backgrounds—can best develop the full measure of their talents in a program fitted to their needs. Many educators feel that individualized instruction makes better use of students' time. Students do not study what they already know, nor do they suffer from the knowledge gaps that may occur in a large group, which can inhibit educational progress (Manlove and Beggs 1966).

CONVENTIONAL SCHEDULING

The conventional or traditional schedule remains popular and is used in the majority of secondary schools today. Its simplicity is an attractive feature for school administrators, many of whom, after experimenting with other models, return to this type of class planning, often because of its uncontroversial character.

Figure 7.1 presents a conventional scheduling model. (Letters of the alphabet used here and in the remaining schedules represent hypothetical academic classes.) Note that each period is structured exactly like the preceding one, and the days do not vary. The basic flaw in such a model is the limitation placed on the adoption of new programs or courses. In schools where curriculum offerings have increased dramatically and the traditional scheduling model has been retained, music offerings, particularly band, are likely to be found outside of what is considered to be the "normal" school day. Vocal music classes are probably scheduled during the lunch period.

Figure 7.1. Traditional schedule

Period	Monday	Tuesday	Wednesday	Thursday	Friday
1	A	A	A	A	A
2	B	B	B	B	B
3	C	C	C	C	C
4	Lunch	Lunch	Lunch	Lunch	Lunch
5	D	D	D	D	D
6	E	E	E	E	E
7	F	F	F	F	F

ROTATING-PERIOD SCHEDULE

Principals who continue to use the conventional scheduling models often introduce variety and a degree of flexibility to their students' schedules by rotating or interchanging periods to add an additional class without lengthening the school day. In essence what results is a seven-period schedule in a six-period day. By dropping one class each day, so that each class meets six times in seven days, an additional class can be accommodated. In such a system, a student taking four or five major subjects is still able to participate in music and other electives. Figures 7.2 and 7.3 represent examples of this innovative approach to traditional six-period scheduling. The boxes marked with Xs can be used as study or activity periods.

In his study of the American high school, James B. Conant (1959) suggested that students with a special ability or interest would be wise to take music theory in place of a foreign language. The schedules diagrammed in Figures 7.2 and 7.3 provide for just such an option; however, colleges and universities across the United States are beginning to mandate a foreign language as a requirement for admission.

Figure 7.2. A seven-period schedule in a six-period day (vertical sequence)

Period	Monday	Tuesday	Wednesday	Thursday	Friday
1	A	G	E	D	B
2	B	A	F	E	C
3	C	X	G	X	D
	Lunch ————————————————————→				
4	D	B	A	F	E
5	E	C	B	G	F
6	F	D	C	A	G

Figure 7.3. A seven-period schedule in a six-period day (horizontal sequence)

Period	Monday	Tuesday	Wednesday	Thursday	Friday	Monday	Tuesday	Wednesday
1	A	B	C	X	E	F	G	A
2	B	C	D	E	F	G	A	B
3	C	X	E	F	G	A	B	C
	Lunch							↑
4	D	E	F	G	A	B	C	D
5	E	F	G	A	B	C	D	E
6	F	G	A	B	C	D	E	F

CONVENTIONAL MODULAR SCHEDULE

A number of secondary schools call their scheduling models "modular," but the models are actually traditional schedules in modular schedules' clothing. For example, with very few exceptions, all classes meet for the same number of mods, or periods, and the schedule is repeated on a daily basis, removing the flexibility originally intended for modular scheduling. Figure 7.4 shows a modular schedule that is actually a conventional or traditional schedule, with fifteen modules offered in twenty-five-minute periods. In this type of model, music classes must be scheduled against multiple sections of required classes to avoid or reduce schedule conflicts.

Other variations of traditional or conventional scheduling offer more choices and are included in the next section, "Flexible Scheduling." While it will become evident that the greater a schedule's flexibility, the more hospitable it is to music education, in reality it is not so much the type of schedule that affects the music education program as it is the attitude and philosophy of the music educator and the school administrators.

Figure 7.4. Conventional modular schedule

Module	Monday	Tuesday	Wednesday	Thursday	Friday
1	Algebra	Algebra	Algebra	Algebra	Algebra
2	Algebra	Algebra	Algebra	Algebra	Algebra
3	English	English	English	English	English
4	English	English	English	English	English
5	Study	P.E.	Study	P.E.	Study
6	Study	P.E.	Study	P.E.	Study
7	Sci. Lab	P.E.	Sci. Lab	P.E.	Study
8	Sci. Lab	Science	Sci. Lab	Science	Science
9	Sci. Lab	Science	Sci. Lab	Science	Science
10	Lunch	Lunch	Lunch	Lunch	Lunch
11	German	German	German	German	German
12	German	German	German	German	German
13	Study	Study	Study	Study	Study
14	History	History	History	History	History
15	History	History	History	History	History

FLEXIBLE SCHEDULING

Perhaps no other study in the history of American education had greater impact on public school curriculum and scheduling than did the work of James B. Conant (1959), which took place in the late 1950s. His recommendations to improve secondary public education resulted in expanded curriculums and experimental scheduling models intended to facilitate increased curriculum demands. Conant maintained that all students should be urged to include art and music among their electives. He felt that talented students were hindered by a traditional six-period schedule from pursuing a varied academic program and at the same time electing to study art and music. His study pointed out that academically talented students who did not take two or more years of art and music in high school were enrolled in schools with a six-period schedule format.

Thus the demand for scheduling flexibility was created across the United States. As the schedule process became increasingly flexible, a wide proliferation of curricular

Figure 7.5. Flexible schedule

Time	Monday	Tuesday	Wednesday	Thursday	Friday
8:30	A		A		A
		E		B	
9:30					B
	B		F		C
10:30					
		A			F
11:30					
	Lunch			Lunch	
12:30	C				
		Lunch	Lunch		Lunch
1:30	F	D	C	A	
					D
2:30			F		
	D	F	R	F	F

offerings kept pace. What follows are descriptions of the most popular flexible schedule options. These schedules are designed to provide appropriate course offerings for effective instruction and the flexibility to meet the individual learning needs of the students.

When scheduling rehearsals for large music ensembles in any type of flexible scheduling, one thing should be understood: they must receive high priority in the total scheduling process. This is not because music educators have inflated egos but because no other high school course offering involves students from every class in the school. In a four-year high school, bands, orchestras, and choirs are likely to have members from all four class levels. For this reason, those ensembles cannot be successfully scheduled against single-section classes. Computer scheduling makes it a relatively simple task to give schedule priority to ensembles involving a cross section of student members. The extent to which this is allowed to happen in a given school is a reflection of the role music plays in the total school program.

As mentioned earlier, a schedule can be flexible but may not necessarily be based on a modular concept. Figure 7.5 gives one example. The music staff sets the specifications for ensemble time requirements in this schedule, based on their judgment as to the most effective way to meet with their students. They may decide, for example, that the traditional daily large group rehearsal is less effective than three weekly meetings of the entire group and two independent rehearsals for each section per week. Again, computer scheduling allows reasonable requests for class time to be met. This type of scheduling is flexible only to the point that succeeding daily schedules do not repeat. Changes in the total five-day format are often made at the end of quarter and/or semester grading periods. The letter "F" in Figure 7.5 represents unscheduled time for independent study or enrichment purposes.

Modular schedule

Without a doubt, modular scheduling has dominated the movement toward increased flexibility in secondary school curriculums. When applied in its strictest sense, modular scheduling is the only truly flexible schedule in that it changes schedule patterns on a weekly as well as a daily basis. Modular scheduling can generate up to forty percent of unscheduled student time for enrichment and independent study. This advantage theoretically provides music educators with an opportunity to meet individually with students on a weekly basis. Students respond favorably to independent study time, and they like the variability of the schedule because it adds a sense of adventure and freshness to the week.

Module lengths stay the same for the entire length of the schedule, and although actual mod lengths vary from ten to thirty minutes, the average is twenty minutes in length. Note that as mod length increases, schedule flexibility decreases.

Figure 7.6. Modular schedule: six-day cycle. (Note: *** indicates unscheduled time. The total time allotted for music combined with unscheduled time represents thirty-one percent of independent study and enrichment time.)

Module	Day 1	Day 2	Day 3	Day 4	Day 5	Day 6
1	English (Lg. grp)	***	History	Biology	Spanish	***
2		Geometry			↓	***
3					***	English
4	↓	↓	↓	↓	***	↓
5	Music	Music	Music	Music	Music	Music
6						
7	↓	↓	↓	↓	↓	↓
8	Geometry	Spanish	***	History	Biology	***
9	↓	↓	Geometry	↓		***
10	Spanish	English		***		Biology
11	↓	↓	↓	***	↓	
12	***	Lunch	Lunch	***	History	
13	Lunch	↓	↓	Lunch		
14	↓	***	English	↓	↓	***
15	***	History	***	Geometry	Lunch	Lunch
16	Biology		***		↓	↓
17			Spanish		***	Geometry
18	↓	↓	↓	↓	English	
19	P.E.	***	***	***		↓
20		***	P.E.	Spanish	↓	***
21		Biology Lab.			***	Spanish
22				↓	Geometry	↓
23	History			***		***
24	↓	↓	↓	***	↓	***

Modular scheduling appears to offer the most advantages to music education because of the independent study time available and because greater flexibility is possible in scheduling rehearsal time for large ensembles. A creative music educator who understands the scheduling process and a competent, sensitive, and skillful school principal who possesses an in-depth knowledge of computer scheduling techniques can work together to provide sophisticated and rewarding music education experiences for all students in their school. Figure 7.6 represents a modular schedule with one music class. This schedule involves a six-day cycle that creates both daily and weekly schedule variety. The time allotted for enrichment and independent study is just over thirty-one percent, somewhat less than the ideal total of forty percent for those purposes.

BLOCK SCHEDULING

Since the early 1990s, secondary schools have been changing from a traditional daily six-, seven-, or eight-period schedule to a more nontraditional scheduling form known as block scheduling. The rate of growth in the number of schools implementing this new format has been dramatic. Some studies suggest that nearly fifty percent of high schools in the United States are presently using or are considering using some form of block scheduling.

Block scheduling is also known as the four-by-four (4/4) plan, the accelerated schedule model, or the Copernican plan. No matter the title, the plans or models all call for a student to take four classes or subjects each semester, totaling eight

Figure 7.7. Block schedule

Semester 1		Semester 2	
Term 1	Term 2	Term 3	Term 4
Subject 1	Subject 2	Subject 5	Subject 5
Subject 2	Subject 2	Subject 6	Subject 6
Subject 3	Subject 3	Subject 7	Subject 7
Subject 4	Subject 4	Subject 8	Subject 8

classes or subjects in one year. Because the classroom time for each of the periods is significantly increased, a course is completed in one semester, with students receiving the equivalent of what had been thought of as a year's credit in that one semester.

Each semester is generally divided into two equal nine-week terms for grading and conferencing purposes. Figure 7.7 shows an example of a block schedule in its purest form.

Modified block schedule

Any form of block scheduling that deviates from the model presented in Figure 7.7 is known as a "modified block" schedule. Blocks can be modified in different ways, but the characteristics common to all forms of block schedules are (1) longer class periods (approximately ninety minutes in length), (2) only three "passing times" between class periods (because there are fewer class periods they are usually ten minutes long), (3) no study hall periods, and (4) four classes/credits per semester (totaling eight classes/credits per year).

The alternate day form of block scheduling (also known as A/B, odd/even, and day 1/day 2) involves following a prescribed block of four courses on day one and a different set of four courses on day two, thus establishing an alternating daily schedule for the entire year. Students still earn eight class credits for the one academic year of work but are exposed to the course work on an every-other-day basis during extended class periods. Figure 7.8 is an example of an alternate day form of block scheduling.

Figure 7.8. Alternate day block schedule

Semester 1   Semester 2

Day 1	Day 2	Day 3	Day 4
Subject 1	Subject 5	Subject 1	Subject 5
Subject 2	Subject 6	Subject 2	Subject 6
Subject 3	Subject 7	Subject 3	Subject 7
Subject 4	Subject 8	Subject 4	Subject 8

The split block model

This model takes one of the four blocks and divides it into two equal sections of time. The shorter period of time is called a "skinny." Any skinny that is longer than one-half of the original block period is known as an "expanded skinny." The split block model can be used to accommodate any class that does not necessarily require the time available in a full block but must meet a full year to earn one class credit. Classes such as music and other arts classes tend to find the split block model more "user friendly" than any full block or modified block schedule models. Examples of split block schedules appear later in Figures 7.10 (p. 147) and 7.11 (p. 148).

Other modified block schedules

There are several different variations of block scheduling. A transitional model has students attending eight classes per day on Monday, Tuesday, and Wednesday. The first four classes (morning classes) attend four expanded blocks on Thursday, the second four classes (afternoon classes) have class in four expanded blocks on Friday. An example of a transitional block schedule is shown in Figure 7.9. This type of schedule is generally used when a school is in the transitional period between a traditional schedule and block scheduling.

Figure 7.9. Transitional block schedule

Period	Monday	Tuesday	Wednesday	Thursday	Friday
1	Class A	Class A	Class A	Class A	Class E
2	Class B	Class B	Class B		
3	Class C	Class C	Class C	Class B	Class F
4	Class D	Class D	Class D		
5	Class E	Class E	Class E	Class C	Class G
6	Class F	Class F	Class F		
7	Class G	Class G	Class G	Class D	Class H
8	Class H	Class H	Class H		

A trimester plan involves students taking three core classes in an expanded block format, earning three class credits. Nine class credits may be earned in one full year of three trimesters.

Extending the School Day

Some music educators have solved their scheduling problems by starting a rehearsal one-half hour before school, then continuing into the first twenty to thirty minutes of the school day. Others extend a rehearsal period at the end of the school day. After-school rehearsals, however, may conflict with athletic programs, and busing of students can create additional problems.

A visit to most secondary schools early in the morning will find many nonmusic classes and activities already taking place before the official school day begins. Many educators and activity advisors have found that the only way to reduce scheduling conflicts is to offer activities before the start of the school day. Concerned music educators would do well to accept these scheduling options if it will remove the possibility of forcing young student musicians to make difficult participation choices. Music educators certainly have the right to seek assurance from school administrators that any music rehearsal scheduled before school will receive protection from potential or already-existing scheduling conflicts.

In some schools where a six-period schedule is in effect, early-morning seventh periods have been added. The seven-period day may be helpful for those students who can benefit from the enriched learning experience of an extra class period. Typically, schools adopting a seven-period schedule run from 8:00 AM until 3:30 PM. The first period is optional and offers extra enrichment opportunities. A music rehearsal would certainly qualify as an enrichment opportunity. Teachers are in the classroom for five periods with one preparation period, and those teachers beginning work at 8:00 AM complete their school days at 2:30 PM. Through this type of school day extension, college preparatory and honor program students can increase elective choices. This type of schedule is more expensive but makes better use of school facilities. The primary goal of this type of schedule modification is to increase opportunities to meet the needs of *all* students.

The Controversy Surrounding Block Scheduling

Change is difficult. A music educator working with a high school performing group is comfortable with the forty-five-minute daily rehearsal schedule. For the most part, the rehearsal periods are conflict-free under the traditional method of scheduling academic classes; there is little overlapping with other classes, and, for the most part, students who want to participate in the music program can.

Then the dreaded words "block schedule" are heard, and the rumors begin to circulate: everything is going to be changed, and the comfortable school day will be turned topsy-turvy. The music educator reads in professional journals about "The Perils of Block Scheduling" and begins to fear the worst.

The best-attended sessions at recent national in-service conferences have dealt with block scheduling and its resulting negative impact on performing arts organizations at the secondary level. Presenters make dire statements, such as "The prevailing adiministrative approach to scheduling at the secondary level is, 'If it ain't broke, BREAK IT!'" The music educator at such a conference hears how block scheduling "is an educational fad that won't work," how it "shortchanges students in all subject areas," and how it "has completely destroyed some music programs." The educator never learns exactly which schools were "destroyed" and how they were ruined, but the impression remains.

Rather than becoming a negative activist when you learn that your school is being converted from a traditional scheduling model to block scheduling, follow the steps below to become fully informed about the effects of block scheduling on music programs. Share that information at every opportunity with colleagues and administration. The administrative decision has already been made, and there is really nothing you can do now to alter that decision. Neither covert activism nor open opposition will do anything more than harm relationships and could ultimately cause permanent damage to the school's music education program.

What to do

If you find yourself faced with the prospect of your school's converting from a traditional schedule to a block schedule, there are a few things you may want to consider doing. First, check out the video *Block Scheduling and the School Music Program,* produced by the Wisconsin Music Educators Association. To order a copy, write to Block Scheduling Video, Wisconsin Music Educators Association, 4797 Hayes Rd., Madison, WI 53704. The video is available in two forms: as a full-length version for music teachers and as an abbreviated version more suitable for viewing by administrators, school board members, and parents. The cost of the video is currently $29.95 for MENC members.

Second, purchase a copy of the MENC publication "Scheduling Time for Music." Most pertinent to block scheduling and music education are two chapters, one written by four Wisconsin music educators and music administrators, and the other based on an Alamosa State College in Colorado master's thesis by Gary Hall dealing with the effects of the four-period day on music performance and retention rates.

Third, contact colleagues in the music education profession who have dealt successfully with the change from traditional to block scheduling. Success stories abound. Learn what they did and how they handled the change. What were the "tough questions" asked and answered?

Finally, get involved locally. Volunteer to be a member of the scheduling committee. The committee needs input from music representatives, particularly if it is well-informed input. In short, be proactive, be informed, be involved in a positive manner. Positive results just may happen.

The manner in which music performance is treated during the scheduling process is directly related to how important a balanced arts education is to the top administrators in the school district. If they believe adequate time for music ensemble rehearsals is an important ingredient in the education of high school students, that time will be found in the block schedule.

Advantages and disadvantages of block scheduling

There are strong feelings, both pro and con, when it comes to assessing the effectiveness of block scheduling over the more traditional six-, seven-, or eight-period scheduling models. Music educators need to become well acquainted with both the perceived advantages and disadvantages to block scheduling and how such a change can influence their programs.

Perceived Advantages of Block Scheduling	*Perceived Disadvantages of Block Scheduling*
Reduced teacher class loads	Class size will have to increase
Students work with fewer teachers	Absences from school will mean missing more of a subject
Fewer class changes, resulting in a cleaner and quieter school	Schools could have trouble finding additional classroom space
Concepts can be studied in greater depth with longer class periods	Students may be forced into classes they don't want — they have fewer options
Discipline problems reduced by fewer passings between classes	Generally there are no study halls in block schedules
Teachers and students have two "fresh starts" each year	

Advantages, cont.	*Disadvantages, cont.*
Less time necessary for administrative duties (roll taking, etc.)	Difficult to schedule music lessons — must pull students out of classes
Teachers see fewer students each day	Difficult to stay on task for a ninety-minute class period
Reduces number of teacher preparations per day — they can prepare more effectively	Longer class periods mean that teachers must schedule breaks during class
Longer preparation period (up to twenty-five minutes longer)	Retention problems can exist when sequence classes are taken (Algebra I and II, for example) with a one-semester break between classes
Students can retake a failed class next semester	
Longer classes create opportunity for greater variety of classroom activities	Longer classes are inappropriate for some courses
Depth of learning is greater	Block scheduling causes dropouts and reduced enrollment in performance classes
Music students can get twenty-five percent of their total graduation credits in music and still graduate with twenty-four credits in four years	Students can't participate in both choral and instrumental ensembles
Provides opportunity to all school staff to reexamine curriculum for priorities	

The most accommodating block schedule

Of the various forms of block scheduling (four-by-four, alternating day, trimester plan, modified block, and split block), only the split block plan holds any reasonable hope of leaving the music department relatively unscathed in the transition to block scheduling. Research done as part of Gary Hall's master's thesis has shown that under any other form of block scheduling, participation numbers have decreased, in some cases dramatically so.

In a study completed in 1993 involving school districts in Kentucky, Indiana, and Michigan, ninety-one percent of schools using the strict four-period (4/4) day form of block scheduling experienced some degree of enrollment decrease in performance classes, whereas only fourteen percent of the schools that used the modified split block form of scheduling showed a decrease. This is a significant difference! This same study showed that smaller schools (those schools with fewer than 500 students in grades nine through twelve) indicate a much higher level of conflict between music performance classes and other academic class offerings. This finding makes sense, in that the larger the school, the more sections of all classes appear in the curriculum, thus reducing the potential for conflict.

The Kentucky, Indiana, and Michigan study also showed that the split block scheduling model works best for music performance classes, even in smaller schools. The alternating-day form of block scheduling could be considered second best in terms of the degree to which it can accommodate music performance classes with a minimum of class conflicts while providing an acceptable student retention level.

While it may be considered difficult, it is possible for music education to thrive in a block schedule setting. Figure 7.10 gives an example of a split block schedule that appears to accommodate music education in a positive manner.

Each full block on the schedule is eighty-five minutes long. The music class period begins at 8:00 AM, twenty minutes before the first block begins; therefore, the

Figure 7.10. A sample split block schedule with two music classes for upper-level students

	Term 1	Term 2	Term 3	Term 4
8:00–8:50	Band	Choir	Band	Choir
8:55–9:45	Choir	Band	Choir	Band
9:55–11:20	AP Physics	AP Physics	AP Physics	AP Physics
11:20–11:50	LUNCH	⟶		
11:50–12:15	STUDY	⟶		
12:20–1:45	Spanish 4	English 3	⟶	
1:55–3:20	Precalculus	World History	⟶	America & the World Today

first two music periods can be termed expanded skinnies. Choir and band alternate every term between the 8:00 AM and 8:55 AM starting time for each expanded skinny so that no one group has to begin the school day earlier than the other for an entire year. The orchestra meets at 8:55 AM throughout the year. During Term 1, the marching band meets at 7:30 AM, resulting in a total daily rehearsal time of two hours, fifteen minutes for that ensemble.

Note that other academic classes meet during the first block each day (which begins at 8:20 AM); this does not appear on the sample schedule. It should also be noted in this schedule, as well as in Figure 7.11, that a short study period has been included. This may be handled as a "home room" period in some schools.

Again, each full block period is eighty-five minutes long. During the fall term, marching band meets at 7:30 AM, plus the entire first period. Freshman and sophomore instrumentalists split off from the upper level students during the second, third, and fourth terms to rehearse for a full block of time. Freshman and sophomore choir and orchestra students have a full block of music throughout the entire academic year.

Directors must share students who wish to participate in two ensembles during the eighty-five-minute period. Those students who participate in only one performance class rehearse for the entire eighty-five-minute block. Those participating in two performance classes rehearse with each one for half of the block period. In the

Figure 7.11. A sample split block schedule with two music classes for lower-level students

	Term 1	Term 2	Term 3	Term 4
7:30–8:10	Marching Band	→		
8:20–9:45	Marching Band	American History	Speech	English
9:55–11:20	Vocal	Band Vocal	Band Vocal	Band Vocal
11:20–11:50	LUNCH	→		
11:50–12:15	STUDY	→		
12:20–1:45	French 1	French 2	Biology	Biology
1:55–3:20	Algebra 1	Algebra 2	P.E./ Health	P.E./ Health

days prior to an important performance, these students might spend an entire block with the vocal or band group.

Lower-level students can be in band, orchestra, and chorus, but all directors of those performance classes must be flexible. This need for instructional flexibility is not unlike what would be necessary under any scheduling model when students wish to participate in three ensembles.

Figures 7.10 and 7.11 offer examples of block scheduling that could be favorable to music performance classes. Individual solutions will vary from school to school. When faced with a change to block scheduling—or any new scheduling plan—music educators should proactively learn as much as possible about the new plan and be involved in the decision-making process.

ROTATING-LESSON SCHEDULE

Earlier in the chapter we discussed how rotating the periods in a school's master schedule can provide an opportunity for increased curriculum flexibility. The use of this concept to schedule private and group lessons, sectional rehearsals, and small ensembles can be one of the most effective tools at the disposal of the music educator as an administrator. Unfortunately, many teachers fail to avail themselves of this opportunity for increased personal contact with their students. A rotating schedule for music students works equally well at both the elementary and secondary education levels. (An implementation of a rotating schedule at the junior high school level was used as an example of administrative function nine, "Changing," in chapter 1 [pages 15 and 16]. Readers should refer to this practical application.)

Gaining access to students for lessons and rehearsals is one of the major problems facing orchestra, choral, and band instructors. Classroom teachers are legitimately reluctant to excuse students from classes for weekly music lessons. Music educators should not even consider requesting that students be released from regular class time unless they are prepared to excuse them from their rehearsals once a week for gymnastics, drama, or some other academic pursuit. Student lessons can be scheduled during the students' study periods, but that time can fluctuate, which often leaves music educators with unnecessary free time when no students are available to them.

With the rotating-lesson schedule concept, students miss a class or a portion of a class only once every few weeks. In Figure 7.12, the rotation time is eight weeks. Each letter on the schedule represents one of eight individuals or small groups. The example represents one day of a music educator's week. Other days of the week could be similarly scheduled, creating personal contact with forty individuals or groups. From an efficiency standpoint, it is suggested that group instruction rather than private instruction be placed on a rotating basis. Groups could consist of two or three like voices or instruments, and in this way one educator could make personal contact with 120 students during a one-week period.

Implementing a rotating-lesson schedule

Classroom teachers may oppose any rotating music schedule plan because they fear the burden of getting students to their lessons will fall on them; they may also be hesitant to face the possible classroom disruption of students moving to and from their appointments. School administrators generally are in favor of any process whereby instructional efficiency is increased, but they are sensitive to the concerns of their classroom teachers as well. On the other hand, parents are likely to favor a rotating-lesson schedule proposal because it will increase student-teacher contact in music, and the portion of a class that is missed every eight weeks or so can be considered nominal. Students usually support the idea and readily accept

Figure 7.12. Rotating-lesson schedule

Hour	1st	2nd	3rd	4th	5th	6th	7th	8th
9:00	A	H	G	F	E	D	C	B
9:25	B	A	H	G	F	E	D	C
9:50	C	B	A	H	G	F	E	D
10:15	D	C	B	A	H	G	F	E
10:40	E	D	C	B	A	H	G	F
11:05	F	E	D	C	B	A	H	G
11:30	G	F	E	D	C	B	A	H
11:55	H	G	F	E	D	C	B	A
12:20	LUNCH							→
12:45	LUNCH							→
1:10	FREE							→
1:35	FREE							→
2:00	BAND							→
2:25	BAND							→

the challenge to observe the appointment times. Classroom teachers thus are the key to the acceptance of a rotating-lesson schedule.

To implement such a schedule, you will first want to submit a written request to the affected administrator to implement a rotating schedule on an *experimental* basis. Highlight and underline, if necessary, the advantages this schedule holds for both the school and the music education program. Request a personal meeting to explain the proposal in greater detail and answer administrative questions. Also ask that a meeting of the classroom teachers be called to explain the rotating-lesson concept to the involved teachers in the presence of that administrator.

Second, meet individually with the teachers prior to the group meeting, soliciting their support for the program. They must be assured that the responsibility for appointment punctuality and discreteness in leaving and returning to the classroom is that of the music students. Be sure that they understand that the rotating-lesson schedule is an experimental project and that if teacher opinion is unfavorable at the end of the experiment, the schedule will be abandoned in favor of other scheduling options. If the program is properly administered and the affected music students accept their responsibility, the classroom teachers will be more than willing to continue the rotating music schedule on a permanent basis.

Prepare the schedule with each group of students identified with a letter assignment, such as Group A, Group B, and Group C. Group assignments appear at the top of the page followed by the rotating schedule itself, as shown in Figure 7.12. Mail copies of the schedule to parents, along with a letter requesting their support in reminding their children about the rotating meeting times and explaining the level of student involvement and responsibility in making a worthwhile project successful.

Meet with music students and carefully explain the schedule and their role in making it effective. Students must understand that no disruptive behavior will be tolerated when they are leaving or returning to their classrooms. Encourage each student to attach the schedule to his or her lesson book and make extra copies available, including posting one on the bulletin board in each room. Classroom teachers need a copy only for role-taking purposes to determine if absent students are scheduled for a lesson at that time.

Any music educator who possesses some degree of organizational and administrative skills will find a rotating-lesson schedule a pleasant challenge to administer and an effective and efficient means of providing musical instruction to students involved in a crowded educational curriculum.

OTHER SCHEDULE CONSIDERATIONS

Up until now, the scheduling process has been dealt with on a daily/weekly basis. There are two other important considerations that involve scheduling and an organized approach on the part of music educators.

Yearly schedule

The full-year schedule, or "school calendar," includes such things as starting and ending dates of the school year, vacation periods, and dates for drama and speech presentations, athletic contests, music events, and so on. For even the smallest school there may be at least one event scheduled every night of the week. Many communities have one night, generally Wednesday, that is designated "church night," and no school activities are scheduled then.

As early as possible in the school year, place concert, contest, and festival dates on the calendar. Before assigning dates, obtain a copy of the activities calendar at the state level. All-state athletic events and tournaments, drama and declamatory contests, state and regional music contests, all-state music events, professional association conferences and meetings, and similar activities need to be considered. If rehearsal time is needed in a performance location, that time must be scheduled in addition to the actual performance date. Additionally, other school music events that occur at different grade levels must be considered. Meeting with all music staff in the school district prior to scheduling major events can eliminate the need for schedule changes.

Realistically, once the school calendar is established, it is practically impossible to change calendar dates without affecting your colleagues in a negative way. Occasional schedule conflicts are acceptable and are bound to occur, but recurring conflicts and change requests become annoying to school administrators and represent a disorganized approach to event planning. For that reason, extra care must be exercised when placing music dates on the annual school calendar, with an eye to avoiding potential scheduling conflicts.

Personal schedule

Be sure to keep an accurate calendar of all school-related, professional, and personal activities. Do not trust your memory regarding activities that occur days, weeks, or months later. Every school event, along with state-level activities that could even vaguely influence your own schedule, should be included on a personal wall calendar. Efficient and successful educators, business leaders, and other professionals recognize the influence such an organized approach has on their lives. They realize that meeting deadlines and avoiding schedule conflicts are an important part of being considered a professional in their chosen career field.

SUGGESTED ACTIVITIES

1. Obtain a copy of your own high school's class schedule and interview your former music educators for their impressions about the effect that schedule has had on the music program. Share the results with the class.

2. Research periodical literature for three articles dealing with scheduling. Summarize the articles and report to the class.

3. Invite a middle school, junior high school, or senior high school principal to class to discuss problems associated with the scheduling process in his or her own school as it relates to music education. Compile in advance a list of questions based on the materials presented in this chapter to promote class discussion.

4. Work in cooperation with a local elementary, middle school, or junior high school music educator and develop a one-day, experimental rotating private or group lesson schedule for his or her school.

5. Interview a local secondary school choral music educator and determine the effects, both positive and negative, that some type of rotating-lesson schedule would have on his or her program. Report the results to the class.

6. Select five of the "advantages" or "disadvantages" relating to block scheduling as presented in this chapter. Take the opposite view on each one to lead a class discussion.

7. Obtain a copy of the calendar of events for the local secondary school. Determine examples of apparent scheduling conflicts and discuss in class how such conflicts could better be anticipated in the scheduling process.

8. Recently some support has surfaced among educational leaders for year-round public school. Open-enrollment options are also being studied and instituted in a number of states across the country. Research these topics and lead a class discussion on one of them to determine the advantages and disadvantages for general education in your geographic area, as well as the implications year-round school and open-enrollment hold for music education programs.

CHAPTER EIGHT

THE MUSIC
LIBRARY

INTRODUCTION

This chapter examines the organizational and administrative concerns associated with an effective public school music library. As with numerous aspects of any program administration, the more effort and careful attention that is devoted to the organizational aspects of a music library, the less time the music educator must spend in dealing with the daily work involved in its administration. What at first glance may seem like an overwhelming organizational web can become a clearly accessible and functional library if the procedures presented in this chapter are followed.

The chapter first introduces you to copyright law, so you can be sure to follow the correct procedures when making copies of music from the library. Next, two types of libraries are described: the central music library, serving an entire school system, and the individual library, located in a single school, with the pros and cons of each type discussed. An in-depth look at how to organize your music library, including how music should be stored, indexed, numbered, and processed, is the heart of the chapter. Specialized equipment that is useful to the music librarian is described, as well as the role of the student music librarian.

In organizing and operating a music library, students can be extremely helpful. They can make positive contributions, and they have the youthful patience necessary to see a project through to completion. In turn, students gain a positive, supervised work experience. The music library is the heart of the music department, and those students who collaborate with a dedicated music teacher in organizing it will gain a great sense of accomplishment and increased self-worth.

COPYRIGHT AND THE MUSIC EDUCATOR

It is appropriate to begin a chapter devoted to the music library with a few words about copyright law. Over the years, music educators have perhaps been among the most flagrant violators of U.S. copyright laws, and in doing so they deprive authors, composers, and publishers of a source of income that is justifiably theirs. Technology is part of the problem. Fast and inexpensive duplicating and photocopying machines are easily accessible; it is not uncommon to find a photocopier as standard equipment in a music educator's office. It's too easy to break the law!

Far too often a band director buys one set of a published marching band arrangement and then makes sufficient copies for a 120-piece band. Too often a choral director, in an "emergency," takes one copy of a choral arrangement and makes forty or fifty complete copies for his or her choir. Both of these music educators have violated the copyright law. Those copies deprive a rightful portion of the revenue due to the source that made the original copies available in the first place: namely, the composer and the publisher.

THE COPYRIGHT LAW

The first new legislation affecting copyright law in sixty-seven years was enacted by Congress in 1976 and put into effect in 1978. The purpose of the law was to encourage creative members of our society by assuring them that the results of their creativity would be fully protected within the legal limits of the law. It also reflected the impact of new technologies, such as photocopying machines, on the dissemination of copyright information. The 1976 law was the first attempt in U.S. legal history to reconcile the interests of copyright owners with the legitimate use of copyrighted material by nonprofit educational institutions, defining "fair use" so that educators and scholars could continue their research without violating copyright.

In determining fair use of material under copyright, four criteria established by previous court action were included in the 1976 law:

1. The purpose and character of the use, whether such use is of a commercial nature or is for nonprofit educational purposes.
2. The nature of the copyrighted work.
3. The amount and substantiality of the portion used in relation to the work as a whole.
4. The effect of the use upon the potential market for or value of the copyrighted work.

Section 107 of the law should help music educators clarify what can be considered fair use as it pertains to the reproduction of copyrighted material for instructional purposes, defining several key factors in making this determination.

Spontaneity. A band director distributes a work from the music library and suddenly realizes that one of the second flute parts is missing. Reproducing a copy of

156 WITHIN THE SCHOOL ENVIRONMENT

an existing part can be considered fair use under the spontaneity concept, provided that the director orders a replacement copy from the publisher within a reasonable time period.

Brevity. Congress, under the 1976 copyright legislation, never intended that it be legal to mass copy complete musical works. However, using a brief excerpt to establish a point in an educational setting can be considered fair use, but using someone else's work to build a whole course or a major unit of that course is not permissible. As it concerns music, the key factor is the performable unit. Making multiple copies of ten percent of a performable unit is acceptable, while copying the entire movement is prohibited.

Cumulative effect. The concept of cumulative effect is closely related to brevity. Reproducing several sections of a piece of copyrighted music cannot be considered fair use. Legislative reports clearly state that anthologies are not fair use, and in such cases permission must be secured from the copyright holder.

It is permissible for a teacher to make a single copy of a chapter from a book, an article, a short story, an essay, a poem, and other similar copyrighted materials for that teacher's use in doing research, teaching, or preparing to teach a class. Multiple copies for classroom use can be made only if proof is provided that the copying meets the concepts of spontaneity, brevity, and cumulative effect. Also, notice of copyright must be indicated on any reproduction. Any copying to avoid purchase or to reproduce consumable materials such as workbooks or worksheets is strictly prohibited.

The copyright law is also very clear on the subject of sound recordings. It states that a teacher may legally make a single copy of copyrighted recorded music if the recording is owned by the teacher or the school and that copy is to be used for classroom use or examination. The copyright law does not deal effectively with videotaping off-the-air for educational purposes, but it is widely felt that the fair use doctrine can be liberally applied to such activity.

Under the 1976 law, authors and composers are protected from copyright infringement for their lifetime plus fifty years. This is a considerable increase from the previous twenty-eight-year protection period, which was also renewable for an additional twenty-eight years. Those holding copyright under the old law can extend it during its first twenty-eight-year period for forty-seven more years simply by applying for renewal. Thus all copyrighted material is now protected for a minimum of seventy-five years under the 1976 copyright law. Theoretically, any piece of music over seventy-five years old has fallen into the public domain. However, arrangements of public domain material can themselves be copyrighted, so reproducing an orchestral score for Beethoven's Ninth Symphony, for example, might still be breaking the law if the arrangement is copyrighted.

Charles Gary (1977) stated, "It is part of a music educator's responsibility as a professional to know about copyright and to use protected materials in the most effective, *legal* way possible to improve learning opportunities for students." The fact that materials appropriate for educational use are copyrighted does not mean that they cannot be made available to music educators. What it does mean, however, is that teachers, to remain within the guidelines established by Congress, must contact publishers, producers, or other copyright holders and request permission to use these materials for educational, nonprofit purposes. Copyright owners are generally quite generous in granting reproduction permission in these cases.

Remember, Congress has been very liberal in considering the needs of all educators in allowing them the freedom necessary to do the jobs for which they receive their salary. At the same time, they are sending a message to educators that illegal reproduction of copyrighted material that deprives the copyright owners of their income is an unfair and illegal act, punishable by law.

Gary's article in the April 1977 issue of *Music Educators Journal* entitled "What Music Educators Should Know about the New Copyright Law" provides the "do's" and "don'ts" that music educators must become aware of in order to abide by the Copyright Act. That article should be on the must-read list of every active and prospective music educator. For additional information regarding music education and the copyright law, consult Jay Althouse's *Copyright: The Complete Guide for Music Educators*. This paperback book is listed in the MENC *Professional Resources Catalog,* and the cost to MENC members is currently $8.00. A copy of the 1976 Copyright Act is available free of charge by writing to Information and Publications Section, Copyright Office, Library of Congress, Washington, DC 20559.

THE NEED FOR A MUSIC LIBRARY

A large percentage of a music education department's annual budget is spent on music or some type of instructional aids. The storage and subsequent protection of music and associated library materials are the direct responsibility of the individual who purchased the items. In schools with separate orchestra, band, or choir directors, each director is generally in charge of a specific portion of the music library. In smaller, one-teacher music departments, that music educator must accept sole responsibility for the entire vocal and instrumental library holdings.

When music is poorly stored and organized, teacher efficiency is compromised and the possibility that music will be lost, damaged, or destroyed is increased. The prevention of music being lost or damaged is simply good management on the part of a music educator in an administrative role.

The remainder of this chapter is primarily devoted to managing the music library and outlining how to create a maximum level of efficiency for the benefit of both students and staff. In addition to housing music for large performing groups, the music library can serve as a holding facility for scores, recordings, tapes, films, filmstrips, transparencies, videotapes, and other instructional materials.

TWO MUSIC LIBRARY CONCEPTS

Central music library *popular in Texas*

Large school districts with multiple junior and senior high schools often combine music library resources in a single, central music library system. Choral and instrumental directors at all levels can check out materials from that one central facility. The school district saves money by avoiding duplicate purchases of music and other resource materials and, at the same time, provides a more diverse library collection from which directors representing various schools within the district may request material. The central library concept has become even more attractive in recent years with the advent of computer software that allows total library holdings to be recorded on disc, creating easy and rapid access to the collection. It is now possible for band, choir, and orchestra directors to access a listing of the central library's holdings on their office computers.

While the central music library concept is cost effective for the school district and provides a wider diversity of materials to music educators, it is certainly not time effective for teachers. They must plan far in advance to borrow materials or music they may want to use in classes and rehearsals. To a degree, the central music library removes a certain element of instructional flexibility. Busy teachers are more likely to make use of a wider variety of library materials when the facility is located in or near their own class or rehearsal rooms.

An efficient alternative to the central music library system is to keep a master inventory on computer of all choral and instrumental music owned by the school district that is housed in each of the schools within that district. It would be available either online to all teachers through their individual computers or copied to disc for them and updated periodically. This approach would allow all group directors to be aware of available materials within the school district and to borrow music and other resources from sister schools. This policy would at least deliver a degree of financial savings to the school district through a reduction in unnecessary duplicate purchases.

Single music library

The single music library system is nearly always found in small schools, but often in larger schools as well. In a single music library, all the instrumental and choral music and other instructional aids, such as films, tapes, slides, and recordings, are kept at a particular school. The materials may be divided into categories such as band, orchestra, or choir and housed in or near the respective rehearsal rooms for those ensembles. The system can still be considered a single library as long as the materials are kept within the school, even though they are placed in several rooms. For convenience, it makes sense to store choral music near the choral rehearsal room; it also enables the choral director to maintain and update the collection on a regular basis.

ORGANIZING THE MUSIC LIBRARY

There are four specific reasons to create and sustain an organized music library. First, a well-organized library enables a teacher to determine with very little effort exactly what music is housed there. Second, the music educator can quickly locate a desired piece of music. Third, he or she can distribute music to students in an efficient manner, thereby saving precious rehearsal time. Finally, music and other instructional materials represent a substantial financial investment; the music library provides the teacher with the opportunity to preserve and protect this investment.

Storage of music

There are many ways in which music can be stored. Some music educators prefer file cabinets rather than open shelving; some prefer boxes rather than envelopes. Common sense dictates that, when space and funding permit, file cabinets should be used. They provide the most protection and security for both instrumental and choral music. However, open shelves are a viable and less expensive alternative and are more efficient from the standpoint of space. Figures 8.1 and 8.2 show two storage systems.

If instrumental or choral music is stored on shelves, it should be placed in storage boxes; if it is stored in file cabinets, envelopes or file folders should be used. Boxes on open shelves better protect the music than do envelopes and give the storage area a neat and organized appearance. However, when boxes are used in file cabinets, valuable storage space is lost; sheet music stored in envelopes consumes far less space. Boxes and envelopes designed specifically for the storage of music can be ordered through any music store. They are available in a variety of thicknesses, shapes, and sizes. Figures 8.3 and 8.4 show a variety of storage containers.

Music stored on shelves should be placed vertically rather than stacked one piece on another. The title of the music and the library number should be readily visible. A point in favor of shelf storage is that, as the library grows, it is less expensive to build shelves than it is to purchase file cabinets.

Figure 8.1.   Choral music storage

A case can be made for the use of regular office-type file folders or manila en-velopes, particularly to store choral music. However, if file folders or envelopes are used, steel file cabinets are a must. The expense of the cabinets generally negates any savings realized by obtaining folders from the school's main office.

Preferably, music should be stored in an area separate from the rehearsal room, but readily accessible from that room. In situations where music must be stored in the rehearsal room, the organization of that storage area takes on increased signi-ficance. The music educator has an obligation to students to provide a positive

Figure 8.2. Instrumental music storage

Figure 8.3. Storage containers for instrumental music

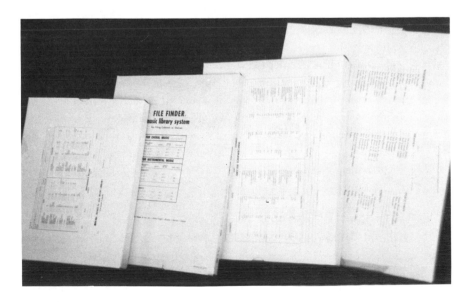

Figure 8.4. Storage containers for choral music

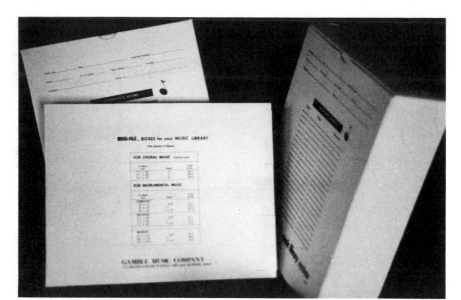

rehearsal environment, including music stored in a neat and organized fashion. A music room with pieces of music stacked haphazardly about the room, with single copies of parts found on top of the piano and folio cabinet, projects negative expectations from the teacher to the student.

Music filing systems

There are four filing systems (plus variations of each) that are being used in high school and college music libraries today. Each filing system has certain advantages and disadvantages. Quite often a music educator inherits a filing system (or lack of one) that is a source of frustration. If you find yourself in such a situation, explore the alternative systems and take the initiative to reorganize the music library. Students are eager to help in such a project, and the end result can be a source of pride for both the students and you. Of course, separate filing systems are necessary for choral, orchestra, and band music.

Alphabetical by title. This system is perhaps the most common method of filing music, particularly in smaller school music libraries. Music is simply filed alphabetically by the title of the piece. The alphabetical-by-title system is the only music filing system where a card file is not absolutely mandatory. Still, it is a good practice to establish card files with the system, especially to cross-index the pieces by composer and classification.

The principal disadvantage of the alphabetical-by-title system is that music must repeatedly be shifted. When new music is purchased, for example, there may be no space available in the file drawer or on the storage shelf for that piece of music to be filed alphabetically. If that is the case, it may be necessary to shift music down through the alphabet to create space for the new music. One solution to this problem is to allow extra space on each shelf and in each file drawer for future library growth, but this can also be a waste of storage space.

Alphabetical by composer. This music filing system is rarely found in junior or senior high school band or choral programs. For that matter, it is unusual to find it in college or university band and choral departments. It is most generally used by orchestral programs with ability levels ranging from student to professional. The existence of the alphabetical-by-composer system was undoubtedly sparked by an interest on the part of orchestra conductors to keep the works of the great masters together in one part of the music library. Orchestral works are often known by the composer's name rather than the title of the piece. For example, Symphony no. 5 by Beethoven is more commonly referred to as "Beethoven's Fifth." Band and choral literature is generally known by the title rather than the composer, and this is particularly true at the high school level. There are, of course, exceptions, such as Handel's *Messiah,* the Hindemith Symphony, the Brahms Requiem, and Persichetti's Divertimento. Choral and instrumental music educators should consider selecting a music filing system other than alphabetical by composer. The composer card file is optional with this filing system, while the title card file is mandatory and the classification card file is highly recommended.

Consecutive number system. This is an accrual filing system that is simple to initiate and maintain. It is becoming a popular system of filing music at all performance levels. Very simply, new music is assigned a consecutive number in the order it is purchased. For example, if the number of the most recent, previously purchased piece of choral music is #232, the next acquired piece would be assigned #233. The greatest advantage of this filing system is that no shifting of music in drawers or on shelves is ever necessary. Another advantage, of course, is the simplicity of the system to initiate and maintain. A severe drawback is that card files are an absolute must. The title card file is mandatory, and the composer and classification card files are strongly recommended.

Inclusive numbers need to be placed in the identification slot on each file drawer or on the edge of the storage shelves. For example, the numbers 212–241 on a drawer or shelf would indicate that that a piece of music that has been assigned a number that falls between those two parameters will be stored there. The consecutive number system works equally well in choral and instrumental music libraries, particularly when a large amount of music is involved.

Letter-number system. Perhaps the most popular accrual method of filing music is the letter-number system. Upon purchase, a piece of music is assigned an identification number, such as A3-22b. The capital letter indicates the file cabinet, the first number identifies the drawer of the file cabinet, the number following the hyphen indicates placement in the drawer, and the small letter denotes classification. An identification number of A3–22b indicates that the music will be located in the "A" file cabinet, third drawer, near the back of the drawer, and the "b" suggests a previously determined classification.

This system works equally well for instrumental and choral music, and the classification code can include more than one letter. For example, perhaps a choral director determined that "a" was the letter to indicate piano accompaniment and that the letter "b" was the classification for spiritual. That particular piece of music would receive a library code number that would include the letters "ab" following the drawer position number. The same double-letter classification could hold true for band music. For example, a band director might assign the letter "e" for transcriptions and the letter "h" for multi-movement works. Therefore, a band transcription of six of Dvorak's "Slavonic Dances" would carry the classification "eh" following the drawer position number.

The letter-number system demands a title card file; the composer card file is strongly recommended, and the classification file is optional, but encouraged. As in the previously discussed accrual system, no shifting of music is necessary, but with the letter-number system, music is more quickly located, and classification information is provided as part of the identification code. If you are in the position of organizing a new music library filing system or revising an established system, strongly consider the letter-number system. Filing music in this way, once the system is in place, can become an enjoyable routine for both student librarians and you.

Processing new music

Before new music is given to students, it should be cataloged by the music librarian. This process includes placing a stamp of identification on each piece of music. Choral music should have an identification stamp on the cover and the first page of the music, because if the cover becomes misplaced, the music will still bear identification. Each piece of music should also be numbered consecutively. In choral music, an assigned number can relate directly to the number on the student folder. In some choral programs, music is assigned by chair number. When the seating arrangement changes, the folder stays and people move. In band and orchestra situations, directors often ask that individual parts be consecutively numbered; in case of loss or damage, the numbering makes it easier to determine the responsible (or irresponsible) party.

File cards must be prepared *before* new music is distributed. If this is not established as a policy, an opportunity exists for confusion to occur when the music is retrieved, and chances increase that the music will be permanently filed without the proper file cards being completed. A file folder, envelope, or box needs to be prepared with the appropriate information, including identification number, title, and composer/arranger. Boxes and envelopes designed especially for the storage of music provide space where additional information can be included, such as the publisher and an inventory of parts or copies (see Figures 8.3 and 8.4). For choral music, the number of available copies of a particular piece of music should already be listed on the file card, which makes it an option to include that information on the file folder or box. If a composition from the band library is being loaned to another school, it is a good practice to inventory the parts prior to mailing them to ensure the return of all borrowed parts. A separate instrumentation sheet (Band Music Inventory Sheet), with the appropriate number of each part can be included with the music when it leaves the library on a loan basis. An example of this type of inventory sheet can be found in Figure 8.13 at the end of this chapter.

Index cards

Commercially printed file cards are available for the purpose of indexing instrumental or choral music. Examples of several types of these cards appear in Figures 8.5, 8.6, and 8.7. Depending on the type of information desired, a music educator can also use standard three-by-five-inch cards and either type the pertinent information on each card or print a set of cards to fit those specifications.

The three major categories of card files that support a music library are title, composer, and classification. Only one card each is necessary for the title and composer categories, but it is entirely possible that a single piece of music may be classified in two or more styles, requiring additional cards. With few exceptions, all school music libraries have a title card file, and many of those also have a composer file, but very few have a classification file. Once in place, the classification file can save a great deal of time when the music director is looking for that one special piece that will top off a concert program.

Choral music is usually filed by voice arrangement; thus categories include SA, SSA, SAB, TTB, TTBB, and SATB. Band music is generally divided into march and concert size, with music matching those size requirements filed accordingly. (Pop music can be found in both sizes also, as can "concert marches." This small bit of confusion underscores the practicality of the classification card file.)

Both instrumental and choral music can be classified in numerous other categories as well. Instrumental categories could include marches, concert marches, Broadway show tunes, novelties, suites, solos, and ensembles with instrumental accompaniment, transcriptions, overtures, and symphonies. Choral classifications

Figure 8.5. Instrumental music index card

Title_____   Library
                                                            Number _____

☐ Band ☐ Orchestra ☐ Ensemble
☐ Quickstep ☐ Octavo ☐ Concert

Composer and/or Arranger _____

Type of Number_____(Classification Guide)_____

Publisher_____ Original Cost_____ Date Added_____

Playing Time:_____   Condensed Score _____ Full Score _____

(List performance dates below.)

PEPPER LIBRARY SYSTEM CARD #10-1
©1965, J. W. PEPPER & SON, INC.

J. W. PEPPER & SON, INC.
VALLEY FORGE — ATLANTA — DETROIT
TAMPA — LOS ANGELES

Figure 8.6. Choral music index card

TITLE_____   Library
                                                            Number _____

☐ OCTAVO   CANTATA OR
☐ EXTENDED   ☐   COLLECTION
   WORK   (BOUND BOOK)

COMPOSER AND/OR ARRANGER

LIBRARY NO. _____

TYPE OF NUMBER_____*(for Classification purposes)*

NO. OF   PERFORMANCE   INSTRUMENTAL
COPIES_____ TIME _____ SOLI _____ ACCOMPANYING PARTS _____

                                               DATE ADDED
PUBLISHER_____ COST_____   TO LIBRARY_____

NOTES ON SPECIAL PROBLEMS_____

(List performance dates on back of this card)

PEPPER LIBRARY SYSTEM CARD #10-2
©1965, J. W. PEPPER & SON, INC.

J. W. PEPPER & SON, INC.
VALLEY FORGE — ATLANTA — DETROIT
TAMPA — LOS ANGELES

Figure 8.7. Ensemble music index card

Library Inventory	**ENSEMBLE MUSIC**

Composer _____ No. _____

Title_____ Classified_____

Edition_____ Score _____

	List each part of ensemble	Difficulty of parts
1	_____	_____
2	_____	_____
3	_____	_____
4	_____	_____
5	_____	_____
6	_____	_____
7	_____	_____
8	_____	_____
9	_____	_____
10	_____	_____
11	_____	_____

No. 5603, Schmitt, Hall & McCreary Company   MINNEAPOLIS, MINN.

might include a cappella, piano accompaniment, instrumental accompaniment, secular, sacred, spirituals, show tunes, folk tunes, Christmas, and other seasonal music. It is easy to see how a particular piece of either band or choral music could comfortably fit into several classifications. The number and type of classifications that can be used in any music library filing system is limited only by the ingenuity and creativity of the music educator. The reader should be warned, however, that if too many classifications are used, the system loses a degree of practicality.

Mandatory information on all three types of index cards are the title, composer, publisher, and library inventory number. Optional information includes the date of purchase, date of last performance, group performing, and the availability of a recording. Additional information pertinent to the choral library is the number of copies, voice arrangement (SSA, SATB, and so on), and the type of accompaniment necessary (piano, instrumental, a cappella).

The title index cards should have the title of the music located at the top of the card, and the composer cards should have the composer or arranger (last name first) in that position, followed by the title of the piece. The classification card should state the classification of the music at the top of the card, followed by the title and composer.

In addition to index cards, there are now database and card file computer programs that offer "virtual" indexing systems. Particularly where a central library is used by several different schools, a computerized filling system may be more practical. It certainly will be faster to use, and most music students are computer literate and would enjoy helping to maintain or initiate such a system.

MUSIC LIBRARY EQUIPMENT

In addition to the files, shelves, or cabinets necessary to store the music and maintain the card files, a limited amount of other equipment is needed. A typewriter (or word processor or computer), tape and a dispenser, a paper cutter, labels, scissors, a

Figure 8.8. Instrumental music sorting rack

worktable, a sorting rack (instrumental), and folio and general storage cabinets are all necessary for the efficient operation of a music library. Much of this equipment and supplies are available through the main office of the school. There are pieces of equipment, however, that are specific to the music library.

Sorting rack. No instrumental music library should be without a sorting rack that allows for orderly dispersion of music from and subsequent return to the music storage area. (Figure 8.8 shows one type of sorting rack.) Too many student librarians waste time trying to arrange instrumental music in score order by placing music around the rehearsal room on music stands, on the floor, or both. The music sorting rack solves this dilemma. When placing several compositions in a band or orchestra folder at the same time, a librarian simply needs to arrange the music folders on the sorting rack in score order and place a copy of each composition on the appropriate folder. When all parts have been distributed, the librarian can place the new music inside folders, collect them in score order, and return the folders to the folio cabinet. Music that is collected and placed in score order before being returned to storage is handled in the reverse order. Band and orchestra directors should provide their librarians with this simple labor-saving piece of equipment.

Folio cabinets. Folio cabinets serve two important functions. First, they provide the most efficient means available for the daily dispersal and collection of music used in choir, orchestra, and band rehearsals. Second, commercially manufactured cabinets, finished in bright colors, contribute to the total positive environment of a rehearsal room. Folio cabinets should rest on wheels sufficient in size to withstand the weight generated by the large volume of music normally present in any large musical ensemble's rehearsal and performance folders. They should be located near the rehearsal room door to allow students easy access as they enter and leave the room. Figures 8.9 and 8.10 show two types of music folio cabinets.

Music storage

If a school district is unwilling to furnish steel filing cabinets, consider using wooden shelving combined with cardboard storage boxes. Construction is relatively inexpensive, and the final product can create an impressive appearance when all the music is cataloged and in its proper place. Shelving of this sort is cost-efficient and makes storing music easy and safe.

Auxiliary library storage

If recordings, cassette tapes, CDs, filmstrips, movies, videotapes, photos, slides, and transparencies are to be housed in the music library, the music educator should

Figure 8.9. Instrumental music folio cabinet

consult with the school librarian to locate catalogs that specifically deal with storage cabinets and other aids for audiovisual materials.

If phonograph records are to be stored, they must be kept in an upright position to avoid warping. Special shelves with dividers six to eight inches apart can be purchased or constructed for the purpose of storing old phonograph records. Compact disc recordings can be stored in any variety of commercially produced storage products. For ease of filing, recordings can be divided into such classifications as classical, jazz, ethnic, folk, pop, rock, solo, musical theater, and avant-garde. Card files based on the classifications selected can be completed and filed in alphabetical order for each category. Should a music educator elect to file CDs by number, multiple classification cards should then be used. There are also commercial software packages available for indexing a CD library on computer.

Other audiovisual materials are also fragile and should be protected by cases or cabinets designed specifically for that purpose. They should be indexed on file cards and cross-referenced according to author, title, subject, and media. In the

Figure 8.10. Choral music folio cabinet

case of extended-play videotapes, cue numbers should be included on the file card to expedite the search for a particular subject. Again, these indices can be maintained on PC as well as on file cards.

MANAGING THE MUSIC LIBRARY

After the school music library has been organized for efficiency, it must be administered in a professional and effective manner. The most carefully structured, best-organized venture of any kind will fail unless it is accompanied by sound management practices. As a music educator, you can set an example for students regarding the careful treatment of school-owned music by the manner in which you manage the library holdings.

Music librarians

The most important resource in any music library is the student librarian. Too many music educators fail to recognize the administrative advantage in *selecting* students to serve as music librarians. Be sure to choose the librarians yourself rather than allow them to be elected by other students. Select at least two from each class or major ensemble. If at all possible, choose librarians from different grade levels in school so that there is always a veteran involved in library work; this promotes continuity and avoids the need for repeated training of students.

The duties of the music librarians include cataloging new music on file cards; distributing, collecting, and filing music; repairing music; and in general doing all the clerical work associated with the music library. If the music library is carefully organized and administered, a tremendous burden of time and responsibility will be taken over by the music librarians.

Music folders. When in the hands of either choral or instrumental students in a rehearsal setting, music needs to be adequately protected. Office file folders, envelopes, or cardboard folios available from music stores all provide a limited degree of protection. The selection of music folders for performing groups is another relatively inexpensive way to advance, in a small way, the image of a musical organization. Colorful, fiberboard music folders, personalized with the name of the school and performing organization on the outside, adds a degree of professionalism to the group and at the same time offers maximum protection for the music. Figure 8.11 shows examples of music folders.

These more permanent types of music folders can be bought at any good music store. Two factors must be kept in mind when ordering folders for both choral and instrumental ensembles: (1) The inside pockets where music is placed should be expandable and (2) each folder should have a pencil "pocket" to neatly store a rehearsal pencil. After all, professional musicians use pencils in rehearsals to mark their music; music students should be allowed—and encouraged—to do the same.

Distribution and collection of music. The process of distributing and collecting music is perhaps the most important task performed by music librarians. Except in emergency situations, music should *never* be distributed or collected during the rehearsal period. The time music educators spend with their students discussing and preparing music is too precious for that type of secretarial activity. Music should always be distributed in advance of the rehearsal period by the librarians. This is a very simple task when a sorting rack and folio cabinet are available.

When music needs to be collected, the music educator should write the appropriate titles on the blackboard and ask the students during rehearsal to place the music, in the order the title appears on the board, on top of their rehearsal folder

Figure 8.11. Personalized rehearsal folders

prior to returning it to the folio cabinet. The music librarian can then collect the music (in score order for instrumental groups), place it on the sorting rack, and, with a minimum of effort, organize the music into numerical or score order and return it to the storage area.

It is a good idea to leave the file box, folder, or envelope in its normal place in the cabinet or on the shelf while the music is out of the library. This applies to both choral and instrumental music. This policy creates an additional source for cross-referencing and ensures that the music will be returned to the correct place within the storage system.

Students appreciate this display of efficiency and attention to detail. The organized distribution of music is another factor that contributes to a positive rehearsal environment.

Filing scores. All complete instrumental scores should be stored separately in a file in the director's office. No matter which library filing system is being used, the scores should be placed in a manila office file folder and filed alphabetically by title. A typewritten label should be placed on the tab of each file folder and include the title (in capital letters), the composer/arranger, and the library identification code number. Single copies of every piece of choral music available in the music library should be placed in alphabetical order by voice arrangement in a file cabinet in the choral director's office. Each copy should also be placed in a manila file folder, with the title, composer/arranger, and library number typed on a label that is then placed on the folder tab.

The advantages of this procedure are evident. There isn't an experienced band director who hasn't distributed a piece of music for rehearsal and then learned that the complete score is missing. Storing the scores in the director's office helps prevent misplacing them, particularly at the point when music has been collected and is being prepared for storage. The greatest advantage to the music educator, however, is that instrumental scores and choral music are readily available when music is being considered for rehearsal and performance. Single copies of choral music used for this purpose should have DIRECTOR'S COPY stamped on the cover to preserve any special notations written on the music for future use. Self-inking rubber stamps are inexpensive and easy to obtain, and choral directors are encouraged to avail themselves of this simple aid.

Numbering music. All choral music should be numbered consecutively. The number on the music should correspond with the number on the rehearsal folder. This procedure aids dispersal and collection of music and determines responsibility for missing or damaged choral music. Band music can also be numbered according to the system in Figure 8.12. Publishers of band music have not yet agreed on the total number of copies of each part to include with a publication; therefore, it is necessary to adopt a flexible system similar to the one in Figure 8.12. A similar table could be developed for numbering orchestral publications.

The numbering of music, both choral and instrumental, enables music librarians to exercise a greater degree of inventory control over music in the folders and expedites the determination of parts or copies missing after music has been collected.

When adopting a numbering system for an instrumental ensemble, always begin an instrument or section with the same number. For example, first B-flat clarinets

Figure 8.12. Suggested numbering system for band publications

Number	Part
1-9	Flutes and piccolos
10-14	Oboes and English horns
15-19	Bassoons
20-22	E-Flat clarinets
23-43	B-Flat clarinets
44-48	Alto clarinets
49-53	Bass clarinets
54-56	Contra-bass clarinets
57-59	Soprano saxophones
60-66	Alto saxophones
67-71	Tenor saxophones
72-74	Baritone saxophones
75-76	Bass saxophones
77-87	Cornets
88-94	Trumpets
95-99	Fluegelhorns
100-110	French horns
111-121	Trombones
122-126	Baritone horns
127-137	Tubas
138-140	String basses
141-150	Percussion

always begin with number 23; the first cornet part is assigned the number 77, and so on.

Loaning and borrowing music. The music publishing industry has certainly not been exempt from the devastating effects of inflation in recent years, and the result has been a significant and at times astronomical increase in the cost of published music. Many band publications now sell for $100 or more, and it is not uncommon to find choral music priced at $1.25 to $2.50 per copy. This increase in the cost of music comes at the same time music budgets in schools across the country are being cut.

The increased expense involved in the purchase of music, combined with reduced school music budgets, has resulted in less music being purchased and more being borrowed at the secondary school, college, and university levels. The result of this backlash has been the collapse of small music publishing firms.

If you intend to loan materials from the music library, you must take certain precautions to ensure the protection and subsequent return of all parts. Keep on hand a supply of heavy cardboard (box weight), cut to octavo size for choral music or concert size for instrumental music. When mailing music, always place cardboard on

Figure 8.13. Band music inventory sheet

Bea Flat Public School

Music Library

Band Music Inventory Sheet

Title of piece_____

Composer/Arranger_____

Loaned to: _____

Address:_____Zip_____

Date out:_____   Date in:_____

Number of copies	Part	Number of copies	Part
_____	Piccolo	_____	1st Cornet
_____	1st Flute	_____	2nd Cornet
_____	2nd Flute	_____	3rd Cornet
_____	1st Oboe	_____	1st Trumpet
_____	2nd Oboe	_____	2nd Trumpet
_____	English horn	_____	3rd Trumpet
_____	1st Bassoon	_____	Fluegelhorn
_____	2nd Bassoon	_____	1st French horn
_____	E-Flat Clarinet	_____	2nd French horn
_____	1st B-Flat Clarinet	_____	3rd French horn
_____	2nd B-Flat Clarinet	_____	4th French horn
_____	3rd B-Flat Clarinet	_____	1st Trombone
_____	Alto Clarinet	_____	2nd Trombone
_____	Bass Clarinet	_____	3rd or Bass Trombone
_____	Contra-bass Clarinet	_____	Baritone horn
_____	Soprano Saxophone	_____	Baritone horn
_____	1st Alto Saxophone	_____	Tuba
_____	2nd Alto Saxophone	_____	String bass
_____	Tenor Saxophone	_____	Timpani
_____	Baritone Saxophone	_____	Mallets
_____	Bass Saxophone	_____	Other percussion

both sides of the music and secure it with rubber hands. Boxes are generally difficult to find, but padded envelopes are readily available in a variety of sizes. These envelopes provide more than adequate protection for music when enclosed with cardboard on two sides. Do not send the file box, envelope, or folder with music that is being loaned to another school. As mentioned earlier, that item should remain in its proper location in the storage system.

A music inventory sheet should be enclosed with loaned instrumental music indicating the total number of copies of each part that are being sent. (Figure 8.13 shows a sample inventory sheet.) Enclose the original sheet with the loaned music and retain a copy for your files. A notation should be made on the back of the library title file card as to whom the music was loaned, the date out, and the expected return date. The librarian should compare returned music with the music inventory sheet, noting any discrepancies. The borrower should be contacted and informed of any missing music. Missing music more than likely will be located, but if not, the borrower should be expected to purchase replacement parts.

If a music inventory sheet has not been enclosed, it is a good administrative policy for the borrower to have the music librarian complete one before distributing the music. A copy can then be sent to the lending school with a short note indicating that the included sheet is an accounting of the music received. Upon collection of the music and prior to its return, the music librarian should refer to the music inventory sheet to ensure all borrowed copies are being returned. Borrowed music should receive the same protection when it is being returned to the owner.

The borrowing and lending of music can result in significant budget savings. However, if adequate funding is available for the purchase of music, it is better to buy than to borrow. Purchasing music supports an extremely important chain in music education: the publishing companies and the composers whose music they publish.

Computers in the music library

In the music education computer software market, management programs are now readily available, specifically designed to accommodate the indexing and record-keeping needs of a music library. Not all available software adapts well to all music filing systems, so card indexes should be maintained as a backup in case of program loss or damage. Because most music educators have access to computers, the computerizing of the music library is an extremely practical organizational aid.

Music educators who observe copyright guidelines and make use of the technology and equipment available to them will find management of their music library resources a professionally rewarding process and experience.

SUGGESTED ACTIVITIES

1. Invite a local orchestra, band, or choir director to class and ask that individual to describe how music is filed, distributed, collected, loaned, and borrowed as part of his or her responsibility as an ensemble director.
2. Visit a local secondary school and develop responses to the same points listed in activity number one. Report to the class.
3. Invite a local lawyer to class to discuss current influences the 1976 Copyright Law has had on *all* types of music in the country. Prepare questions relating to international copyright infringement and foreign policy in relation to unauthorized production of compact disks and video tapes which originated in this country.

CHAPTER NINE

ASSESSING AND
GRADING MUSIC
PERFORMANCE

INTRODUCTION

Assessing and grading students is one of the most difficult and controversial areas of music education. Yet in today's performance-oriented environment, educators increasingly must justify their programs through concrete measurements. Music, like any other academic subject, has to produce "results," and these results are measured in terms of student achievement.

This chapter begins with a discussion of why assessment is important in music education. The new National Standards for Arts Education developed by the Consortium of National Arts Education Associations, through a grant from the Music Educators National Conference (MENC) have helped establish a national model for local educators. Whether or not these standards are appropriate for every music program, they do establish a groundwork on which programs can be measured.

To help readers understand how assessment works, the chapter introduces and defines basic terminology. It then reviews developing objectives for a music program, which is a key element of establishing assessment, because goals cannot be assessed unless they are defined from the start. The chapter goes on to examine several measurement tools, from standardized tests to video assessments, progress charts, learning contracts, and portfolio assessments.

The problem many music teachers face is how to grade a student's achievement in a performance situation. Subjective qualities—such as tone quality, depth of interpretation, and involvement with the music—are very difficult to quantify. To answer this concern, the chapter introduces and explains grading methods, along with some of the criteria that can legitimately be used in evaluating a student's performance in a group setting. Sample written tests are provided that can help establish objective measures. The chapter includes an assessment of different measurement tools, from individualized evaluation scales to negative and positive point scales. Not to be overlooked are student self-evaluations and evaluations of the class and the teacher, which can be useful in formulating objective measures of individual and group achievement.

The chapter concludes with an overview of the history of musical aptitude testing and the use of these tests in the music classroom. Industry-developed tests are also discussed, with some guidelines as to their usefulness and effectiveness.

The Need for Assessment

Since the early 1980s there has been a rush to assessment among music educators at the national level. Boards, commissions, advocacy groups, and task forces of all types have advanced the need for new and upgraded assessment techniques and have prescribed both short- and long-term solutions to satisfy that need. In the last fifteen years, numerous articles have appeared in the *Music Educators Journal* dealing with assessment in music education in one form or another.

There is a great desire on the part of music educators and their supportive professional organizations to see that music is recognized as a bona fide discipline in the curriculum of public schools in this country. In 1994, Congress passed "Goals 2000," the Educate America Act. The arts were included among the disciplines in which Congress determined every young American should be able to demonstrate competence. To determine competence, assessment criteria were required. The push for such criteria resulted in the nine National Standards for Arts Education and the MENC publication *The School Music Program: A New Vision.* (More information regarding the MENC National Standards is given in chapters 13 and 14.) Readers are urged to become well acquainted with the national standards and their accompanying assessment strategies.

As music educators, if we wish to have our efforts seen as genuine parts of a complete curriculum, we must be accountable, and that means accepting assessment. Some music educators look at the standards and deem them unattainable. There are teachers, for example, who meet their elementary general music students for only a half hour each week. They feel there is simply no time to teach the material necessary to satisfy MENC's assessment strategies. Similarly, a choir director whose group meets twice weekly may cite a lack of time to satisfy the strategies associated with the choral performance standards.

Music teachers should not view the national standards as an indictment of their efforts and abilities. They are *voluntary* and intended to be adaptable for local situations. As constructed, the standards and their accompanying strategies for competency are meant to be examples, not prescriptions.

It is important that the outcomes of any assessment based on the national standards be shared with others. If the results are positive, they should be made public. Unfavorable assessment results should serve as the foundation for local advocacy involving parents and school officials. No self-respecting administrator would want a local music program to fail miserably when measured against a national assessment model. A temporary negative result can often lead to a long-term positive effect, particularly when assessment evidence is so strongly supportive.

Assessment, no matter how difficult to do, has become a part of music education. Standards of any kind are meaningless without some sort of system for assessment. Some colleagues in the music education profession continue to resist it, citing the lack of time, the nuisance factor, and the disruption of their work. It is important, however, that these teachers come to terms with the changing assessment scene.

More and more states are mandating measurable curriculum objectives for public schools. The only way music teachers can accommodate these requirements is through the process of assessing student achievement and classroom content on a regular basis. Because of this emphasis on performance achievement as well as teacher accountability, how students are assessed and by what measurement techniques must be a paramount concern for all music educators.

UNDERSTANDING THE TERMINOLOGY

Before we examine the purposes of assessing and grading music performance and look at some examples, we need to define the terms associated with measurement methods.

Standardized tests

Tests with fixed content that are devised so that they can be administered to different groups of people at different times are called standardized. The method of administering such tests must be specified so that they will be given in an identical manner on different occasions. Scoring procedures for standardized tests also must be established. William E. Whybrew (1972, p. 15) defined standardized tests as those that have been devised so that they can be administered and scored in a uniform way upon different occasions by different persons.

Norms

Test norms can be defined as scores that have been established as typical for a population, that is, typical for all persons grouped according to common characteristics and/or criteria. Standardized tests can exist without norms, but a very important value of standardization is eliminated if norm scores are not present. After all, comparison of the test group with scores of previously tested subjects is one of the most attractive aspects of standardized testing. Norm scores are often presented in terms of percentile ranking. For example, if a subject's raw score on a standardized test is 122, and if that test score is found to rank in the eightieth percentile, it means that eighty percent of the test scores for that group are below 122. Test norms in the form of percentile ranking allow you to make a group comparison when using a standardized test. For example, when comparing two raw test scores of 35 and 45, it's impossible to tell how much better the raw score of 45 is than 35. But if the raw score of 45 ranks in the ninetieth percentile and 35 ranks in the thirtieth percentile, it can then be said that the score of 45 is three times better than 35.

Reliability

Test reliability refers to the consistency with which a test measures actual knowledge. Reliability is reasonably easy to determine by using the test-retest method, through administration of a test on two separate occasions to the same group under identical conditions. If two sets of scores from the same test were to match exactly, the reliability score, or coefficient, would be a perfect 1.00. An acceptable indication of score similarity is a reliability coefficient of 0.85.

What makes a test reliable? First of all, a test that is too easy for the level of the group will yield a high reliability score; a test that is too difficult will involve an abnormal amount of guessing, which creates poor reliability. Care must be exercised on the part of the music educator to select a standardized test that is suited for the grade level to which it will be applied, which should ensure optimum reliability for the instrument. The length of a standardized test affects reliability: the longer the test, the higher its reliability. Again, a test that is lengthy with high-reliability scores when applied to ninth-grade students could lose much reliability when the same test was administered to fourth-grade students because of the fatigue factor.

A test's objectivity influences its reliability. The standardized tests with the highest reliability coefficients have eliminated any possibility of student interpretations or viewpoints. The clarity of the exam and its instructions affects reliability, as do the conditions of administration. Test scores are more reliable when the test is administered in familiar surroundings. Test items also need to be independent of one another so students can't determine answers to some questions from information contained in other questions. The arrangement of test items in order of difficulty can also positively affect test reliability. Finally, the scope of the test must be considered: the more limited the field to be covered, the smaller the range of item difficulty. Questions too easy or too difficult are of no help in determining potential knowledge or skill (Lehman 1968, p. 14).

Validity

When determining the validity of an aptitude test, you should ask, "Does it measure what it is supposed to measure?" If it can be said that an aptitude test measures an individual's potential for some type of musical achievement, then validity may be determined as the truthfulness of that test. Although a good test must be valid, measurement of that validity is complex. There's no minimum acceptable validity coefficient score. Coefficient scores relating to validity are generally lower than those for reliability and are determined through less objective research. A test can be reliable yet not valid for the use for which it is being considered, but a test cannot be valid without also being reliable.

A standardized test should be selected based on reliability scores and an examination of the test for apparent validity. For example, if the main use of the test will be to predict future success of beginning instrumental students, the content of the test must accurately measure aptitude in the areas of pitch and rhythm discrimination, sense of time, and musical sensitivity. If the test is to predict success in sight-singing, different criteria will assume increased significance. Any standardized test must be judged against its specific purpose (Lehman 1968, p. 1015). That is validity.

Measurement

Refers to the use of tests and performance rating scales that are designed to produce a specific grade. It applies to the collecting of quantitative information. Any information gathered through measurement generally provides a basis for making a judgment or evaluation.

Evaluation

Involves determining the value of something. An evaluation employs a number of tools, such as appraisals, interviews, observations, and checklists, to reach a conclusion. To be effective and useful, an evaluation must be comprehensive, and more importantly, systematic. As it pertains to music education, it involves the judgments that music educators make relating to their students and student efforts and can be considered the result of assessment. Evaluation is used to satisfy the question "Are students attaining the instructional objectives established for them?"

Assessment   a collage of a bunch of different stuff

Guides instruction and is the means by which educators can gather information about their students' level of achievement. The process of assessment emphasizes discernment and discrimination and is best carried out by using a variety of techniques (Music Educators National Conference 1996, p. 1).

Musical aptitude

Musical aptitude may be defined as a predictor of ability to retain, recognize, and reproduce a short musical phrase, and it is an indicator of the potential of capacity for musical achievement (Lehman 1968, p. 7). Those qualities are likely to develop over time, resulting in higher aptitude scores, although they may then cease to improve beyond a certain level in spite of additional training. Music scientists and psychologists feel that musical aptitude is a product of innate potential and early environmental influences (Gordon 1971, p. 7). When all of these qualities are considered, it is easy to understand why musical aptitude is so difficult to determine.

Musical achievement

Musical achievement can most readily be defined as a measurement of what has been learned. An achievement test attempts to measure facts, skills, understanding, or other aspects of learning. Yet achievement tests necessarily reflect the initial aptitude that individuals bring to the learning situation. As with any instrument of assessment, music educators must establish what is acceptable evidence of achievement as they establish objectives for their programs. Above all, music educators are warned not to attempt to use musical aptitude tests to determine musical achievement.

Accountability

Accountability coincides with responsibility. School music programs and music educators are accountable to a supervisor and/or administrator, who is in turn accountable to the school district, school board, and ultimately the public (Boyle and Radocy 1987, p. 15). This type of scrutiny ensures accountability in one form or another and will continue to play a major role in the evaluation of education.

ESTABLISHING OBJECTIVES

Music teachers must construct clear and specific objectives that establish exactly what their instruction should achieve and how that instruction promotes achievement (see chapter 1). What is it that music students can be expected to do or accomplish as a result of instruction? What should music students be able to do to demonstrate their competency? These and other related questions should be answered through the establishment of educational objectives.

Music students achieve according to expectations: not their expectations, but those of their teacher. It must be remembered that those same students have expectations as well when they enter the classroom or rehearsal area. If established objectives vary dramatically from student expectations, serious behavioral problems could arise.

Music performance objectives are often difficult to construct with any degree of clarity. Some aspects of music making, such as phrasing, note accuracy, and rhythmic accuracy, are easy to assess objectively; others, such as tone quality, intonation, and musicality, are measured subjectively and therefore are difficult to accurately assess. For example, just how flawed is a student's tone quality? Just how musically expressive was a student's performance? How can a performance actually be measured against what the performer is capable of doing? These are hard questions, with no easy answers. A serious attempt will be made in the following pages to guide readers in the establishment of attainable and practical assessment techniques as they relate to music performance achievement.

TYPES OF ASSESSMENT

Standardized tests

Commercially produced standardized music achievement tests are readily available for use. Published standardized tests provide a music educator with the advantage of comparing local test scores with a large group of students with varying backgrounds through the use of norm scores that accompany the test.

The problem that many educators have with standardized music achievement tests is that they feel the tests do not actually measure what they deem as important and pertinent musical knowledge for their students. It is not uncommon, therefore, in the name of self-preservation, for music educators to "teach to the test" when the administration of standardized music achievement tests are mandated in their school district. The test thus dictates the curriculum rather than measuring the success or failure of what the teacher would ideally feature in the classroom. Many teachers feel that "teaching to the test" is unethical or at the very least counterproductive.

Video assessment

Marching band directors have been using video as an assessment technique for many years. After each marching band show, a video is shown to members of the band, either as a group or in small groups or squads. When done properly, students are encouraged to assess their own performance and the overall quality of the band's performance. They are also encouraged to determine exactly what must be done to improve their performance as it relates to the overall production. The director also evaluates the band's achievement level and outlines areas for improvement.

Directors of concert organizations could take a cue from their marching colleagues by employing a video review of ensemble performances, complete with guided written student comments and critiques. These methods can be great aids in improving student performance.

Progress charts

For many years, particularly in the area of instrumental instruction, student progress charts have been used. Students are given a series of objectives to achieve, and as each one is reached, grades or some indication of achievement (gold, silver, red, or blue stars, for example) are noted on the charts. The charts are publicly displayed, often in rehearsal rooms. Music educators have found this method to be an effective motivator, employing the power of peer pressure to effect improvement. Lately, however, some music educators are removing progress charts from public view on the urging of their administrators, who cite the need to accommodate individual students' right to privacy. Before using progress charts, therefore, you should seek administrative approval.

Learning contracts

Learning contracts have been on the education scene for many years, at all levels, from elementary schools through graduate programs. In a typical system, students and parents enter into a contract with the music teacher, outlining the criteria on which grades will be awarded. Based on the criteria, students can contract for an A, B, C, or so on. Some music educators are using contracts as an indication that their curriculum is based on the national standards. This is not a bad idea. Many music educators also feel that an assessment system based on contracts is a clear and simple method of assigning and explaining grades.

Portfolio assessment

Portfolio assessment is perhaps the hottest assessment technique today. The term is often used interchangeably with *authentic, alternative,* or *performance assessment.* These comparisons are not exactly accurate, but nonetheless are quite frequently made. Basically, alternative assessment is any method that deviates from the more traditional form of standardized, multiple-choice items to measure achievement. Music educators often support portfolio assessment, not because they believe so strongly in this form of alternative assessment, but because they react negatively to standardized testing.

Proponents of portfolio assessment feel that any type of analytical activity can be easily assessed with written exams; however, they feel that such things as a student's interpretation and evaluation of a concert performance can best be reflected through the use of written student critiques.

Those in favor of using portfolios in assessing student understanding and achievement also feel that test scores all too often play a part in political and economic decisions affecting the quality of education in today's schools. They point out that tremendous pressure can be felt by school districts and teachers to produce high scores on standardized tests. Furthermore, they argue, these achievement scores are not a reflection of the attainment and retention of knowledge on the part of students.

A music portfolio is basically a container for evidence, a work in progress, so to speak. Advocates feel that an opportunity exists within the portfolio system for process and product to share equally in importance, an opportunity which does not exist in other forms of assessment. Opponents of portfolio assessment argue that no correct way has been determined to design a portfolio. They point out that most portfolios include examples of typical and best work, but offer doubts as to whether a student should be rewarded for typical work.

There is no consensus of opinion as to what exactly should be included in portfolios of performance class members. Ensemble music folders could provide examples of work completed, work in progress, and problems identified and solved. Some music educators feel that instrumental or choral ensemble members should be required to listen to an audiotape or view a videotape of a concert performance and write a critique of the performance following guidelines established by the instructor. The critiques could then be included in student portfolios. Solo and ensemble adjudication forms, audition results, news articles and photos, worksheets completed, performance and written test results, and individual and group audiotapes are all examples of items that could be included in individual student portfolios.

In portfolio assessment, music teachers make all the judgments as they evaluate the progress of their students. But students need to be involved in the process, and both teachers and students should jointly write a statement that defines guidelines for items to be included in a portfolio. Note that serious grading of portfolios involves a high level of subjectivity and is extremely time-consuming.

GRADING AND MUSIC PERFORMANCE

The accountability process in music education continues to cry out for a more valid, organized, and systematic approach to assigning grades to performance classes. Music educators owe it to themselves as well as the talented youth under their direct supervision to develop a grading process that disassociates itself from the long-standing tradition in music performance of assigning grades based primarily on attendance and attitude.

Music performance loses respectability in the eyes of school administrators because of the lack of viable grading criteria. More important, many music educators feel that serious repercussions can result from the lack of an educationally sound approach for assigning music performance grades. They feel that grading on non-musical criteria such as attendance and attitude can be seen as an indication of weakness in the total music education program.

Many music educators see the process of grading their performing groups as a nuisance, an encroachment on the valuable time they spend leading their orchestras, choirs, and bands. The problem with this attitude is that students seem to place the same level of importance on their performance grades as the teachers do. Any grading procedures should be seen by students as fair and appropriate, or barriers can arise between them and group directors. Unfortunately, many music educators and their students appear to function comfortably within the current system. Change to more comprehensive assessment and grading is on the horizon, though, and music educators must be prepared to make necessary adjustments in how they assess achievement and assign grades to their performance classes.

A scenario

"Attitude and attendance," replied a nervous first-year music educator when questioned in his choir room by a mother concerned about the grading criteria that led to her daughter's C for the recently completed grading period in choir.

The mother persisted, and the embarrassed choir director could not offer an educationally sound and valid rationale as to why attendance, or class participation, and attitude were the sum total of consideration given to assigning quarterly grades for choir, other than that was the way he was graded in high school.

The mother requested a three-way meeting between herself, the choir director, and the school's principal to discuss the matter. As a result of the meeting, the grade was changed by one level, and the distraught teacher was faced with the prospect of establishing some type of performance-based evaluative process for the purpose of assigning choir grades during the next nine-week quarter. An awesome task! No one would relish this experience. Once again, proactivity provides a more professional as well as comfortable manner in which to resolve conflict.

Grading participation

Participation and student attitude play a significantly larger role in performance classes than in other academic classes. Because music classes are performance-oriented, teachers and class members alike rely on one another to create a successful and musically satisfying ensemble performance. Students who miss algebra class harm only themselves, not the rest of the class, but those who fail to attend rehearsals or, even worse, a performance, can have an extremely negative impact on the group's efforts.

Because music performance classes are elective, it is only natural that a student's participation level be included as part of the criteria for assigning a performance grade. It should not, however, be the only criterion. Grades should be awarded based on some type of merit, and participation levels can justifiably be considered in the determination of that merit.

Conversely, student attitude and personality have no place in the grading process because of the level of subjective judgment involved. Music teachers must find alternate means of dealing with poor attitudes in their performance classes. After-school, one-on-one conferences, detention, work with a school counselor, and suspension from the group are but a few ways of dealing with less-than-desirable attitudes exhibited by a student.

COMPREHENSIVE GRADING SYSTEMS
FOR MUSIC PERFORMANCE

In preparation for this chapter, the author reviewed ten years' worth of issues of a leading choral journal, a prominent instrumental music publication, and *Music Educators Journal* for articles dealing with grading music performance. Not one article dealing solely with performance grading was found in any of the issues. The choral and instrumental publications had no articles dealing with assessment. *MEJ* had numerous articles on assessment of music programs, instruction, and musical achievement, as well as assessment based on the national standards, but no articles dealing specifically with assigning grades to members of performance classes.

Popular textbooks tend to offer platitudes on the problem of assessment, such as, "Solutions to the grading dilemma in music education are not simple, but teachers should nevertheless have some valid bases for grades assigned to students," but offer no suggestions. Why are the solutions not simple? What are some valid bases for assigning grades? Experienced music educators as well as students preparing to become music educators need some "for examples" to help them address the grading dilemma.

When developing a plan for assigning performance grades, consider using a multiple-based system. That is, use participation level in the grading process if it can be systematically assessed, but supplement it with two other techniques that measure achievement in performance. What follows are grading strategies that move toward more objectivity in the process, along with accompanying examples on grading bands, choirs, and orchestras.

Written tests for performing groups

The saying "Teach the music, test the music" comes to mind when music directors attempt to construct written tests based on one or more compositions that are in the folders of their ensembles. Test questions can be developed pertaining to a particular composition: for example, questions relating to the style of the piece, the composer, specific performance problems faced and solved, a variety of musical terms, rhythmic and melodic motives, the tonality of the piece, tempo indications and meanings, expression markings, and dynamic indications.

Figures 9.1 and 9.2 are examples of written tests for either instrumental or choral ensembles using one piece of music in the groups' rehearsal folders. The multiple-choice format was selected in these examples because of ease of scoring, an important consideration when dealing with a large choir, band, or orchestra. Multiple-choice tests also are more objective than tests that require short essay-type responses.

The music for Figure 9.1 is found in Appendix A and for Figure 9.2, in Appendix B. Readers are urged to compare each test with the music on which it is based, and perhaps even take the test themselves. Only those pages of *And Nature Smiled* that are applicable to the test are included in Appendix B.

Figure 9.1. Sample written exam based on instrumental literature

---

BEA FLAT MIDDLE SCHOOL

Written Exam on *Regenesis*

Place an *x* in the blank to the left of the answer that is the
BEST response to each of the following statements and questions.

1. How fast should the tempo be on the first section of *Regenesis?*
   _____ a. Slow tempo.
   _____ b. Moderately slow tempo.
   _____ c. Rapid tempo.
   _____ d. Very fast tempo.

2. Which of these terms refers to the style of a piece of music?
   _____ a. Allegretto.
   _____ b. Freely.
   _____ c. Largo.
   _____ d. Andante.

3. The word "dynamics" refers to
   _____ a. how fast the piece should be performed.
   _____ b. the range that the instruments are expected to play.
   _____ c. how smooth and connected it should be performed.
   _____ d. degrees of loudness or softness at which the ensemble is expected
       to play.

4. In measures 7–10, to be musically correct, where should a breath be taken?
   _____ a. After count four in bar 7.
   _____ b. After the dotted quarter in bar 8.
   _____ c. After count three in bar 9.
   _____ d. After the eighth note in bar 10.

5. What do the curved lines mean in bars 11–12?
   _____ a. Play as smoothly as possible.

_____ b. Play with a slight separation between the notes.

_____ c. Play softer as the notes descend.

_____ d. Play with a vibrato, if possible.

6. How loud should the dotted quarter note be played in measure 15?

_____ a. Approximately medium-loud.

_____ b. Approximately medium-soft.

_____ c. Somewhat louder than *f.*

_____ d. Somewhat louder than *ff.*

7. In an ensemble setting such as *Regenesis,* what does the abbreviation "rit." in measure 25 mean to you?

_____ a. Suddenly slower.

_____ b. Suddenly faster.

_____ c. Maintain steady tempo.

_____ d. Look at director for indication of tempo change.

8. What two keys could be represented by the key signature at measure 27?

_____ a. G Major and e minor.

_____ b. F Major and d minor.

_____ c. E Major and c# minor.

_____ d. B Major and g# minor.

9. How fast should the tempo be at measure 27?

_____ a. Very slow tempo.

_____ b. Moderately rapid tempo.

_____ c. Rapid tempo.

_____ d. Very fast tempo.

10. The notes that appear in measures 29–36 represent

_____ a. an accompaniment figure.

_____ b. an accompaniment figure based on a rhythmic motive.

_____ c. an accompaniment figure that should be performed in a smooth and connected manner.

_____ d. a composer's way of testing the musicians' sight-reading ability.

11. The words and symbol at the end of measure 47 are an indication

_____ a. to jump to the coda on the second time through this section.

_____ b. that if the next page is too difficult, the band may choose to skip to the last three lines.

_____ c. to return to measure 27, play to measure 31, then skip to the last three lines.

_____ d. to return to the beginning and play to measure 27, then stop.

12. In measures 74–77, to be musically correct, where should the breath be taken?
_____ a. After the dotted quarter in bar 74.
_____ b. After the dotted half note in bar 75.
_____ c. After count four in bar 75.
_____ d. After the eighth note in bar 77.

13. What does *sff* mean to you?
_____ a. Watch the director.
_____ b. Play the note very loudly, with a strong attack.
_____ c. Play as loud as you can.
_____ d. Play loud and tongue as hard as you can.

14. In measures 90–96, a breath is indicated by a comma in bar 91. To be musically correct, where should the next breath be taken?
_____ a. On count one of bar 96.
_____ b. After dotted quarter note in bar 92.
_____ c. After count four in bar 92.
_____ d. After count four in bar 93.

15. What measure number reflects the use of syncopation in *Regenesis*?
_____ a. Bar 74.
_____ b. Bar 15.
_____ c. Bar 102.
_____ d. Bar 106.

16. How fast should the tempo be at bar 82?
_____ a. Slowest tempo possible.
_____ b. Very slow tempo.
_____ c. Moderately slow tempo.
_____ d. Moderately rapid tempo.

17. What do the two diagonal lines at the end of measure 89 mean to you?
_____ a. Pause longer than normal, watch the director.
_____ b. Move directly to measure 90, watch the director.
_____ c. A tempo change is imminent, watch the director.
_____ d. Take a deep breath, watch the director.

18. What do the abbreviations and words at the end of measure 103 mean to you?
_____ a. Repeat back to the beginning, play to measure 31, then skip to measure 48.

_____ b. Repeat back to the symbol at measure 31, play through measure 47, then skip to measure 104.

_____ c. Go directly to measure 104 with no repeat, but at a faster tempo.

_____ d. Repeat back to measure 48, play to measure 103, then stop.

19. In measure 102, using the 1-e-&-a counting system, what count does the fifth note appear on?

_____ a. 2-e.

_____ b. 4-&.

_____ c. 3-&.

_____ d. 2-a.

20. When a piece of music is called "program music," it is because

_____ a. it should be performed as part of a home concert program rather than at a music contest.

_____ b. the title looks nice in the printed program for the concert.

_____ c. the music tells a story.

_____ d. a computer program can be purchased to aid in the preparation of the music.

Figure 9.2. Sample written exam based on choral literature

BEA FLAT MIDDLE SCHOOL

And Nature Smiled Written Exam

Place an *x* in the blank to the left of the answer that is the
BEST response to each of the following statements and questions.

1. The word *legato* is a performance style indication and means that music
   should be performed
   _____ a. at a slow tempo.
   _____ b. with distinct diction.
   _____ c. smooth and connected.
   _____ d. in a strict rhythmic manner.

2. In music performance, the word *simile* means that the music that follows
   should be performed
   _____ a. in a similar style.
   _____ b. in a happy manner.
   _____ c. at a slower tempo.
   _____ d. at a slightly faster tempo.

3. The word *rubato* indicates that the music should be performed
   _____ a. in a rubbery and elastic style.
   _____ b. at a slow and strict tempo.
   _____ c. at a moderately fast tempo.
   _____ d. in a tempo that gradually slackens.

4. The poem on which this piece of music is based is allegorical in nature.
   This means that
   _____ a. the poem tells a story in which people and things have another
              meaning, as in a fable.
   _____ b. the poem is spoken at a rather rapid tempo.
   _____ c. every other line in the poem must rhyme.
   _____ d. a breath is taken at the end of each line of the poem.

5. The abbreviation ♩ =72–80 at the beginning of this piece is an indication
   that
   _____ a. there are between 72 and 80 quarter notes in each musical phrase.
   _____ b. quarter notes can get up to 72 to 80 counts in this piece of music.

_____ c. the tempo of this piece of music should be initially established at 72 to 80 beats per minute.

_____ d. even measures are performed at a tempo of 72 beats per minute, and odd measures are performed at a tempo of 80 beats per minute.

6. The word *dynamics* refers to

_____ a. how fast a piece should be performed.

_____ b. the range that the voices are expected to sing.

_____ c. how smooth and connected a piece should be performed.

_____ d. degrees of loudness or softness at which the choir is expected to sing.

7. What does the term *through-composed* mean to you?

_____ a. There is no a cappella singing in this piece.

_____ b. There are numerous tempo changes in this piece.

_____ c. There is piano accompaniment throughout.

_____ d. There is new music provided for each verse of the poem (text).

8. In measure 32, to what does the term *horsetail* refer to?

_____ a. A wild-growing weed.

_____ b. A wild-growing flower.

_____ c. The rear area of a horse.

_____ d. A story about a horse.

9. In measure 21 of the second soprano part, using the 1-e-&-a counting system, on what count does the last note in the measure appear?

_____ a. 4.

_____ b. 4-&.

_____ c. 3-a.

_____ d. 4-a.

10. In measure 32 of the soprano part, using the 1-e-&-a counting system, on what beat does the third note appear?

_____ a. 2-e.

_____ b. 2-&.

_____ c. 2-a.

_____ d. 1-a.

11. The process of changing from one key to another key in a piece of music is called

_____ a. transposition.

_____ b. modulation.

_____ c. modification.

_____ d. transformation.

12. In a large ensemble setting such as *And Nature Smiled,* what does the term *accel.* mean to you?

_____ a. Take one step forward.

_____ b. Suddenly slower.

_____ c. Suddenly faster.

_____ d. Look at director for indication of tempo change.

13. What does the symbol over the first note in the alto part at measure 30 mean to you?

_____ a. Sing the note just a little bit on the high side.

_____ b. Take a breath after the note.

_____ c. Sing the note broadly, with full value.

_____ d. Sing the note shorter than indicated, with a marked accent.

14. In measure 62–64, where should the breath(s) be taken?

_____ a. On count 3 of bar 62 and after the half note in bar 64.

_____ b. On count 3 of bar 62 and after the last note in bar 63.

_____ c. On count 3 of bar 62 and after the second eighth note in bar 64.

_____ d. On count 3 of bar 62 and sing until bar 69 without another breath.

15. If you didn't have a director, when should you normally release the whole note in measure 72?

_____ a. On count 4.

_____ b. On count 4-&.

_____ c. On count 4-a.

_____ d. On count 1 of the last measure.

If written tests are to be used to measure the achievement of performance classes, it is recommended that they be administered twice each school year to each class. Each test grade should be combined with grades from two other assessment techniques to determine a final grade for that particular term.

The downside of written exams based on performance literature is that there is little or no possibility for reuse of the test with future performance classes. Each time a written test is to be administered, a new test must be created, because it is highly likely that it could be several years, if ever, before a piece of literature will again be used in a particular performance class.

It takes approximately one hour to construct a twenty-item, multiple-choice music performance test. Subsequent tests will involve creating similar questions. When individual test items are stored on computer, minor adjustments to those items can be accomplished quickly, thereby reducing the total time involved in preparing a test for a different piece of music.

Self-grading as assessment

An example of a form that students can use to evaluate their own performance during a given grading period can be found in Figure 9.3. This same form could easily be adapted for bands or orchestras by making an adjustment in item number 5 to reflect actual time practiced each week. Figure 9.3 is based on a self-grading form included in the article "Management Systems for Music Educators" by Kirk Kassner, which appeared in the March 1996 issue of *Music Educators Journal.*

Figure 9.3. Self-grading form

Bea Flat High School Music Department
Choral Ensembles Self-Grading Form

Quarter: ___1 ___2 ___3 ___4   Academic year_____
Date_____

Name_____
Ensemble_____

Reflect back on this quarter and assign a numerical value to your performance in each category. If the teacher rating differs from the student rating, that number will appear next to that of the student.

ELEMENT   Student   Teacher

1. Courtesy: Rating on this grading element   _____   _____
Outstanding=8, Generally=6, Average=4, Seldom=2

2. Responsibility: Rating on this grading   _____   _____
                 element
Brought to class all materials and supplies needed for learning
Every day=8, All but 2 days=6, All but 3 days=4, All but 4 days=2

3. Dependability: Rating on this grading   _____   _____
          element

Learned to perform all music properly and participated in concerts, rehearsals, and other ensemble activities, during and outside school hours.

Always=8, Usually=6, Sometimes=4, Seldom=2
Indicate 15 for an unexcused absence from a performance.

4. Helpfulness: Rating on this grading element   _____   _____

Performed services necessary for the good of the ensemble. Examples include serving as a musical tutor, helping take care of music, serving as an ensemble officer, helping with equipment for rehearsals and performances, planning group activities. (List helpful activities on the back of this paper.)

Helped in many ways=8, Helped at least once a week=6,
Helped once each month=4, Helped once during the quarter= 4

5. Personal practice away from rehearsal: _____   _____
    Rating for this grading element

Two or more times per week= 8, At least one time per week=6,
Once every other week=4, A few times times during the quarter=2

6. Improvement in skills and concepts: _____   _____
    Rating on this grading element

Improved abilities in understanding music notation, how to use the singing voice, musical style, and gaining mastery of other musical elements necessary for contributing musically to the choral ensemble.

Outstanding=16, Good=8, Average=6, Fair=4

7. Extra credit: Rating on this grading element   _____   _____

Attended other musical events and completed a concert review form for each, participated in music performance other than with school ensembles, took private lessons, wrote a paper on current musical topic, etc.
(List on back of this paper.)

Four or more extra-credit activities per term=8, Three activities per term=6,
Two activities per term=4, One activity=2

TOTAL POINTS   _____   _____

Scale: A=56 points or above, B=41-55 points,
      C=26-40 points, D=11-25 points

FINAL GRADE   _____   _____

Students can be asked to complete a self-grading form at the close of each term. It is not unusual for students to rate themselves more harshly than an instructor might rate them. As indicated on the form, if a music teacher's rating is different (either higher or lower) than the student rating, the teacher places that rating in the blank to the right of the student rating. Points are totaled for both the student and teacher categories, and if there is disagreement in the point totals, the two scores are averaged and the grade given based on the scale found at the bottom of the page.

Individual performance ratings

Grades determined through the use of performance rating scales gained widespread popularity in the music education profession in the 1990s. The use of performance rating scales is a definite step toward making a subjective evaluation process objective.

For use in a four-year high school, individual performance rating tests would be divided into four different levels. Figure 9.4 is an example of a level-one test for an average group of freshman instrumentalists. The difficulty of each level is determined by requirements, including the music that students are asked to perform. In this case, the chromatic scale is only two octaves; two relatively easy major scales are required; and a sixteen-measure melodic etude designed for ninth-grade musicians is included, along with a twelve-measure rhythm etude that is played on one pitch throughout. The music was developed from etude number 6 in Form A of the Watkins-Farnum Performance Scale.

Figure 9.4. Example of a level one performance scale for instrumental music.

INDIVIDUAL PERFORMANCE RATING

Level One: Instrumental

Name _____
Year in school _____ Date _____

1. Scale requirements: Two-octave chromatic, E-flat and A-flat major scales and arpeggios, as indicated on the scale sheet.

Rating (Consider accuracy of: a. Tempo b. Pulse c. Notes)

_____ 5 Performed all elements accurately and correctly.
_____ 4 Performed two of the elements accurately with the exception of _____ .

_____ 3 Performed one of the elements correctly, but had
          problems with _____ .

_____ 2 Performed none of the elements with total accuracy.

_____ 1 All five of the elements were poorly and inaccurately performed.

2. Music etude

Watkins-Farnum Performance Scale. Winona, MN: Hal Leonard Music, Inc.
Etude #6, Form A.

Musical rating (Consider accuracy of: a. Tone b. Articulation
c. Notes d. Phrasing e. Dynamics)

_____ 5 Performed all five of the elements accurately and correctly.

_____ 4 Performed nearly all elements correctly with the
          exception of _____ .

_____ 3 Performed some elements correctly, but had some
          problems with _____ .

_____ 2 Performed few of the elements accurately, most
          specifically _____ .

_____ 1 All five of the elements were poorly and inaccurately performed.

Rhythmic rating (Consider accuracy of: a. Tempo b. Pulse c. Rhythm
d. Accents)

_____ 5 Performed all four elements accurately and correctly.

_____ 4 Performed nearly all elements correctly with the
          exception of _____ .

_____ 3 Performed some elements correctly, but had some
          problems with _____ .

_____ 2 Performed few of the elements accurately, most
          specifically _____ .

_____ 1 All of the elements were poorly and inaccurately performed.

3. Rhythm etude

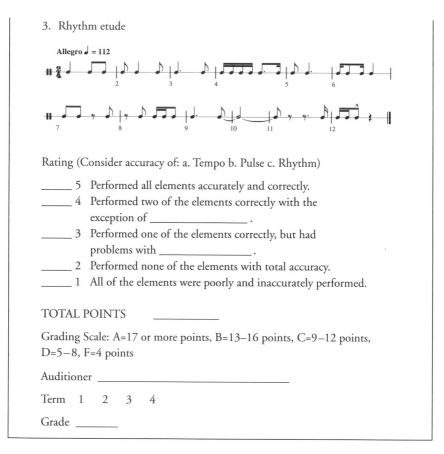

Rating (Consider accuracy of: a. Tempo b. Pulse c. Rhythm)

_____ 5 Performed all elements accurately and correctly.
_____ 4 Performed two of the elements correctly with the
          exception of _____ .
_____ 3 Performed one of the elements correctly, but had
          problems with _____ .
_____ 2 Performed none of the elements with total accuracy.
_____ 1 All of the elements were poorly and inaccurately performed.

TOTAL POINTS   _____

Grading Scale: A=17 or more points, B=13–16 points, C=9–12 points,
D=5–8, F=4 points

Auditioner _____

Term   1   2   3   4

Grade _____

Figure 9.5 is an example of a level three choral individual performance rating test. It is constructed to be administered to high school junior choral musicians. Again, the level of the test is determined by the test requirements. For example, in addition to singing scales in solfège, students are asked to perform their scales in thirds and fourths. The required folk song is also of a difficulty level appropriate for an average eleventh-grade choir member.

Figure 9.5. Example of a level three performance scale for choral music

INDIVIDUAL PERFORMANCE RATING

Level Three: Choral

Name _____

Year in school _____ Date _____

1. Scale requirements: One-octave major scale in appropriate range, scale in 3rds, scale in 4ths, one octave natural relative minor scale. Sung in solfège.

Rating: (Check the highest level attained)

_____ 5 Performed scales accurately with precise pitch.

_____ 4 Performed scales almost accurately, but there are some missed pitches.

_____ 3 Performed scales somewhat accurately, but had problems with _____ .

_____ 2 Had difficulty with all requirements, most specifically _____ .

_____ 1 Performed poorly on all requirements.

2. Folk song: Sung in solfège

Crowe, Edgar, Annie Lawton, and W. Gillies Whittaker, ed. *The Folk Song Singing Series, Book VI.* New York: Oxford University Press, 1933, p. 2.

Tonal rating (Consider the accuracy of: a. Tone b. Notes c. Pitch)

_____ 5 Performed all elements accurately.

_____ 4 Performed most elements accurately, with some variation in _____ .

_____ 3 Performed with some consistency, but had significant problems with _____ .

_____ 2 Performance lacked accuracy in all required elements.

_____ 1 Did not use a singing voice and made numerous errors.

Rhythm rating (Consider the accuracy of: a. Tempo b. Meter c. Melodic rhythms)

_____ 5 Performed all elements accurately.

_____ 4 Performed most elements accurately with some variation in _____ .

_____ 3 Performed with some consistency , but had significant problems with _____ .

_____ 2 Performance lacked accuracy in all required elements.

_____ 1 Performance severely lacked accuracy in all required elements.

3. Elements to be evaluated throughout the performance

Rating (Consider: a. Breathing process b. Diction c. Posture
d. Musicality and expression)

_____ 5 All elements in place during the performance.

_____ 4 Most elements in place, but _____ need(s) attention.

_____ 3 Some elements in place, but _____ need(s) attention.

_____ 2 All elements need some degree of attention,
             most specifically _____ .

_____ 1 All elements somewhat weak, most specifically _____ .

TOTAL POINTS   _____

Grading Scale: A=17 or more points, B=13–16 points, C=9–12 points,
D=5–8, F=4 points

Auditioner _____

Term   1   2   3   4

Grade _____

When blanks are included after a particular rating, the instructor should indicate which performance elements were problematic. For example, in Figure 9.4, under the rating that is worth four points in item number 2, perhaps the student performed the etude with most of the elements in place but had a little trouble with articulation accuracy and dynamic contrast. The teacher would write the letters "b" and "e" in the blank. The same would hold true for the choral performance rating test in Figure 9.5. The examiner would write the letter that corresponds to an element that needs attention in the appropriate blank at the end of a particular rating.

Each of the performance rating tests can be administered in only a few minutes, making this move toward an objective process attractive to instrumental and choral directors who deal with large numbers of students. The students would be given the music and informed of other requirements as much as two weeks in advance of the test. For that matter, it is also a good idea to provide the students with a copy of the test in advance so they understand how and on what they will be evaluated.

Readers are encouraged to adjust any of the requirements listed in Figures 9.4 and 9.5 to their own teaching situation. The figures in this chapter are meant as examples only.

Participation evaluation system

As mentioned earlier, participation levels are one factor in determining a final grade for a music performance class. A Participation Level Evaluation Form is shown in Figure 9.6. It is similar to a cumulative point system used for years by

Figure 9.6. Example of a participation evaluation system for instrumental music

Bea Flat High School
PARTICIPATION EVALUATION FORM
Instrumental Music

This point system is designed to enable all students in the ensemble to attain a sufficient point total that will result in an "A" letter grade for the marking period.

Students are expected to complete their own point sheet total on a weekly basis and submit it to Mr. Kleff on the last class day each week. Failure to do so will result in a zero point total for that week.

_____ 1. Rehearsal attendance with proper equipment and materials: 5 points (4 points if tardy).

_____ 2. Attendance at extra rehearsal scheduled for your ensemble outside of school time: 6 points (5 points if tardy).

_____ 3. Attendance at a sectional rehearsal scheduled before or after school: 6 points (5 points if tardy).

_____ 4. Lesson taken with instructor or outside of school with private instructor: 3 points. (If taken outside of school, list date, the teacher, and material covered.)

_____ 5. Attendance at a public performance for your ensemble: 20 points (15 points if tardy). Deduct 40 points for unexcused absence.

_____ 6. Solo performance at a community or church event: 3 points.

_____ 7. Small ensemble performance at a community or church event: 2 points.

_____ 8. Solo performance at a music contest. (Superior: 4 points, Excellent: 3 points, Good: 2 points)

_____ 9. Small ensemble appearance at a music contest. (Superior: 3 points, Excellent: 2 points, Good: 1 point)

_____ 10. Complete a playing audition (All-State band, All-District band, talent show, etc.): 3 points. (Specify date and type of audition.) _____

_____ 11. Concert attendance (limited to instrumental music concerts and recitals outside of school hours and/or ANY Bea Flat High School concert performances): 2 points per event. Attach a completed concert review sheet (available from Mr. Kleff).

_____ 12. Point makeup report. Up to 25 points may be earned each term on a contract basis by submitting a written report prior to the last day for reporting grades each term. Written report requirements and approved topics for this term are available from Mr. Kleff.

_____   TOTAL POINTS

Scale for the term: A=280 or more, B=220-279, C=160-219, D=100-169, F=99 or below

Name _____ Date Submitted _____

music educators for the purpose of making year-end awards to student musicians. This and similar systems are valuable in assessing the participation levels of students involved in music performance classes.

Record-keeping associated with student participation points can seem overwhelming. The system presented in Figure 9.6 removes a great deal of that burden by having the students complete their own sheets on a weekly basis. Students must be aware that individual sheets will be randomly checked for accuracy. Intentional discrepancies can result in a score of zero for the week in question. Student assistants can place the weekly scores in a grade book or enter the scores into a computer as part of the record-keeping program. At the end of the quarter, there are only eight or nine numbers to total in order to determine a score and final grade for each student.

As with the other rating systems in this chapter, any grade earned for participation must be combined and averaged with two other grading techniques.

Point systems

There are basically two types of point systems, with variations. One is a cumulative system, similar to that shown in Figure 9.6, in which a student begins the year (or term) with zero points. Points are then earned for rehearsal and performance participation, auditions, practice time, concert attendance, and a variety of other possible performance-oriented activities during the course of the year. Points earned determine the type of award a student receives.

The other type of point system has each student beginning the year (or term) with a set number of points, generally 100. As the year or term progresses, points are deducted according to a list of possible infractions. This is known as a deductive, negative, or discount point system. Figure 9.7 shows an example. Such a point system can also be used for grade determination as long as it is averaged with two other grading techniques to determine a final grade for the marking period.

In Figure 9.7, each student begins the academic year with an "A" letter grade in the performance class and 100 points. It is the individual's responsibility to avoid any of the eleven listed infractions to maintain that A grade until the end of the term.

Music educators who adapt such a system should assume the responsibility of placing their own emphasis on the importance of each point system item. This is done by weighting each item by the number of points assigned to it. Music educators must also determine exactly which items they wish to include in the point system, based on their individual philosophy. Figures 9.6 and 9.7 serve only as models for point systems.

STUDENT EVALUATION OF INSTRUCTION

Any music educator who received an undergraduate degree in the last twenty years or so probably was involved in a campuswide student evaluation of faculty. University

Figure 9.7. An example of a discount point system

DISCOUNT POINT SYSTEM
Bea Flat High School Band

Each student begins the term with 100 points and a letter grade of A. Points will be discounted (deducted) from the total of 100 for any violation of the concert band policies as they appear below. At the end of the term, grades will be assigned based on the discounted point totals as follows:

Unexcused absence from rehearsal	deduct	5 points
Unexcused lateness from rehearsal	deduct	1 point
Failure to have necessary materials at rehearsal (Instrument, music, pencils, schedule, etc.)	deduct	2 points
Talking or otherwise disrupting rehearsal	deduct	2 points
Poor posture during rehearsal	deduct	1 point
Playing another person's instrument	deduct	2 points
Chewing gum in rehearsal room during rehearsal	deduct	1 point
Unexcused absence from extra rehearsal	deduct	5 points
Misconduct while in uniform (see band handbook)	deduct	5 points
Failure to return fund-raising monies on time	deduct	.5 point (per day)
Unexcused absence from performance	deduct	10 points

Scale: A=94–100, B=87–93, C=80–86, D=73–79, F= 72 and below

faculty are often evaluated by students in their classes based on criteria on which they have little or no input. The value of these assessment measures has been strongly debated, but the present consensus of opinion seems to indicate that, no matter how flawed the evaluation instruments are, instruction levels have improved on college and university campuses through the semiannual process of student evaluations. These evaluations are, by all intents and purposes, administered as an instrument reportedly designed to improve instruction.

The downside of the student evaluation process is that some administrators feel that an element of grade inflation has crept into the system. Some professors, consciously or subconsciously, are reluctant to award low grades to students even when they are deserved, for fear of receiving low scores on their student evaluations in turn.

It is, of course, another matter when music educators on the secondary level develop and administer their own student surveys. The music instructor is the only individual who has access to the survey results, and he or she also controls the questions included in the survey. This practice appears to be based on a genuine desire on the part of teachers to improve their classroom instruction performance.

Music educators who are not currently using student surveys to evaluate their effectiveness are encouraged to consider doing so on a trial basis. Student comments relating to repertoire, overall organization, discipline, and so on, can be very revealing. Figure 9.8 is a sample of questions that can be included in such a survey. The questions used will depend on the information that is important to the individual instructor.

Again, all of the examples offered in the last part of this chapter are an attempt to assist practicing and prospective music educators with some concepts and ideas to aid in the difficult, and as seen by some, uncomfortable process of assigning grades to students involved in performance classes. Readers are reminded that if they elect to adopt any of the preceding systems in their process of assigning grades, it is recommended that they select three systems and average the grades.

Any comprehensive grading process will be time-consuming, but the long-term return on the investment of additional time can be vast for music educators and the students with whom they work.

Aptitude Tests in Music Education

The study of the psychology of music and music tests and measurements has traditionally been reserved for graduate school. If the subject is presented at all at the undergraduate level, it is in the form of a brief reference to the fact that published tests are available to measure aptitude and musical achievement. The faculty of schools of education tend to feel that their own educational measurement classes provide prospective music educators with all the knowledge they will ever need to be successful teachers. This position regarding tests and measurements cannot be professionally justified. Music educators need to understand the use of tests and measurements to help them better select those that can serve their purposes in different teaching situations. This author's experience has shown that many music educators are not equipped with that basic information (Whybrew 1972, p. viii).

It is the obligation of every music educator to identify and nurture musical talent. Frequently even the most experienced teacher will fail to recognize the presence of outstanding musical ability in a shy or stubborn child. If this talent can be discovered through the use of a good test, it may be the basis of helping a child to a better life by capitalizing on previously unrecognized abilities.

A brief history

The measurement of traits and abilities began to gain popularity in the United States in the late nineteenth century. During this period reformers expressed concern about the welfare of the mentally retarded. This concern resulted in the estab-

Figure 9.8. Sample student survey form

MUSIC DEPARTMENT
Instructor Evaluation Form

Music Ensembles

For each item mark the number that
corresponds to the rating scale below.

	1 (Best)	2	3 (Average)	4	5 (Poor)
1. How do you rate this year's contest and festival repertoire?	0	0	0	0	0
2. Rate your instructor's general effectiveness and efficiency in rehearsal technique.	0	0	0	0	0
3. Rate the instructor's clarity of conducting patterns.	0	0	0	0	0
4. To what extent is the instructor organized and prepared for rehearsals?	0	0	0	0	0
5. How well does your instructor identify and correct errors by making specific suggestions?	0	0	0	0	0
6. Rate your instructor's attitude toward students.	0	0	0	0	0
7. Is your instructor fair and consistent in the manner in which students are treated?	0	0	0	0	0
8. How helpful is the instructor in solving individual student performance problems?	0	0	0	0	0
9. Rate how you feel the instructor is genuinely interested in you as a person.	0	0	0	0	0
10. To what extent does the instructor explain membership, attendance, performance, and grading requirements for your ensemble?	0	0	0	0	0

11. List what you see as the instructor's major weaknesses.

12. List what you see as the instructor's major strengths.

lishment of special institutions to provide for the care of this population and thereby created a need for some type of uniform means of identifying and classifying such cases. Early work on the part of physicians and physiologists associated with the classification and treatment of the mentally retarded gave rise to the school of experimental psychology. Scientists were at first interested in measurements such as sensitivity to visual and auditory stimuli and simple reaction time. Their attention gradually turned to measurement of the rate of learning, perceptual span, and timing of various mental tasks (Whybrew 1972, p. 3).

The 1920s saw increased interest in the measurement of specific aptitudes. Psychologists and educators focused their efforts on the measurement of the potential for an individual's accomplishments in a wide variety of fields. Early studies listed the traits that the authors considered to be important elements in musical talent. Most of these studies involved analysis of the abilities and personalities of individuals known to be gifted musicians (Whybrew 1972, p. 6). The earliest and best-known test of musical talent was Carl E. Seashore's Measures of Musical Talent, published in 1919. No test in the history of music has been examined with more careful, and often biased, scrutiny than was the Seashore battery. Measures of Musical Talent will be examined in more detail later in this chapter.

The period of greatest development in the testing movement took place during the 1920s not only in the number of tests produced, but also in the wide extent to which they were administered. Unfortunately, early results of tests, including Seashore's, were often accepted uncritically and were applied universally. Persons using the tests lost sight of the fact that the measures were very crude and that care in interpreting the results was necessary.

After Seashore's test was revised in 1939, other musical aptitude tests began to appear. As each test came along, it was accompanied by numerous studies relating to the use and potential of the instrument. There was little activity in the designing of new measures during the 1950s, but in 1965 Edwin Gordon released his Musical Aptitude Profile, and Arnold Bentley published his Measures of Musical Ability in 1966. These two batteries touched off an unprecedented flurry of scholarly activity associated with musical aptitude testing. Over a ten-year period, the measurement studies involving musical aptitude became an extremely popular topic of doctoral dissertations. You need only look at copies of *Journal of Research in Music Education* from this period to get a sense of the activity level in the area of musical aptitude. Few issues were published in the late 1960s and early 1970s that did not include a new study dealing with some aspect of musical aptitude testing.

By the early 1980s, the amount of research associated with musical aptitude drastically subsided and was replaced with research in computer-assisted instruction, music needs in special education, musical achievement, comparison of instructional methods, and musical perceptions in early childhood. This change may reflect general trends in educational research as well as new demands on music education.

Purposes of musical aptitude tests

An examination of doctoral dissertations and other studies of musical aptitude tests indicates that far and away the most popular use of these tests has been to predict the success of students enrolling in instrumental music programs. As mentioned earlier, the most recent research took place in the 1960s and early 1970s and involved Gordon's Musical Aptitude Profile and Bentley's Measures of Musical Ability. The bulk of the research indicates that musical aptitude tests have a reasonably high level of success in predicting future musical achievement of instrumental music students. The accuracy of predictability increases significantly when aptitude test scores are combined with intelligence scores and classroom achievement. Thus, the principal use of aptitude tests in this country has been associated with elementary-level instrumental music students.

Another purpose for musical aptitude tests is to encourage musically talented students to participate in a music program. Aptitude tests help the music educator adapt classroom music instruction methods to meet the ability levels and individual needs of students. Determining musical aptitude helps in formulating teaching strategies and gives parents objective information regarding their children's potential for future achievement in music. When used correctly and on a regular basis, musical aptitude tests become a music educator's most valuable, practical, and objective diagnostic tool (Froseth 1971, pp. 98–105).

PUBLISHED MUSICAL APTITUDE TESTS

There are a number of excellent published, standardized musical aptitude tests available for use by music educators, but by and large music teachers do not employ them. The reasons may include the fact that many music educators don't understand them and their purpose, or simply do not know what is available. The following list highlights five published musical aptitude tests. Essential information about each test—author, dates of publication and revisions, age or grade levels, and time required to administer—has been included. The information is taken from work by Paul R. Lehman, William E. Whybrew, Paul R. Farnsworth, and J. David Boyle. The tests appear in alphabetical order by author.

Arnold Bentley: Measures of Musical Ability

Publication date: 1966
Administration time: 25 minutes
Age level: Elementary grades,
   ages 7–14
Includes: Recording, instructions, manual,
   twenty-five answer sheets, and key

Publisher and distributor:
George G. Harrop & Co., Ltd.
Educational Department
Box 70, 182–184
High Holburn, Holburn,
London, England WCIV 7BR

Measures of Musical Ability is presented in four separate tests: Pitch Discrimination, Tonal Memory, Chord Analysis, and Rhythm Memory. Sounds produced on the accompanying recording are made by an oscillator and electronic organ. The record presents thorough instructions, with numerous examples offered throughout the test. The pitch discrimination test asks the student to determine if the second of two successive pitches moves up or down. The tonal memory test asks, "Which tone in the second playing of a melody is changed?" Students are asked to determine the number of tones in a chord as part of the chord analysis test, and the rhythm memory test involves determining in which of four beats is the rhythm altered in the second playing of a pattern. Some music educators feel indicated that the British accent of the narrator might prove to be distracting for elementary school children.

The answer sheets provided for use with the test are easy to read and uncluttered, and they provide ample space for responses. They must be hand-scored with a master key provided with the test set. Evaluation of the test scores is accomplished through the use of a five-place system of norms that accompanies the test. A separate scale is provided for each age group from age 7 to 14.

The test boasts high validity (0.94) and reliability (0.84) coefficients. It is one of only three musical aptitude tests designed specifically for the elementary grades. Due to the technical level of the battery, Bentley's test fulfills the assessment needs of many elementary school teachers.

Raleigh M. Drake: Drake Musical Aptitude Test

Publication date: 1954, revised in 1957
Administration time: 80 minutes
  (both test forms)
Age level: Age 8 through adult
Includes: Cassette tape, manual,
  and 100 answer sheets

Publisher and distributor:
  Raleigh M. Drake
  711 Beach Road
  Sarasota, Florida 33581

Two test forms of equal difficulty are provided, with each form comprising twelve items. The two forms (Form A and B) of the musical memory test are equivalent; however, in the rhythm test, Form B is more difficult, and it alone is recommended for use with students who have at least five years of musical experience. When testing unselected subjects, both forms are recommended. The musical memory portion involves determining whether or not the key, time, or notes are changed in a subsequent playing of a melody. As part of the rhythm test, subjects are asked to listen to an established tempo and then count silently after the metronome halts until they are asked to stop counting. The number a subject is counting at the moment the voice says "stop" is his or her answer.

The answer sheets are scored by hand, a process that is somewhat complicated by the lack of scoring stencils. Norms are provided for both musical and non-musical subjects for each test form and the combined forms. Norms are provided for the musical memory test by two-year steps for ages 7–8 to 19–20.

The reliability of both forms for students without musical training is positive, with a coefficient of 0.85 for both tests. Reliability scores were somewhat higher for those students indicating past musical experience. Validity scores, on the other hand, are somewhat problematic. Validity coefficients are based on teacher ratings, with median scores of 0.55 for the musical memory test and 0.58 for the rhythm test. Nonetheless, Drake's test battery is well prepared, well standardized, and can be regarded as an important and positive step in the identification of musical talent.

Edwin Gordon: Musical Aptitude Profile

Publication date: 1965

Administration time:

  Sessions of 50 minutes each

Age level: Grades 4–12

Includes: Three tapes, manual, scoring

  masks, 100 answer sheets, record-keeping files

Publisher and distributor:

Houghton Mifflin Company

One Beacon Street

Boston, Massachusetts 02107

Gordon's Musical Aptitude Profile consists of three separate tests: Tonal Imagery (Melody and Harmony), Rhythm Imagery (Tempo and Meter), and Musical Sensitivity (Phrasing and Balance). In the tonal imagery test, two versions of a recorded melody are played: an unembellished version and one with additional notes. The listener is asked to determine whether the second melody would be the same as the first if the added notes were removed. In the tempo test, students are asked to compare the tempo of two examples, and the meter test requires students to determine if the "accents" in two recorded melodies are the same or different. The musical sensitivity subtest asks subjects which of two performances of the same musical excerpt, endings to a melody or an entire melody, "sounds better."

Reliability coefficients are provided separately for each of the nine grade levels, for each of the three tests (0.80–0.92), for the subtest (0.66–0.85), and for the composite score (0.90–0.92), all of which are unusually high. Validity coefficients for homogenous groups for the three tests, seven subtests, and composite scores range from 0.19 to 0.97, with the composite scores and main test scores running generally between 0.60 and 0.70. Percentile norms are provided for all standard scores at the nine grade levels (4–12). The test can be scored manually with the accompanying scoring masks or sent to the publisher for machine scoring. The test manual is the most complete and helpful guide included with any musical aptitude test. For example, it offers a useful section on the interpretation of test results. The MAP is noted for its thoroughness and care and has become one of the most important contributions to the field.

Edwin Gordon: Primary Measures of Music Audiation

Publication date: 1979

Administration time: 20 minutes

  for each of two parts

Age level: Grades K–3

Includes: Two tapes, 100 tonal and 100 rhythm

  answer sheets, manual, scoring mask

Publisher and distributor:

G. I. A. Publications, Inc.

7404 South Mason Avenue

Chicago, Illinois 60638

The Primary Measures of Music Audiation is intended to help teachers and parents evaluate tonal and rhythmic aptitudes of young children. *Audiation* is a term coined by Gordon and refers to sound recalled or imagined without the source of the sound being physically present. It is similar to the phenomenon referred to as "imagery" by other test designers and music psychologists (Gordon 1971, p. 7).

The PMMA consists of two parts, Tonal and Rhythm, and is administered through the use of two tape recordings. As with tests designed for older children, the subjects need to determine if two phrases for each of forty items are the same or different. Because each child responds by drawing a circle around pictures on the answer sheet, it is not necessary to be able to read language, music, or numbers. This test can be administered by a music specialist, classroom teacher, or interested parent. A profile card is provided for each child as well as a class record sheet for each group of children.

Composite scores, in addition to Tonal and Rhythm scores, are presented through percentile norms for each of the four grade levels for which the test was designed. Reliability scores are quite good, especially when considering the difficulty in distinguishing between aptitude and achievement at such a young age. Validity scores for younger test subjects are understandably difficult to determine, but the composite scores of the PMMA and Gordon's MAP correlate at the 0.61 level.

Directions in the test manual and the explanations included in the verbal commentary to the children are very clear and easy to understand. Reviewers have found the test to be an interesting and meaningful experience for young children and feel it will probably serve an important need for that particular age level.

In 1983 Gordon released an advanced version of the PMMA entitled "Intermediate Measures of Music Audiation," which was intended for grades one through four. The test is similar in every way to the PMMA except the difficulty level of the test items.

Carl E. Seashore: Seashore Measures of Musical Talent

Publication date: 1919, with
 revisions in 1939, 1956, and 1960
Administration time: 60 minutes
Age level: Grades 4–16 and adult
Includes: Recording, manual,
 scoring key, and 50 answer sheets

Publisher and distributor:
 The Psychological Corporation
 757 Third Avenue
 New York, New York 10017

The Seashore test is valued today more for its historical significance than for assessing musical aptitude; it set the standard by which all other musical aptitude tests have been measured. Its construction and thoroughness of testing procedures have been recognized, even by critics, to be of the highest quality. This recognition is certainly well founded when you consider that Seashore had no established format or precedent to follow.

Seashore's battery contains six separate subtests measuring pitch discrimination, loudness, rhythm, time, memory, and timbre. In the pitch tests, the subject must determine if the second of two tones is higher than the first, and in the loudness test if the second of two tones is stronger than the first. The rhythm test asks if the second of two rhythm patterns differs from the first. As part of the time test, a subject identifies if the second of two tones is longer or shorter than the first, and in the timbre test if the timbre of a recorded tone differs from the first. In the memory test, subjects respond to the question "Which tone in the second playing of a melody is changed?"

Percentile norms are available for three grade levels; 4–5, 6–8, and 9–16. Reliability coefficients are provided for the three levels and range from 0.62 to 0.88. Difficulty in sustaining the attention of the test subjects is thought to negatively influence reliability coefficients. In the manual, Seashore discusses the validity of the battery exclusively in terms of logic or content. Much research associated with determining accurate validity coefficients of the Seashore test has taken place over the years, and the resulting figures have been quite low. An enormous body of literature exists dealing with the use of the test in studies concerned with faulty speech, hearing, foreign language accents, and other selected fields.

The manual provides clear and concise instructions for administering the test, and the answer sheets can be either machine or hand scored. For each subject taking the test, a profile sheet can be made that shows that person's standing in each of the subtests. When it is properly administered and when the results are properly interpreted, the battery is a useful tool in determining musical aptitude.

INDUSTRY PROMOTIONAL TESTS

Through the years several instrument manufacturers have designed their own tests of musical aptitude that measure with some degree of accuracy potential skills in rhythm, pitch, melody, and chordal recognition. These tests are in no sense serious evaluative devices, but they do determine a degree of relative ability and can often be useful to an instrumental music educator under certain circumstances.

Promotional tests can create a sense of identification of the student with the instrumental music program. They are short, easy to take, and very inexpensive. The principal motivation for a music educator to use promotional tests is to create interest in the program. These tests are designed for administration in grades 5 through 8.

Few promotional tests are standardized, and they are offered without norms or validity and reliability information. The following is a list of available industry promotional tests. In general, these tests can be obtained through the music dealers or by contacting the companies whose addresses follow.

Talent Quiz

Cost: Teacher cards, $.50 each; student worksheet/answer forms, $.30 each; text booklet and scoring "masks" free

G. LeBlanc Corporation
7019 30th Avenue
Kenosha, WI 53141

In Tune: A Recruiting Program for Band

Cost: $29.95 for Music Profile with
video for use in administering;
100 scorecards (additional scorecards
no charge), text correcting "masks,"
sample letters, manual, and more

United Musical Instruments, Inc.
P.O. Box 727
Elkhart, IN 46515
Available from: Any UMI retail dealer
(Armstrong, Conn, Artley, King, Benge)

Music Guidance Survey

Cost: $7.50 per 100 student answer
forms, $.50 for score key, $.30 for
instruction form, $6.75
for cassette recording

The Selmer Company
Box 310
Elkhart, IN 46515

SUGGESTED ACTIVITIES

1. Secure one of the musical aptitude tests referred to in this chapter and administer it to a group of children in your local public school on a test-retest basis. Determine its reliability and compare it with that of the coefficients found in the test manual. Compare the scores of the local subjects with national norms found in the test manual.
2. Compile a list of factors that can affect how musical aptitude correlates to music history, applied music, and music appreciation grades. Lead a class discussion on the topic.
3. As class project, develop a musical aptitude test with ten items in each of the following areas: pitch discrimination, rhythm, melody, and tempo. Administer the test in the test-retest manner and compose reliability coefficients for the instrument.
4. Compile a list of considerations that serve as restrictions for the author of a group test that do not necessarily inhibit the author of a test for an academic class. Lead a class discussion on the topic.
5. Summarize three studies presented in *Journal of Research in Music Education* that are indicative of three different uses of musical aptitude tests in research in music education.
6. Compile a list of principal differences and similarities of the six musical aptitude tests presented in this chapter. Lead a class discussion on the topic.
7. Work with a local middle school or high school band director and compile a written test based on one of the pieces in the band's folders. Administer the test and share the results with the class.
8. Work with a local middle school or high school choir director and compile a written test based on one of the pieces in the choir's folders. Administer the test and share the results with the class.
9. Invite local music educators to visit the class and ask them to share how they determine letter grades for their performance classes.

OUTSIDE THE SCHOOL
ENVIRONMENT

CONTESTS
AND FESTIVALS:
FRIEND OR FOE?

INTRODUCTION

Contests have been part of music education since the late nineteenth century, although their scope and format have changed considerably through the years. Perhaps nothing has generated more discussion than the question of whether or not contest participation has any value for specific music programs and music education in general. The consensus is that moderate competitive or noncompetitive music contest participation is of some benefit to music education programs. Moreover, noncompetitive contests are more in line with the general philosophy of music education. In recent years, overemphasis on marching band field competitions, with a corresponding decrease in the quality of other facets of the instrumental music program, has been a source of concern for many music educators. There has been a recent trend toward noncompetitive contests in both the jazz and marching band areas, which has met with favorable reaction from the music education community.

Noncompetitive contest rating systems tend to project an inflated image of performance quality, because only the first three ratings are generally used in a five-tier system. This is a subject that needs to be realistically dealt with at both the state and national levels of music education professional organizations.

Music festivals have provided an alternative for performance experiences outside the school for those teachers electing not to participate in contests. A festival format that offers both clinic and performance experiences for participants is usually the most acceptable to music educators, although honor-type festivals provide quality performance opportunities for talented and interested student musicians. No matter the format, the key to success of any music festival is in the establishment of worthwhile objectives and the organization and management practices enacted by participating music educators. Festival participation should be an annual event on the calendar of all junior and senior high school performing groups.

As will be noted in chapter 11, the music contest movement, and more specifically the National Music Contest, profoundly influenced the acceptance of music education as a legitimate offering in public school curriculums. Indeed, large-group contests were organized before music education acquired any degree of curriculum status. Over the past forty years, controversy has intermittently surfaced regarding the relative value that music contests hold for music education. The purpose of this chapter is to outline for readers the strengths and weaknesses, the advantages and disadvantages, and the administrative concerns of contests and festivals and to provide an understanding of their role in contemporary music education.

The chapter begins with a brief definition of terminology and a description of the controversy surrounding music contests and the possibility for their abuse. Recommendations are given for the appropriate amount of contest participation for different groups, from marching bands to choirs and string orchestras. The advantages and disadvantages of contest participation are considered, along with some objectives for participation. The process of rating and ranking performers is discussed, along with some aids that will make adjudication more equitable. The chapter focuses next on the three most common types of music festivals—massed, honor, and clinic—and offers guidelines for selecting one and organizing a local music festival. It concludes with a discussion of commercial festivals.

UNDERSTANDING THE TERMINOLOGY

Before going further, it is necessary to become acquainted with some terminology. An event that is called a "contest" in one section of the country is called a "festival" in another. Events that are called festivals can be highly competitive in one state and noncompetitive in the next. To avoid confusion, the following definitions are supplied.

Competitive music contests

When the word *competitive* is used in conjunction with the term *music contest,* it may be assumed that individual or group participants will be ranked. In other words, a winner will be determined. "Nonwinners" are often ranked from second place to last place based on scores they receive from a panel of adjudicators. Some competitive music contests simply determine the first-place entry and do not attempt to rank the remaining entries.

Noncompetitive music contests

Music events that provide constructive criticism as well as unranked ratings can be considered noncompetitive contests. In these events, contestants are awarded a number, a grade, or a similar rating, and several contestants can receive a top rating. Entries are awarded ratings based on the subjective opinion of an individual judge or panel of judges. When several contestants receive a Division I rating, for example, no winners of the contest are established: hence the term noncompetitive music contest.

Music festivals

In this chapter, the term *music festival* is defined as an event that includes one school or several schools, and involves some type of performance activity that is not rated and not ranked. The festival may involve performance critiques without ratings for participants, or simply consist of a performance by a group made up of students from several schools.

Commercial festivals

There are numerous festival opportunities for school music performance groups throughout the country. Any music festival organized on a for-profit basis will be termed a *commercial festival* in this chapter. Such events are often sponsored by companies that handle festivals throughout the United States. Their purpose in sponsorship is to make a profit. In most instances that goal is accomplished handsomely.

THE CONTROVERSY

Early music contests that determined winning entries in a variety of categories at the local level, with subsequent winners progressing on to regional, state, and national competitions, provided student music ensembles with a high degree of personal and community motivation, as well as notoriety, which positively influenced the progress of the total music education movement. Participation in solo, small-ensemble, and large-group competitive contests became the rationale for the existence and continued support of many programs. As music began to be accepted as part of the school curriculum in the 1950s, many educators began to question the validity of competitive music contests. Competitive contests involving choirs, orchestras, and bands were gradually replaced by noncompetitive events that offered an opportunity for several groups to be judged "superior," several more to be judged "excellent," and so on. This adaptation seemed reasonable and in keeping with established educational goals and objectives. These events continue to this day on an annual basis throughout the country.

Controversy still exists regarding noncompetitive music contests (rated, but not ranked); some critics question whether even these events are in the best interest of music education. By and large, however, music teachers have embraced a noncompetitive contest structure for orchestras, bands, and choirs, as well as associated solo and small-ensemble participants, and feel that these events support their programs.

A discussion of the advantages and disadvantages that contest participation holds for music directors and their students will be offered later in this chapter.

MUSIC CONTEST ABUSE

Probably no other area in music education offers the potential for abuse of sound teaching principles than marching and jazz band competitive contests. Contest participation for other school concert organizations has generally become noncompetitive (rated, but not ranked). It took years of program examination and evaluation to reach that stage. However, there continues to be a near mania on the part of many marching and jazz band directors to win competitive contests.

It is not uncommon for student musicians to spend countless hours practicing, then traveling hundreds of miles, all to perform in marching band contests. Many educators have become concerned with this overemphasis on contests and the out-of-balance participation level of student musicians.

Limited music contest participation can be a stimulating and effective means of sustaining student and community interest and, as mentioned earlier, does provide a certain degree of program evaluation. But a problem exists when young educators get caught up in the contest craze before they have the teaching experience to develop a philosophy or establish the goals of the program. It takes an experienced teacher to approach music contests so that participation is an educational experience. Unfortunately, many young instrumental music educators burn out without ever knowing the rewards and joy of teaching music to young people and of providing those students with quality educational experiences.

How sad it is that bright student musicians are placed in a situation by their band directors of viewing their counterparts in neighboring schools as enemies. Contests with such titles as "Battle of the Bands" and the "Tournament of Champions" help promote the importance of beating the competition. Those same events, if addressed in a professional manner, could provide student participants with an enjoyable educational experience. Disturbing as it may seem, the directors who create a fever to win are themselves the ones who are reluctant to face the reality of losing. How much better it would be if those same directors taught their students to be the best they can be, rather than stressing the importance of beating the students in a neighboring school.

With the possible exceptions of swing and jazz choirs, choral music educators have generally avoided being absorbed by the competitive contest mania. Jazz band directors are not as likely to be guilty of abusing contest opportunities as their marching band colleagues. However, competitive opportunities are generally fewer for jazz bands and, more than likely, the marching band director in a school is also responsible for the jazz band. Any band director who overemphasizes one aspect of the program is not likely to have the time or energy to devote to all of its other parts.

Commercial motivation

The number of competing marching bands, as well as the number of students participating in those bands, has increased significantly since the early 1970s. This growth pattern coincides exactly with the direct involvement of marching band equipment manufacturers and distributors in promoting competitive contests. Some branches of the industry have realized substantial sales gains for their companies by promoting and sponsoring competitive regional contests for high school marching bands, which culminate in an annual national competition. A similar pattern was seen earlier in this century in instrumental and solo contests, as well as drum and bugle corps competitions.

The relationship between band directors and the marching equipment suppliers has been a mutually beneficial and satisfying one. Companies have gained new markets and increased sales, and many band directors, eager to build support for threatened music programs, have been quick to take advantage of any opportunities for increased exposure and public awareness. However, those same directors who previously worked so hard to justify music education's existence can now upon occasion allow themselves to get caught up in a process that contradicts basic educational goals.

Competitive marching contests can provide a variety of benefits for student participants, but many music educators consider marching contests to be extracurricular activities. Moderate involvement in these activities can be beneficial to a music education program, but caution must be exercised to avoid overemphasizing one portion of the program at the expense of another. Music education programs and associated art forms should not be based on or supported by nonmusical reasons or competitive spirit or director ego.

Toward noncompetitive contests

Contest events for solo, ensemble, and large-group concert participants moved toward noncompetitive formats years ago. That philosophy is slowly beginning to appear in jazz and marching band contests as well. Generally, competitions sponsored by state activity associations or professional music education organizations provide for rated but not ranked adjudication for participants. Competitions sponsored by equipment manufacturers, travel agencies, or even many colleges and universities are likely to have a rated and ranked adjudication format.

Leading jazz educators feel that a contest or festival structured so that clinicians' comments replace adjudicators' scores holds the most value for young jazz musicians. They also feel that it is justifiable, and perhaps even important, to recognize outstanding soloists (not *the* outstanding soloist) at such an event through some type of award. (It should be noted here that many jazz contests and festivals are becoming large and impersonal. Music educators are encouraged to carefully select a smaller event, with practical limits on applications, which enables their ensembles to spend more time with guest clinicians.)

Music educators who have established a "winning is everything" atmosphere within their performing groups often discover that they have created a monster. Many of these teachers eventually find it difficult, if not impossible, to maintain the level of instructional intensity, and they either leave the profession entirely or move on to a different music education position that involves little or no performance pressures. This outcome is most certainly an indictment of a process that, when correctly applied, can be a strong component of music education.

PROGRAM BALANCE

It is possible to balance contest participation within the overall objectives of the music education program. Educators need to be aware of their motivation for participation: Why are they participating in the contest? Who benefits? Do the benefits derived by the students justify the effort required for contest participation? Is the event or the music educator the catalyst? These and many other questions need to be answered on a continuing basis to maintain balance within the program.

Marching band contests. Three competitions in any one school year can be considered a maximum number for any marching band. More than three appearances at competitive or noncompetitive events on an annual basis approaches abuse of the program. Whether competitive or noncompetitive, these events can benefit a band program and its student participants in several ways. This depends largely on the philosophy and experience of the director and on whether that director has established viable goals and objectives.

Large-ensemble contests. One annual contest appearance by choral or instrumental concert organizations is strongly recommended and is sufficient to maintain program balance and instructional feedback. On an infrequent basis, a trip to some distant contest or commercial festival is acceptable for school concert organizations. Student musicians certainly can benefit from listening to and comparing their performances with other musical groups away from their own geographical area.

Jazz ensembles. Two contest appearances during an academic year by school jazz bands or swing and jazz choirs can serve as adequate evaluative opportunities for those groups. Colleges and universities sponsor contests and festivals at various times during the year. This allows a director to enter an ensemble at the most opportune and beneficial time.

Solo and small ensembles. One or two actual contest opportunities per year are all that are available to solo and small-ensemble musicians. Because solo and small-ensemble participation can be considered an extremely important component of any quality music education program, as many school-level performance experiences as possible are recommended. Additional solo and ensemble opportunities exist at the local level in the form of recitals and precontest performances that simulate actual contest conditions, including adjudication conducted by another music educator in the district or from a neighboring community.

ADVANTAGES AND DISADVANTAGES OF MUSIC CONTEST PARTICIPATION

Through the years, music educators have recognized a rather specific list of advantages and disadvantages of music contest participation. Those educators who advocate music contests tend to de-emphasize weaknesses in the process, while those opposed to contests are prone to overlook potential benefits.

Advantages of contests

Contest proponents maintain that participation promotes a feeling of cohesiveness within the group and that through that closeness goals are more easily established and worked toward with enthusiasm. Musical groups participating in contests are likely to establish and attain higher musical standards, and through that attainment a long-term interest in good music is developed and strengthened. Contests provide an opportunity to perform outstanding music, and through performance students are given an incentive to work on the most minute musical details with the utmost care. Students participating in contests are evaluated by someone other than their own instructors, and through constructive comments they are helped in the preparation of future performances.

Contest performances give music educators and their students an opportunity to look back and see how far they have progressed, to have that progress evaluated and their accomplishments measured. Proponents argue that an important aspect of music contest participation is that resulting ratings are made public. Parents and school administrators alike will then become more aware of the value and quality of the music program.

Finally, students have an opportunity to hear their peers in performances, both good and bad, and can glimpse a view of musical life in other schools. This advantage, which the music educator can help promote, is an often overlooked benefit of attending music contests.

Disadvantages of contests

Some music educators feel that music contests, whether competitive or noncompetitive, cannot provide an accurate measurement of their instructional efforts. Ten to twenty minutes of exposure to a judge or panel of judges is insufficient time to evaluate the results of several months' work. They believe too much time is devoted to preparing music for contests at the expense of learning a greater and quality variety of music.

Opponents also feel that participation in contests puts the curricular work of music education on a level with extracurricular activities, such as varsity sports. Continued emphasis on competitive and noncompetitive activities could destroy the gains made in placing the study of music solidly in the total educational curriculum. The public relations gains resulting from exposure cannot be allowed to become the primary justification for the existence of music programs. Stressing competition only causes learning to center on using music to win, and many educators frequently compete for the trophy or award rather than using the musical value of the event as the incentive for performance quality.

Too few constructive criticisms are provided by adjudicators in many contests, and too little opportunity is available for hearing the performances of other individuals or groups. Ratings are based on subjective judgments, which makes the idea of determining a "winner" questionable. Educators opposed to competitions also feel that the expense involved in contest participation cannot be justified and that, finally, the standing of the music educator in a community can be jeopardized if local contestants do not receive high ratings.

The advantages and disadvantages of music contests are numerous and vociferously defended by both sides. Yet it is a fact that music contests are increasing rather than decreasing in popularity. They are here to stay, and the number of student participants continues to grow. Prospective teachers are urged to develop an approach to contest participation that is compatible with positive curricular objectives and is in keeping with their evolving philosophies of music education. The level at which a music education program becomes involved in such activities is governed entirely by the music educator charged with administering the program.

Music contests and motivation

Proponents of music competitions suggest that these events motivate students to performance and achievement levels much higher than would be reached otherwise. If students are motivated toward greater achievement, what does contest participation do for the music educator? Exactly the same thing! Granted, many music educators do not need external motivation to provide their students with high-quality music education programs. These teachers approach every performance with the same meticulous care, whether it be a home concert or a state or regional music contest. Unfortunately, there are also a number of music educators who cannot be motivated to excellence regardless of the stimulus. They take their groups to music contests year after year, receive the same poor ratings, return home, and place the blame for their failure everywhere except where it properly belongs.

Many other competent music educators fall somewhere in between these two categories. They are the teachers who are motivated toward higher levels of excellence through music contest participation. They are also dedicated and talented enough to take suggestions resulting from contest performances and use this constructive criticism as a basis for personal and collective musical improvement. Music contest involvement can certainly be a successful, positive, and motivational educational experience for students and teachers alike. The level of that success, as in so many other aspects of administering a music education program, is related directly to the manner in which music educators philosophically approach the event itself.

OBJECTIVES OF MUSIC CONTEST PARTICIPATION

Music educators must provide leadership in establishing objectives for participation in music contests (see chapter 1 for more information on setting objectives and monitoring your progress). Setting objectives is necessary if the experience of entering a music contest is to be considered educationally sound.

A few general objectives of music contest participation are offered here.

1. Establish a positive attitude toward learning and music competitions by reducing emphasis placed on the contest results.
2. Promote a musical learning experience by providing as much appropriate information as possible concerning the material to be performed.
3. Provide an opportunity for students to apply previously learned material.
4. Offer students the opportunity to experience a rise in personal performance standards.
5. Create a greater community awareness of student efforts and their resulting musical performances.

At first glance, these objectives appear to be somewhat lofty in nature, but through closer examination, each one can easily be supported by specific procedures. Consider establishing such goals and objectives in conjunction with music contest participation, and share these goals with students during the preparation process.

CONTEST RATING SYSTEMS

The most prevalent system for rating music contest participants is a five-tier roman-numeral rating scale:

I — Superior

II — Excellent

III — Good

IV — Fair

V — Poor

This system, if used properly, provides for the range of diversity necessary to reflect fairly and adequately an individual or group musical performance. What has happened over the years, however, is that the two lower ratings have almost disappeared. An observation made by Donald Ivey (1966) in an MENC sourcebook published over thirty years ago more accurately describes today's music contest rating system as interpreted by students and educators:

I — Wonderful job, glowing success

II — Not so hot; maybe a mistake to try

III — Ugh! Total failure; give up

IV — Never heard of it!

V — Suicide!

Students, teachers, and the public need to realize that the five-place rating system employed in music contests is synonymous with the A, B, C, D, F system used in most schools. Just as teachers are reluctant to give students a D or an F, adjudicators rarely assign a level IV or V rating on a performance. What in effect is taking place is an inflated impression of the performance quality of student musicians at contests. The manner in which the present system is used is likely to continue but will vary in application from one area of the country to another. Canadian contest hosts have taken a more honest look at rating systems and have established a three-tier approach using the letters A, B, and C. This seems the easiest and most equitable way to handle ratings.

One approach to contest ratings adopted by several state activity associations for contests under their jurisdiction is called the "star system." In such a rating system, contestants receive constructive criticism from an adjudicator based on their performances. If a performance reaches a level of excellence determined by the adjudicator, a star is awarded to that individual or group. Those entries earning star ratings at the district level are then allowed to perform at the state music contest. At both levels, adjudicators are encouraged to limit their star ratings to approximately thirty percent of the entries in each performance area. Extra star ratings may be awarded above the specific number if an adjudicator is willing to complete a form stating the reasons for the rating. Students not receiving star ratings are given constructive comments concerning their performance.

Favorable reaction by music educators to the star system has been quite widespread. Under this system, the stigma attached to not earning the top award in a particular category is not as great as it is in the I, II, III, IV, V or A, B, C rating systems. There is no perfect approach, but the star system appears to support more closely the educational principles expressed most often by music educators in conjunction with noncompetitive contests.

AIDING THE ADJUDICATION PROCESS

Music educators have an obligation to their students, themselves, and contest evaluators to prepare contest music as carefully and thoroughly as possible. They can aid in the adjudication process by numbering the measures of all music submitted for adjudication, choral as well as instrumental. Measure numbers allow adjudicators to pinpoint problem areas more quickly, as well as those passages deserving praise during a performance. Adjudicators are always impressed by the concern of music educators whose students submit solo or large-ensemble scores with the measures numbered. Such consideration is one indication to an adjudicator that a music educator is serious about the process.

All contests have specific rules governing their operation. Educators can aid adjudicators by carefully following the classification and timing rules. To comply with the copyright law, most contests also stipulate that music submitted to a judge be an original, not a photocopy.

There is a wealth of performance material available to all music educators, so reliance on the latest hot number on a recent promotional recording is unnecessary. Many contests now have required, graded music lists. This is a positive step to exposing young musicians, as well as new teachers, to what is considered to be quality musical material.

Some contests have included additional measurements of musicality, such as sight-reading by large ensembles. While it would appear that this requirement would hold some value as an aid to the adjudication process, it has not met with a great deal of favorable reaction from music educators. Some have gone so far as to suggest that a musicianship test be administered to individual students following a contest performance. This test might include listening items, cover a variety of music, some literature, and theory items, but would not exceed fifty minutes in length. It is felt that such a test would recognize and reward musicians instead of performers. However, the complexities of implementing such a test and disagreement as to the needs for objective measurement of musicianship have prevented the test concept from becoming anything more than experimental.

All music educators are aware that contests produce winners and losers. However, the biggest winners come away from contests with a greater depth of musical understanding, accelerated musical growth, a personal sense of accomplishment, and an awareness of the uniqueness of concentrated effort toward a specific set of goals—not a trophy or ribbon.

MUSIC FESTIVALS

Through the years, noncompetitive music festivals have filled an extrinsic performance void for those music educators who made the determination that contests were not in the best interests of their programs or students. Other educators who felt that contests played an important role in the success of their programs recognized the importance of festival participation for enrichment purposes.

A music festival, as described in this section, involves unrated, unranked performances by groups representing two or more schools, culminating in some type of final performance. Many schools sponsor their own festival and bring in an outside conductor to work with students throughout the day, but such a format is more appropriately referred to as a clinic.

Types of festivals

Three basic types of festivals will be discussed. Of course, variations on each festival format are possible and quite common. Each festival type is somewhat unique, but each brings together young musicians from a variety of educational settings under the leadership of an outstanding guest conductor in a day-long schedule of rehearsals and performances.

Massed festival. A massed festival involves several schools, usually three or four, that bring their entire bands, choirs, or orchestras to one location and combine them into one large, "massed" group. Music has been prepared in advance by each performing group, the guest conductor rehearses the group several hours in the morning and afternoon, and a concert is presented in the evening.

While the intent of music educators involved in these festivals is honorable, all too often the benefits to students are somewhat suspect, for two reasons:

1. The music is too difficult. Educators select music for the festival that their own groups would have difficulty performing alone.
2. The groups are poorly prepared. Although much of the selected repertoire is quite difficult, each participating school fails to prepare the music in advance of the festival. It is not uncommon for students to appear at the first rehearsal of a festival having never seen the music. If even one participating school fails to adequately prepare for the festival, the potential for a learning experience for all other students has been severely reduced. When all participating schools fail to

prepare music in advance of the festival, the potential for any musical benefit to the students has been totally eliminated. In these situations, the festival is reduced to a social experience, and for most of those involved (including the guest conductor), an unpleasant one.

Many fine guest conductors and music educators no longer agree to take part in massed festivals because of these two serious problems. A massed festival can be a quality learning experience if involved music educators make a serious commitment to themselves, their students, and the festival concept by establishing educational objectives and preparing music as carefully as time allows. Then, and only then, will students receive musical benefits in proportion to the time spent on the project.

Honor festival. An honor festival involves the best student musicians from each participating school. Such a select group provides the opportunity to experience a higher performance quality than does the massed festival. Students in an honor festival are also generally able to perform more difficult music.

Honor festivals are often citywide in membership, or they involve schools in a particular organized athletic conference, or schools from a specific geographic area, such as the Northwest Iowa Music Festival. For some honor festivals, participants are selected through a strict audition process, but for most festivals students are recommended and selected by local directors. The number of students allowed to participate is usually based on the size of the school and the number of schools involved in the festival. An honor group with membership between 100 and 200 students is recommended, although select smaller and larger groups have proven to be successful as well.

Again, preparation is the main ingredient in the success of this type of festival. One or two schools whose musicians arrive at an honor festival totally unprepared for rehearsal are going to limit considerably the potential learning experience of the other participants. As with the massed festival, the honor festival culminates in an evening performance of music prepared during the day. Due to its select nature, the prospect for performance excellence is considerably greater for an honor festival than it is for a massed festival. The exclusivity of the honor festival is questioned by some music educators, but supporters of the honor concept contend that the musical enrichment that takes place for the more interested and talented musicians outweighs the fact that not all musicians from each school are able to participate in the festival.

Clinic festival. The clinic festival appears to be the most educationally sound type of event. In this type of festival, three or four participating schools combine a clinic-type experience with the massed festival concept. During the morning hours, a performing group from each school plays fifteen to twenty minutes of music for the guest clinician/conductor. The guest writes constructive comments, much the same as would an adjudicator at a music contest. During the remaining time allotted for that group, the clinician/conductor verbally critiques the music performed and works with the ensemble on the musical aspects that need attention. A competent and experienced clinician/conductor can have a dramatic influence on the musical performance potential of a student group during a one-hour period. A sensitive guest is also quick to point out the many excellent musical aspects of the performance.

The morning hours are consumed by clinic sessions with each participating group. Ideally, if travel conditions permit, each performing group has the opportunity to listen to the other performances and clinics. This type of observation is highly recommended and can be an important attribute of the clinic festival.

During the afternoon, all participating groups are combined into a massed ensemble and the clinician/conductor rehearses no more than a total of twenty minutes of music that will be presented as part of an evening concert. During the afternoon rehearsal period, the guest is provided the opportunity to demonstrate rehearsal techniques, illuminating the concepts discussed as part of the morning sessions.

At the evening concert, each school ensemble performs five to seven minutes of music from the clinic session, followed by a massed ensemble performance. The evening concert, including set changes, is less than an hour in length. Participating music educators, their students, and the guest clinician/conductor all go home with a feeling of confidence that through the day's activities, the best interests of music education have been served. Of course, as with other types of festivals, preparation by local directors is the key to success for the event.

Selecting festival music

There are three ways in which repertoire for a music festival is selected:

1. *The guest conductor makes the selection.* This can result in underprogramming or overprogramming, but most experienced conductors are able to make a proper selection of material with which they are familiar. The festival committee has the right and obligation to reject any suggested festival music that they feel is inappropriate in any way for the festival ensemble.
2. *The festival committee decides.* Involved music directors are in a position to know the type and level of music most suitable for their festival groups. The disadvantage in total committee control of festival music selection is that it is possible that some music might be selected that is unfamiliar to the guest conductor. It is understandable that guest conductors are more apt to provide all participants with a quality learning experience when they use music with which they are familiar and music they know to be successful learning and performance vehicles in a festival setting.

3. *A combined decision is made.* The selection of festival music can best be accomplished when the committee and the guest conductor make a joint decision. This decision is likely to produce a repertoire that is familiar to the guest conductor and is within the musical grasp of the massed ensemble.

As previously mentioned, the major flaw in choosing repertoire for a music festival is selecting music that is too difficult for the ensemble, resulting in an uncomfortable and frustrating experience for all parties concerned. Music educators must bear in mind that challenging music need not be frustrating to perform. There is a much better opportunity for musical learning experiences to occur when festival music is too easy than when it is too difficult.

Music festival objectives

As with contests and almost every other aspect of music education, the best learning experiences result from established, achievable, and monitored goals and objectives. Music festival objectives should be established for the event by the participating educators. Objectives might be to:

Broaden student musical growth through the experience of rehearsing and performing with fellow student musicians under an outstanding guest conductor.

Introduce participating teachers to rehearsal techniques that offer long-term musical benefits.

Acquaint students with challenging, developmental, and interesting musical literature.

Objectives such as "Give the kids a treat," "Provide an opportunity to meet others with like interests," or ""Have a pleasant time in a musical atmosphere" are not educational. Making music in a festival setting involves learning. Social interaction must be considered a worthwhile byproduct of that learning experience.

Within several weeks following a festival, the educators who planned it should review its success in terms of meeting objectives and make preliminary plans for the next festival. All too often, educators wait nearly a year before planning, and in that time memories tend to dim; a valuable opportunity to upgrade the festival and improve the learning experience for students has been lost.

Organizing a music festival

Because music contests are generally sponsored by state activity associations, professional music organizations, or colleges and universities, no contest management concerns are offered as part of this chapter. However, because festivals are very often locally sponsored and organized by one or more music educators to meet their specific program needs, it is appropriate that some general organizational considerations be presented. Because festivals are often personal undertakings, some of the organizational and management suggestions may not be appropriate for every situation, but new teachers should find them to be of some assistance in planning a first festival.

Committee meeting. Teachers from participating schools should meet several months before the event and determine the following:

1. Festival objectives.
2. Date, place, format, and festival title. Titles are important to provide a sense of identity for the event, both for present and future use. "Festival for Young Voices," "Tri-State Band Festival," and "Quad-City Chorale" are typical festival titles.
3. Budget.
4. Clinicians and/or conductor. Recommend several in order of preference in case of date conflict.
5. Repertoire. The final determination will likely be a combined decision of the conductor and committee.

Contact clinician/conductor. Several months before the event, call the conductor who is the first choice of the committee. Highly respected clinicians and conductors are in demand and need to be contacted several months to a year in advance of a festival. If the clinician is available, briefly outline pertinent information in addition to the date, such as festival format, hours involved, and the honorarium the committee will pay for the event. Follow the initial contact with a letter. The purpose of the letter is to confirm the telephone conversation and reiterate the date, time, hours, fee, and place; never trust anything to memory. Also, request input for festival music literature and ask that a photo and a brief biographical sketch for publicity purposes be sent within a reasonable period of time.

Festival preparation. *Eight weeks before the festival,* send registration materials to participating schools requesting pertinent information, such as fees, if any.

Submit a festival poster to the printer *five weeks before the event.* Include the name of the clinician/conductor, time and place of the festival concert, a list of participating schools, and where to secure tickets, if applicable, and a phone number for inquiries.

Three weeks before the event, send the following information to participating schools:

1. Festival schedule.
2. Sketch of school with bus parking, unloading area, warm-up, and performance areas clearly marked.
3. Name of the group's host. It's a nice touch to have a local student serve as host and guide for each school group as it arrives at the festival site.
4. Homeroom or storage area as applicable.
5. Equipment that the host school will furnish.
6. Appropriate concert attire required.
7. Meal locations and costs.
8. Reminder to have school identification on all instruments and equipment.
9. Festival posters for participating schools to distribute.

Two weeks before the festival, press releases should be mailed or delivered to appropriate media sources. Include specific festival information, such as clinician/conductor, participating schools, concert program, and other suitable information. At the same time, copy for the festival program should be submitted to the printer. Include a picture and appropriate information (one or two short paragraphs) about the clinician/conductor, the program, program notes (optional), participating schools and their directors, and acknowledgments of any other nonparticipating individuals who made some type of contribution to the success of the festival, such as any local school officials or music parents.

One week before the festival, personally invite the local newspaper to send a photographer and/or arts reporter to the event. Music festivals are newsworthy, and editors are interested in events that affect large numbers of readers.

If possible, have a check ready immediately for the clinician/conductor(s). Meet with the school business manager or other school official at least two weeks before the festival to see what steps need to be taken to expedite the process. Guests appreciate and deserve to receive payment at the close of the event for services rendered.

No more than eight weeks after the festival, the participating music directors should schedule a follow-up meeting to discuss festival objective achievement, determine quality and success levels of the festival, and make preliminary plans for next year's event.

Undoubtedly numerous small details and organizational concerns will arise that weren't mentioned in the previous section, but information has been provided that should allow even the most inexperienced music educator to organize and manage a festival. Remember that careful planning leads to success.

One final thought: A complete notebook or file needs to be compiled with copies of all correspondence and paperwork associated with the festival. These files become extremely valuable when planning subsequent events, particularly if the festival is rotated among participating schools.

COMMERCIAL MUSIC FESTIVALS

Commercial festivals for school music performance groups that are promoted by companies whose sole purpose is the business of festival sponsorship have been around for over twenty years. These festivals offer a variety of performance opportunities, including any number of larger choral ensembles, plus swing and/or jazz choirs. Concert and jazz bands participate, and often there is some type of marching band category, including separate classifications for guard, drill teams, dance teams, and drum lines. String orchestras as well as full symphonic orchestras round out the performance opportunities at most commercial festivals.

Commercial music festivals are often organized around some type of amusement or theme park experience, with the admission to the facilities included in the festival package. Lodging in a high-quality hotel/motel, adjudication, awards, get-acquainted student dances, or receptions are often included in commercial festival packages as well. Some festivals also include a banquet gathering for students and their directors, and/or a reception honoring the director of each participating group. All such festivals have an awards ceremony in which an array of trophies and plaques are distributed to participating ensembles and musically outstanding individuals.

Financial outlay for musical groups attending many commercial festivals is most often determined on a cost-per-student basis, which includes many or all of the above options. Cost figures for commercial festivals can reach upwards of $100 per person in the group. Each performing group is generally responsible for their own travel arrangements to and from the festival city.

Classifications

Participating groups are assigned a performance classification based on their respective school enrollment figures. There is no national festival classification standard that has been established, just as classification standards for music ensembles vary from state to state. To their credit, some commercial festival companies have done research on high school enrollment figures nationwide and developed their ensemble classifications from those figures. For example, if a commercial festival offers three performance classifications, organizers then determine that one-third of the high schools in this country have an enrollment of 350 students or below, one-third have an enrollment of 351 to 825 students, and the remaining one-third have an enrollment of 826 students and higher. (These enrollment figures are for example only; each festival will determine its own breakpoints.) The organizers then establish the three classifications accordingly. This method of determining performance classifications appears to be equitable, regardless of the festival site and the home of the performing group(s).

Ratings and rankings

Many commercial festivals have embraced a system that allows music educators some flexibility when it comes to adjudication. Festival adjudication options include (1) rated (superior, excellent, etc.), (2) ranked (first place, second place, etc.), (3) rated and ranked, or (4) not ranked or rated—groups perform for comments only. All groups are judged and compared with other ensembles in their respective categories or classifications. There are usually other options available to directors of performing groups, but the preceding are the most common. Commercial festival participation offers a level of adjudication flexibility not generally found in regional and state music contests sponsored by high school activities associations.

Selecting a commercial festival

The process of selecting a commercial festival should begin as much as two years before the date of the festival. Music educators are urged to seek and compare information from at least three commercial festival companies that promote events somewhere in the geographic area to which they wish to travel. Personal contact with staff at the commercial festival headquarters is an absolute must. Through a series of phone conversations with festival staff, a music director can learn a great deal about the company.

Questions to pose to festival promoters include:

1. How many years has the company been promoting music festivals? A company that has been satisfying its customers for ten years or more is doing something right.
2. How many festivals does the company sponsor annually? When festival staff seem to be overscheduled and overworked, overpromotion can be a concern.
3. Does the company deliver what it says it will? To determine this, request a copy of a previous festival program, especially one in the area where you wish to attend. It is always interesting to learn how many groups actually appeared at a commercial festival. You may also want to contact by telephone several of the music directors listed on the program for a personal evaluation of their festival experience.
4. What are the adjudication options available to each performing group? Can a group be rated, ranked, rated and ranked, perform for comments only, etc.?

How are performing groups divided into classifications? How many classifications are there?

5. If ratings are used in the adjudication process, what is the percentage of "superior" ratings awarded annually? More than ten percent superior ratings tends to cheapen the rating system as well as the quality of the desired festival experience.

6. What types of awards are presented? Is there a sweepstakes award involved? Are outstanding musician awards presented to deserving students? If so, how many? What are the criteria?

7. Are verbal critiques from adjudicators to performing groups part of the festival adjudication format?

8. What is the quality of the festival performance venue? A music director does not want to take an ensemble halfway across the country to perform in a gymnasium. *That* type of musical experience is available at home!

9. How are adjudicators hired? What are their professional qualifications? Performing groups pay a good deal of money for their commercial festival experience and deserve competent and quality constructive criticism of their musical efforts.

10. What are the nonmusical experiences available to participating students? Which of those experiences is included in the festival package, and which are available for an extra fee?

Commercial festival history

Commercial festivals as we know them have been in existence since the mid-1970s. There are currently more than fifty festivals in the United States. Several new festival companies come on the scene each year and several go out of business—an important reason in itself to check the background of the company before making a commitment to a particular festival.

There are basically two categories of commercial music festivals:

1. Festivals operated by a former music educator, more often than not a former band director. This individual has an in-depth understanding of the needs of music educators, as well of the importance of well-organized and high-quality musical experiences for all participants. The organizer has personal knowledge of and contact with music directors at the university level across the country who are qualified to provide meaningful adjudication. The festival business is this former music educator's entire professional life.

2. Festivals owned and operated by a travel company. Quite frequently, no one associated with a travel company has any experience dealing with music educators or student musicians. Their expertise lies in travel arrangements, tours, lodging facilities,

and meal arrangements. The company must rely on the advice and knowledge of an individual outside the organization to manage and operate the festival at each site on the schedule. Communication can break down, misunderstandings can develop, and important details can be left to chance when the organization and operation of a music festival are not the primary focus of the festival director.

These problems, of course, do not apply to all commercial music festivals sponsored by travel companies; however, the background of the individual a travel company retains to manage its festivals and the degree of influence the company exercises over festival operations are of utmost importance to a music educator considering commercial festival participation. The bottom line is to carefully evaluate festival management, using the questions already suggested as well as posing your own concerns.

Educators who elect to participate in music contests can enrich that experience through local festival participation. Other educators, who for one reason or another do not participate in large-group music contests, find that festivals can provide a valuable opportunity for an enhanced learning experience if the practices presented in the preceding pages are observed. This author recommends, economic and geographical conditions permitting, that all junior and senior high school performing groups participate in at least one music festival on an annual basis. If funds permit, a trip scheduled to a commercial festival every three or four years can be an extremely enjoyable and satisfying experience as well, and, at the same time, perhaps aid recruitment and retention of ensemble members. When properly organized and administered, these events are avenues for excellence in music education, as well as an element of good public relations for the total music program.

Suggested Activities

1. Secure a copy of the rules or bylaws relating to music contests in your state from the governing agency, whether a state activities association or a professional music educators organization. Discuss in class the implications that these policies hold for music education in your area.
2. Obtain a set of adjudication forms (available from MENC). Discuss in class such terms as artistry, influence, instrumentation, appearance, stage presence, and choice of music as they apply to the contest adjudication process.
3. Invite one or more experienced contest adjudicators from your own campus to discuss their impressions of the positive and negative aspects of the music contest adjudication process.
4. Invite an experienced music festival conductor from your own campus to discuss the positive and negative implications of music festival participation.

5. Research periodical literature and determine advantages or disadvantages of solo and ensemble music contest participation for elementary and junior high school students. Discuss your findings in class.

6. Classes for contest-participating organizations (Class A, B, and so on) are generally determined by high school enrollment or the size of the participating ensemble. Discuss advantages and/or disadvantages of those two classification systems.

7. Discuss in class what effect the elimination of jazz contests or festivals would have on jazz ensemble programs in public and private schools.

8. As a class project, assume responsibility for planning, organizing, and managing a music festival on campus or in the community.

9. Pick one of the objectives of music contest participation that appear on page 225 and develop three strategies to aid the implementation of that objective. Use examples provided on page 9 in chapter 1 as a guide for strategy development. Share your strategies with the class.

CHAPTER ELEVEN

PUBLIC

RELATIONS

INTRODUCTION

Public relations is a means of communication between the music educator and the community. A school's music program cannot be considered successful unless it is also looked upon as such by its constituency. Promoting an image of success is accomplished through a certain level of selling on the part of the educator. Active and ongoing public relations efforts establish an atmosphere that allows promotion to succeed. Goal-setting is an extremely important part of any public relations process, as important as it is to any other noninstructional element in music education.

Performances can have a positive or negative effect, or simply no effect, on the image of a music program. Concerts that have been carefully prepared and thoughtfully constructed will undoubtedly convey a positive image to the public if general public relations strategies are employed. The music educator must be constantly alert to new and interesting approaches to concert performance.

Concert promotion can evolve into a routine, but in the early stages, it requires in-depth planning and extra effort on the part of the educator. Any publicity done in conjunction with musical performances is in itself a form of public relations, and the quality must be carefully considered. A variety of ways to promote and publicize musical performance is available. The educator must choose the publicity method or approach that best suits the program's needs. Developing a mailing list is perhaps the most effective means of communicating concert information to the potentially interested public.

The use of photography and video technology in music education as a means of performance evaluation has been on the scene for several years; however, the use of these media as instruments of public relations has yet to gain widespread appeal.

Music educators should make it a point to become involved in the community. They possess special skills that can make them valued assets in community activities.

Their involvement in such activities often leads to greater depth of understanding and support by community members for a music program.

COMMUNICATION AND PUBLIC RELATIONS

Readers may recall the short discussion presented in chapter 1 relating the association of the music educator as an administrator to the thirteenth administrative function: communicating. It was pointed out that communication can influence in a positive or negative manner nearly all of the remaining functions.

Actions that keep the parents and community informed of the purpose, usefulness, conditions, and needs of the music program come under the domain of public relations. Public relations, a two-way system of communicating between the community and the music educator, can promote the public's goodwill and ensure future support of the program. If the public relations approach is well planned, it will reflect the positive qualities of both the school and the music program and result in favorable public opinion and, therefore, acceptance of that program.

It is important that music educators sell their programs and themselves to the broadest constituency possible. The creation of a broad base of support for music education in the community can be of great value, whether for seeking increased budget support or simply greater program support through concert attendance. Two-way communication between the music educator, administrators, parents, and the entire community is a natural part of the sales effort. Far too often public relations is thought of only as a one-way communications channel (from music educator to the public), creating a degree of isolation that is nearly as harmful to the music program as no communication whatsoever.

For some new music educators, the need to promote their programs to both the school and community is distasteful. They feel that music education is a wonderful experience for young people and should stand on its own merits. Such a philosophical approach to developing support for a music program is at best impractical. Of course, it is desirable to touch every student in some manner through the music program. However, the reality is that those students will never be touched unless the need has been created, demonstrated, and communicated to school officials and the community alike. This can best be done by a logical and practical course of action involving public relations.

Broad-based parental and community support can significantly contribute to reducing or preventing program cutbacks, if and when they should occur. Parental advocacy is a natural and important part of the total base of support; if community representatives other than parents endorse the music education program, it has an even greater impact when school budget planners are considering program reductions in music. This broad base of support is most effectively achieved through an active and positive public relations effort. It is not enough to have a good orchestra, choir, or band at either the elementary or high school level. People have to know about it. They must be informed, and in turn must provide feedback to the music educator as well as to students involved in the program. The music educator must be prepared to take action on the feedback offered. Hence, communication results.

Evaluating community needs

The music educator should evaluate the music program in terms of community needs:

How strong is the economy of the community?

Is it a suburban, urban, or rural community?

What is the principal occupation of its residents?

How strong is the tax base and level of support for the school?

The social structure of the community should be considered:

How are the arts accepted in the community?

Is there a community concert series or a community chorus, band, or orchestra?

Are there music stores in the community?

Is there a newspaper, as well as radio and television stations?

Answers to these questions can help determine the depth, focus, and activity level for a public relations program associated with music education. Community attitude toward music should be considered in conjunction with the scope and direction of the music program.

Concerts and public relations

School concerts are an important community public relations vehicle. Generating and sustaining strong concert attendance is an administrative responsibility of the music educator. Getting an audience to a concert involves the element of public relations known as publicity. How the audience is treated, both aesthetically and musically, after arriving at the concert also involves public relations. For example, a two-and-one-half-hour concert generally does not make for positive public relations. When a great deal of time spent at a concert is consumed by set changes or a seemingly endless parading of personnel to and from the stage, public relations suffers.

Parents will tolerate overly long or poorly organized programs; they have no choice. But the general public is a different story. If a music educator really wants to use attendance at concerts as a means of communicating music program quality to parents and the public, then the concerts should be short (rarely over one hour) and organized with the audience in mind.

If a music educator continually finds program length to be between two and three hours, too many people are involved in the production. For example, if the annual band and choir Christmas concert falls into the lengthy category, two choices exist: (1) present separate concerts, either on the same or different evenings; or (2) have each group perform less, but better-prepared, music.

Across the country, school music concerts that are consistently well attended by parents and the general public have several similar characteristics. First, they are well publicized and well promoted; second, they are prepared musically to the best ability of the participants; and, third, the concert itself is a production that makes the most efficient use of audience time and student effort.

The all-school extravaganza is a possible exception to the "shorter is better" rule. It must be kept in mind, however, that the immensity of a major project in no way precludes an efficient and organized approach. Students, parents, and the public alike greatly appreciate this demonstration of efficiency on the part of the music educator. When considering the presentation of an all-school extravaganza, a music educator should be aware that the audience will primarily be made up of families of student musicians. Thus the audience will be somewhat fluid; family members will very likely come and go as the concert progresses. Some music educators promote audience flexibility as a means of attracting today's busy family members to their concert programs.

Promotion

Advertising for a single event is known as promotion. In order for any promotional campaign to be successful, the foundation for this effort must be laid through an ongoing program of public relations. An atmosphere is created by an active public relations plan that allows promotion to succeed. For example, a music educator has an excellent chance to receive positive media coverage for a particular event if the local media have been informed on a continuing basis of past successes and previous community activities and if other prior newsworthy features have been submitted in a professional and informative manner. Public support for a major fund-raising effort is likely to be better when the music program is considered to be an important part of school and community life. Also, as will be discussed later in this book, should some type of fiscal difficulties arise, a solid public relations base will be invaluable.

GOAL-SETTING IN PUBLIC RELATIONS

When working to strengthen a music program's public relations with the school and community, the music educator needs to determine both long-range and short-term objectives. Long-range goals will be few and quite broad. An example of one such goal would be to establish a strong relationship between the music program and the community. Short-term objectives to support that long-range goal could be to increase the visibility of music groups in the community, to better inform the community of music events and achievements, and to become personally involved to a greater extent in the community. The general process of setting, verifying, and monitoring goals and objectives was discussed in greater detail in chapter 1. Bear in mind that the goals and objectives must be achievable and should be monitored and verified.

Beginning teachers often have difficulty establishing goals and objectives because they fail to see themselves teaching in a given situation for more than a year or two. Music educators new to the profession should try to approach their work with a sense of permanency, with the idea that they will be teaching in this new position for a number of years. If a music educator can assume this attitude toward a new teaching position, enlightened and practical goal- and objective-setting in public relations, as well as throughout the entire music program, will be less difficult. In the final analysis, it will be more beneficial to the school, to the community, and to the music educator.

Short-term objectives should be designed to be achievable in the time span of one school year. Using such parameters provides ample opportunity to measure the progress of any public relations effort. Objectives can be renewed, adjusted, and revised each year, but thinking in terms of achieving annual objectives will help motivate the music educator.

Several short-term objectives were just mentioned in conjunction with the long-term public relations goal to establish a strong relationship between the music program and the community. Another short-term objective could be to improve communication with parents concerning (1) performance and special rehearsal dates, (2) student responsibilities, and (3) the total scope of the music program. Note that short-term objectives tend to be more specific than long-range goals. The level of specificity increases when listing means toward objective achievement. For example, in support of the above short-term objectives, several techniques or strategies could be listed.

1. Send a calendar of events to parents, along with a list of student responsibilities associated with those events.
2. Establish a schedule and encourage parent visitation to classes and/or rehearsals.

3. Initiate an annual Parents Night that allows parents to participate in class and rehearsals.

These three strategies are very specific, and the success of each, along with program benefits, can be easily verified and measured at the close of the school year. The strategies that seem to work and to increase communication could be continued, while any techniques deemed unhelpful to the short-term objective could be discarded and replaced with other techniques the following year. Achievement of these objectives is certain to result in greater constituency support. The music educator needs to become involved in providing a quality final product to the school and community and must assume the responsibility for making them both aware that the product exists. Setting long-term goals and short-range objectives can be a means to that end.

PUBLIC RELATIONS THROUGH PROGRAMMING

How the music educator prepares and presents concert programs to the public can be a most effective tool in the total public relations plan. Group directors, caught up in tradition, often ignore the potential to enhance the image of the music program and to increase concert attendance through a creative approach to concert programming. The level of the musical experience achieved by student participants is closely associated with the manner in which the music was taught and not so much the format or environment in which it was performed. Music educators with successful programs are those who are receptive to the needs, wishes, and enjoyment level of their audiences, as well as those of their students.

Dedicated teachers are constantly alert to new concepts and procedures that promote innovative approaches to performance programming. The number of new ideas available to a music educator is proportionately related to the educator's dedication to developing new performance avenues, as well as a willingness to experiment with contemporary performance concepts.

A year-long program built around the music of a particular ethnic group can increase community interest. For example, music from a certain national tradition could be included as part of every concert presented by all performing groups during the year. A "Salute to Scandinavia," involving citizens from the community in authentic costume, could provide an opportunity for a more historical approach to the preparation and presentation of the music and heighten interest on the part of the local media. This effort would increase student awareness of music from another part of the world and make it possible to involve other departments within the school, such as the social studies, speech, and drama departments. This same approach to promoting music from another country could be developed for a single concert featuring music from that country. During a visit to Illinois several years ago, this author learned of one educator's innovative way to handle the Christmas holiday rush. Because of a crowded school calendar and the many obligations on the part or parents during that time of year, a creative middle school teacher in Champaign organized a continental breakfast concert hour. It was scheduled early in the morning, before school, which allowed parents to stop by the school for breakfast and a little music on their way to work. Each group was scheduled to perform two or three selections, so that parents could coordinate their breakfast schedules with their children's performance schedules. Coffee, juice, and rolls were available at a nominal fee, and parents were urged to come and go as their personal commitments permitted. The parents gave rave reviews to the experiment, and it provided an opportunity for students to participate in an exciting and memorable performance setting. An experimental project born somewhat out of necessity will in all likelihood become an annual, noteworthy, and newsworthy affair.

Some music educators schedule a pops concert or program of lighter music in conjunction with an ice cream social. Tables and chairs, complete with checkered tablecloths, are set up, and refreshments are served by music students costumed in vests and straw hats. School jazz ensembles have been known to perform their concerts in nightclub settings, with punch and cookies on the menu. Items served at a concert can often be secured on a donation basis from a local soft drink distributor, a fast-food outlet, or a movie theater. These settings provide a different and attention-getting experience for students and audiences alike.

Madrigal dinners have become popular with many school choral groups. Musically demanding and expensive to produce, this type of production requires a great deal of expertise and organizational and promotional skill on the part of a music educator. After gaining community acceptance and support, an annual madrigal dinner can become a potent fund-raising vehicle and provide a distinctively special performance experience for students participating in the choral program.

Another means of attracting attention to a concert program is to change the location of a performance to another site within the community. Local churches and auditoriums should be considered. A concert in a shopping mall is another option. If a group isn't already performing in a school gym, a performance could be scheduled there and perhaps involve gymnastics in some manner. Outdoor concerts hold some potential, but the possibility of inclement weather must be considered. Performances scheduled inside or outside any public building are sure to attract audience members who have never been exposed to school music performances.

Incorporating local dignitaries and officials in programs as guest conductors, narrators, and even soloists is another way to gain exposure for the program. School administrators and community officials are often honored to be asked to participate in a school music program, and such an event provides a newsworthy public relations opportunity. State and regional political figures, as well as other noteworthy individuals, are other possible concert program guests.

Many schools schedule evening arts festivals to broaden their audience base. A structure for such a program could be an open-house format for all school concert groups. In different areas within the school building, various groups could perform at fifteen- to twenty-minute intervals over a two-hour period. At the same time, work by students involved in art classes could be on display, a fashion show by a home economics class could be scheduled, and projects completed in an industrial arts or woodworking class could be placed on display. The open-house format allows parents and other interested parties to see and hear exactly what they want.

Such efforts generate greater exposure for school performing groups. They also provide opportunities for public display of student projects normally relegated to a classroom showing. More important, they create opportunities for instructional staff and students to work together toward a common goal: displaying their individual and collective talents.

Side-by-side concerts—in which two or more groups perform a portion of a single concert—offer numerous benefits for all participants. The groups involved normally would not share a concert setting. For example, a high school choir concert could include a performance by the sixth-grade choir; the high school band could share a concert with a touring college or university group; a school orchestra could appear as part of a program presented by a community symphony. The public relations benefits are obvious: increased publicity opportunities, increased audience size, and exposure to audiences who normally would attend only the concert of one group or the other. Of equal importance are the personal and musical benefits gained by the participants in hearing and working with other groups. This type of concert can be one of the easiest to organize and can produce unusual and interesting audience composites.

Any music educator can develop innovative ways to present students in unique performance situations. The resulting improvement in image and public relations is well worth the effort.

CONCERT PROMOTION

When answering the usual questions involved when promoting a concert—such as who will be performing, what will be performed, when and where the concert will be given, and how much it will cost—you will need to answer one more question: *Why* would people want to attend the concert? If realistic answers can be provided, then the first major obstacle to concert promotion has been overcome. Without answering this question, you cannot enthusiastically and effectively promote the event. If the "why" is difficult to ascertain, then perhaps the program, from a conceptual as well as a musical standpoint, needs to be reexamined.

Concert publicity efforts can be routinized. Writing press releases, taking photographs, and submitting promotional material to the proper news media need not be difficult and time-consuming tasks once a routine is established. Determining what the media are interested in and what type of material is likely to be used are the first steps in publicizing a concert. The type of articles that are of interest to the local newspaper may surprise you. Determine what kind of material is appropriate and use it as a guide to submitting additional information.

It is wise to make media contacts in person, especially when making these contacts for the first time. Media representatives view personal contacts as an indication of a promoter's concern for detail, and they appreciate the attention. The in-person approach also lets media representatives come to know you as more than a name on a page, and they're able to ask pertinent questions regarding the event.

Even the smallest communities are served by a daily or weekly newspaper. Although the paper may be published in a larger nearby town, the publishers are concerned with providing local news coverage to smaller neighboring communities, and they are aware of the potential for advertising dollars in this coverage. For this reason, news articles and accompanying photographs about an upcoming school concert are generally welcomed by the arts editor or other individual on the newspaper staff charged with overseeing arts coverage. In larger metropolitan areas, it can be more difficult to receive newspaper coverage for a school concert because of the multitude of professional events that compete for attention with amateur performances. That doesn't mean that urban-based music educators should necessarily expect no media interest. News releases and photographs should still be submitted, and on occasion they may be used.

A weekly newspaper in a small community is certain to publish anything available regarding school concerts because every item in the newspaper is of a local nature. Be sure to explore this valuable public relations avenue in promoting all events.

One or two days before a concert, it's a good idea to take out a small ad in the newspaper serving a community, simply to remind the public about the event. To make the ad more distinguishable, consider having the copy set against a black background. A small ad constructed in this manner will compete nicely with larger, more expensive advertising. A newspaper advertising representative will be happy to provide assistance designing the ad.

Radio stations serving a community are another medium for concert publicity. Again, the smallest communities may have only two nearby radio stations vying for advertising dollars. Press releases sent to these stations are likely to be covered as news items, as well as given as public service announcements, particularly if the material is delivered in person. Also, radio advertising is not expensive. A series of ads one or two days before a concert could cost as little as $50 and greatly increase public awareness of the event. Free coverage from both radio and newspapers is more likely to be forthcoming if concert advertising is purchased.

Area television stations can be informed about future music programs via a press release. All radio and television stations are required by the Federal Communications Commission to devote a percentage of their airtime to public service announcements, free of charge to the public. School music productions fall into the public service category. Everyone who listens to radio or watches television will be exposed to numerous daily public service announcements. If a newspaper ad is already developed, it takes no greater effort to submit a copy of the press release to radio and television stations, along with a short note requesting the use of the material as part of a station's public service announcements.

Cable television services provide community access channels. Listings are free and can reach a broad audience. Also, community access channels may be encouraged to televise concerts and other musical events as part of their public service programming. Contact your local cable provider to find out more about community services.

The school newspaper is another source of free advertising for concert productions. Every ensemble in both junior and senior high school is likely to include a member of the school newspaper staff. A choir or band reporter can be the correspondent between the ensemble and the school paper.

Bulletin boards, both in and out of school, can be an avenue for concert advertising. Students can assemble and distribute neat and attractive posters about the event and decorate in-school bulletin boards. Many students relish and excel at this type of responsibility. Be sure to explore this relatively effortless means of concert publicity. One very important detail must be kept in mind, however. Nobody has ever been attracted to a concert by sloppy, careless, haphazard, and generally slipshod poster invitations. If posters are going to be used, take care that the information is presented in a concise manner in a neat, well-designed format. Anything less reflects poorly on the quality of the concert to be presented. Again, image is of great importance in public relations.

Another type of "virtual" bulletin board can be found on the Internet. Your school may have its own Web page that provides parents and other interested people with information about school events. In that case, creating a special music department page would be a simple procedure, and one that computer-literate students would be happy to design and maintain. There are also various bulletin boards servicing different areas and providing access to different types of information; sending out an electronic press release to these groups is easy once a mailing list is established. Newspapers, radio, and TV stations may also have Net sites, so the entire process of contacting media may be easily digitized.

Another effective approach to concert publicity is compiling and using a mailing list to personally invite members of the community. Mass mailing is not expensive and much of the effort involved is secretarial, so supervised students should be able to handle it. The invitation should be printed on letterhead stationery. In addition to the usual information concerning time and place, other data regarding the music to be performed, length of the program, and special features can be included.

The mailing list can be compiled by asking students to submit the names of families and neighborhood friends who do not have students participating in the music program. Additional names of community businesses and political leaders should be included. The list should be revised annually, and although it is not necessary from an information standpoint to include music parents on the mailing list, parents do appreciate the reminder. Administration of the mailing list can be handled via computer. Even simple database programs usually have a mailing-list function; many students will be familiar with the programs and be able to help you design the list if you're unable to do so on your own. Parents who have e-mail addresses can also be part of the list, and announcements can be sent to them electronically.

Students can generally devise unusually creative means of presenting concert publicity in the school paper. Remember, school newspapers are often read by people other than the students in a particular school.

It is not necessary to pull out all the stops in publicizing or advertising every school concert, but once or twice a year, perhaps in combination with some special event, accept the challenge of creating the broadest possible publicity base for a concert performance. The results could be pleasantly surprising.

In helping to design your own publicity system, check out what other educators are doing. Be sure to ask questions of veteran teachers regarding this very important aspect of music education administration. It is also wise to remember that good public relations start with good teaching. Good teaching can often advertise itself with organized assistance from the music educator.

Planning dates

To organize your efforts, make a calendar indicating when certain tasks need to be accomplished in conjunction with concert promotion. Without a reminder, publicity efforts are likely to be haphazard or left undone. For example, three weeks before the event you will need to arrange for photos to be taken, developed, selected, enlarged, and copied. This process could take more than two weeks. Two weeks before the concert, envelopes need to be labeled for the mass mailing and the letters to be enclosed must be written, typed, and printed. Posters must be designed and prepared, press releases must be written, and ad copy for the media must be readied. A week before the concert, letters should be in the mail and ads and press releases should be in the hands of the appropriate parties. Adjunct publicity efforts need to be accomplished as well, but whatever the promotional strategy, the entire effort will come together with greater efficiency and a higher level of success if work begins well in advance of the concert. Successful promotion involves planning dates placed on a calendar.

Press releases

When writing a press release, a few fundamental guidelines must be kept in mind. The basic information to include is who needs to know about the event, what the event is, when it is scheduled (date and time), and where it is to take place. Special features, the concert theme, if any, and the concert type (pops, serious, and so on) can be included. Above all, why people would want to attend must be clear. Concert admission, if any, should be mentioned as well. The information should be written in clear, concise sentences and presented in a double-spaced, typewritten format. Copies should be sent to anyone even vaguely in a position to assist in the promotion of the event.

Use 8 1/2-by-11-inch paper. Odd sizes make an editor's job difficult. Never use onion skin or tissue paper that will not accept pencil marks. Leave wide margins, approximately 1 1/2 inches, on each side.

Give full reference data in the upper-left corner of the first page of the release. This information can be single spaced. List the name of the organization and the name, address, and phone number of the individual submitting the release. Type the release date in the upper-right corner of the first page. If appropriate, stipulate FOR IMMEDIATE RELEASE, which means that the editor or broadcaster can use it at once. If you ask for a specific publication date, it should read: RELEASE TUESDAY, APRIL 10.

Four spaces below the reference material, a few words of explanation should appear. This group of words identifies the story and is called the slug line.

Start the copy of the release a third of a page below the slug line. The space may be used by an editor for a headline or instructions. If the release runs more than one page, type "(more)" at the bottom of each page except the last. Always end each page with a complete sentence or paragraph. When the release runs more than one page, type the organization's name, the slug line, and the number of the page in the upper-right-hand corner of each succeeding page. The copy continues one inch below the three single-spaced identification lines. Do not hyphenate words at the end of a line. A ragged right margin is acceptable. Type END two spaces under the final paragraph. Figure 11.1 shows a sample press release.

The release should be checked for accuracy and the pages should never be stapled together. Press releases are not difficult or time-consuming to formulate and are an often-ignored public relations tool. Releases stored on computer disk can be updated and revised for future promotional use.

Other public relations opportunities

Information regarding contest and festival participation and/or results can be presented in both the local and school newspapers. These events also can provide interview opportunities for the music educator. If the participation is a major event, media coverage is likely to increase. Students receiving scholarship assistance or who are planning careers in music as well as community appearances by soloists and ensembles at hospitals, nursing homes, churches, service clubs, and similar locales are also newsworthy. Ensemble tours and student participation in music camps can be publicity opportunities. In short, anything music students do can be

Figure 11.1. Sample press release

BEA FLAT HIGH SCHOOL CHOIR   FOR IMMEDIATE RELEASE
John C. Kleff
Bea Flat Public Schools
873-2888

(BEA FLAT HIGH SCHOOL CHOIR TO PRESENT SPRING CONCERT)

   BEA FLAT, MN -- The Bea Flat High School Choir
will present its annual spring concert in the school
auditorium on Thursday, April 20.
   The concert is scheduled for 8:00 PM and will
feature music from the Broadway musicals <u>Oklahoma</u>,
<u>West Side Story</u>, and <u>The Music Man</u>. Mary Simmons, an
alumnus of Bea Flat High School, returns to her alma
mater to perform solos selected from each of the
three featured productions.
   According to music instructor John C. Kleff, the
concert will last approximately one hour and will be
followed by a reception for Ms. Simmons in the school
cafeteria. Kleff indicated that the public is invited
to the reception after the program.
   "The students have worked very hard on this program," Kleff said, "and everyone is excited about the
opportunity to perform selections from three of the
all-time great musical productions."
   Tickets may be purchased from any high school choir
member and at the First State Bank. Tickets will also
be available at the door, $2.00 for adults, $1.00 for
students.
   For more information concerning this performance or
for special seating requests, contact John C. Kleff at
the Bea Flat Public Schools, 873-2888.

                    - END -

brought to the attention of some segment of the media. This effort certainly falls within the realm of the music educator as an administrator.

Visual images

Photography is a valuable tool for promotion, publicity, and public relations in general. Music room bulletin boards, scrapbooks, and collages, as well as school display cases, offer broad opportunities for the use of photographs. Quite simply, students like to see themselves and other students. Parents like to see photographs of their children, and the public enjoys the opportunity to see youth involved in worthwhile activities. Good-quality photos that accompany press releases are likely to be published. Candidates for publication are pictures taken in a rehearsal setting in preparation for an event, a teacher assisting a student in preparing for a concert, or a director talking with several students about the future event.

Color slides of specific events can always be shared with parents' organizations, music clubs, or community-service clubs. Black-and-white enlargements can be produced from color slides for publicity purposes. The image quality is not quite as good as if black-and-white film had been used originally, but it is an acceptable alternative if no prints exist.

Often there are students with good equipment who can assist in photography. In all certainty, there is at least one parent of an ensemble member with a whole room full of photographic equipment who would be willing to serve as a photographer for the ensemble. Black-and-white film is not expensive and print choices can be determined from contact sheets, which show a developed positive image in negative size, thus permitting an entire roll of film to be previewed on an 8 1/2-by-11-inch sheet of paper. Funds for photography are a legitimate part of the printing and publicity line item in the music department budget.

All schools in the United States now possess a video camera and playback equipment. Many music rehearsal rooms have such equipment as part of the permanent music room inventory. Music educators should not fail to make use of video equipment, not only for performance analysis purposes, but as a means of communicating music program activities to their constituencies as well.

COMMUNITY INVOLVEMENT

The level of community involvement by a music educator can have a direct effect on how the school's music program is viewed by the public and can provide a substantial base for public relations success. It is helpful if the music educator lives in the community in which he or she works. After all, it is difficult to become involved in community activities unless you reside in that community. The public does notice! Exceptions, of course, are the densely populated urban areas and the sparsely populated rural areas. In either of those cases, a music educator could have difficulty finding housing.

Community involvement can include such activities as forming a parents' group, organizing community events, creating a community musical performing group, directing or participating in a church choir, and teaching adult music classes, such as appreciation, musical theater, or individual instruction. The development of music programs for older and retired adults can be an extremely worthwhile and personally satisfying. There are many opportunities for community service. It does take a bit of courage to leave the security of the school environment and venture out into the unknown realm of public service. Those that do will generally find an amenable and genuinely enthusiastic reception from the community.

Consider joining a service or social club, if this opportunity is available. Many service club activities support youth work in some manner. Social and fraternal groups provide opportunities to meet and become acquainted with community members in a relaxed environment.

Sports activities, such as bowling and golf, are other opportunities to become known to community members other than those associated with the local school. Even if the activity is done with teachers, it is taking place in a community environment. This is a positive image for the school.

MUSIC IN OUR SCHOOLS MONTH

No discussion on the need for public relations in support of music education would be complete without at least a brief reference to Music in Our Schools Month, sponsored by the Music Educators National Conference (MENC). This month-long event provides an imaginative opportunity to expose both school and community to the importance of school music programs and associated activities on a national level. During the month of March each year, special contests, adult involvement, mayoral proclamations, and a general "spreading of the gospel" of the the importance of music education in today's schools occurs all across the United States.

Numerous promotional items such as posters, banners, buttons, bumper stickers, pencils, mobiles, memo pads, balloons, certificates, and program covers are available from MENC for use in any promotional effort. Many of the items can be used throughout the year.

For more information regarding Music in Our Schools Month, contact MENC, 1902 Association Drive, Reston, VA 22091. Order promotional items at least two months before anticipated use. This is a superb manner in which any music educator can become involved in public relations on a grand scale.

Membership in MENC and other professional organizations can help you keep abreast of current trends in the field. Most organizations include in their annual dues a subscription to a monthly periodical. By becoming actively involved in professional organizations at the state and regional levels, you will help to make your career more than a job, but a profession.

You may want to order MENC's *Action Kit for Music Education,* a product of Music Makes a Difference, a campaign by the National Coalition for Music Education to educate the public about the need for music education in today's schools. The kit consists of two video interviews with Henry Mancini and with Tim Lautzenheiser, who address the value of music education. Also included is the National Commission on Music Education's 1991 report, *Growing Up Complete: The Imperative for Music Education,* and the how-to manual *Building Support for School Music: A Practical Guide.* This invaluable resource is available to MENC members for $34.40.

SUGGESTED ACTIVITIES

1. Visit a local radio station and determine its policy on public service announcements and the advertising rates for a school concert promotional effort.
2. Design and put into effect a promotional campaign for a future concert to be presented by one of the major performing ensembles on your campus. Under the supervision of the group director, write the press release, design and distribute posters, write a letter for mass mailing, and so on.
3. Locate and evaluate promotional efforts associated with at least ten events that appear in the next Sunday edition of the newspaper serving your area.
4. Devise a hypothetical long-range goal in public relations and the accompanying short-term objectives used to support the long-range goal. Include support strategies for implementation of the short-term objectives.
5. Invite a local or regional corporate public relations specialist to visit the class and discuss the importance of public relations and image.
6. Evaluate the local community in terms of its needs for music and music education. Then present public relations activities suggested by the evaluation.
7. Invite a local music educator to class and discuss his or her associated public relations and promotional policies, restrictions, and handicaps.
8. Design a hypothetical series of five side-by-side concerts involving public or private school ensembles and evaluate the public relations benefit and promotional potential of each.

CHAPTER TWELVE

PARENTS'
ORGANIZATIONS
AND
FUND-RAISING

INTRODUCTION

Fund-raising and parents' organizations are combined in this chapter because it is difficult to talk about one without involving the other. For example, a widely accepted function of parent support groups is to provide a degree of financial assistance to a performing organization. Booster organizations are frequently involved in an advisory capacity and are a source of willing volunteers for fund-raising projects.

If the trend to reduce the funds allocated by schools for music education continues, the number of parent support groups—and their role in financially assisting music programs—will increase significantly. A parents' organization can also provide strong support for school music education beyond fund-raising. For example, it can become a viable influence in the arts at the community level. It would appear that a comprehensively structured organization provides the greatest overall support for the total music program. When organizing a booster club, music educators should seek administrative approval and keep school officials informed of group activities. A parents' organization needs to be governed by a charter or constitution to maintain the scope and direction of the group.

Fund-raising on the part of school music programs and their support groups has become big business in the United States. As with the initiation of a booster group, music educators should seek the approval of school officials before beginning any fund-raising campaign. Any successful fund-raising effort must be accompanied by a solid organizational base. The establishment of several committees in conjunction with a project removes a great deal of the burden from music educators and allows parents the opportunity to be more effective in managing the project. There are numerous techniques for raising funds for school music groups. Music educators should test-market products for potential sale and consult with colleagues for other ideas for raising money. To maintain a high intensity level of all participants, fund-raising campaigns should be short and efficient. Music educators need to explore expedient and equitable ways in which to distribute moneys raised through the efforts of students and/or their parents. Regardless of the nature or scope of any project, its ultimate success depends directly on the administrative and organizational skills of the music educator associated with it.

THE NEED AS IT EXISTS

The percentage of American tax dollars going to public school education from state and federal governments has decreased gradually, but significantly, over the past twenty years, while inflation has pushed cost per pupil figures higher and higher. The result has been a series of legislative propositions and resolutions placing the burden of financially supporting public school education on local governments. Many city and county commissions were already at or near the maximum allowable tax levy for education. State governments that previously relied on personal property taxes to finance public education have discovered what the citizenry has known for years: personal property taxes are an unreliable and unjust means of financing schools, because wealthier districts can afford better facilities than less-advantaged ones, making for unacceptable disparities in a state's overall educational program.

Because of budget reductions, school administrators have been forced to reduce or eliminate program offerings and postpone plans to enlarge or remodel the physical plants of their school systems. In certain elementary schools in Nevada and California, principals now hold annual fund-raising programs involving students and parents of the district. The money raised from these major efforts provides funds for such projects as reroofing a building, replacing old windows with more energy-efficient models, and adding computer laboratory equipment.

Arts and vocational programs have been caught in the budget crunch in many parts of the country. Parents' groups that were already in place have been called upon for moral and financial support when music budgets were reduced. In many instances parents' organizations hastily organized for budget debates have become a permanent part of the music program.

Some music educators are afraid that parents will become overly involved in running the music program. Horror stories have been told about parents' groups that have attempted to take over the band program or have tried to get the choir director fired. Such cases are isolated and can most certainly be prevented by appropriate anticipation, organization, and action on the part of the music educator. The following material is intended to aid music educators in developing the expertise to carry out with confidence this significant administrative responsibility.

PARENTS' ORGANIZATIONS

A parents' organization, or booster club, as it is often known, can serve as a strong support group in the advancement and better understanding of the music program, and can provide increased visibility and an improved image to that program. A booster organization's main goal should be to promote the education of students in the field of music. An active organization will include not only parents of students presently involved in music but also other individuals within the community who support the work of the music department.

Benefits of a parents' organization

Through participation in a booster organization, parents gain a better understanding of music education. They learn the purpose of the music program and become involved to a degree in their children's education. Through their participation, parents can develop a sense of appreciation for the work that both the students and their director contribute to the music program. Communication between staff and parents is improved. This important link between the school and community can provide an element of strength to the music program that is simply not available in other academic programs.

Through energetic involvement with a parents' organization, a music educator has the opportunity to get to know the students' parents to a greater degree; the parents, in turn, appreciate the opportunity to become acquainted with the individual who affects the musical lives of their children.

A parents' organization can be a great source of assistance for the busy music educator. Parents can help in supervising and chaperoning students on trips made by the performing groups. They can also aid in publicizing events and in building greater audience support for concert performances. When necessary, parents can serve a very productive role in providing financial assistance to music programs through their fund-raising efforts.

Some music educators believe that parents and students should not be involved in raising funds in support of a music program. They feel that, if the program is worthwhile, the school district should support it. This position is idealistic considering the budget cuts and program reductions of the past few years. If parents have come to associate a certain quality level with the music program, they are very often willing to support that program by limited fund-raising efforts. In cases where school districts are unable to totally support the program, music educators would be failing their obligation to their students if they were to neglect parental involvement and fund-raising as a source of moral and financial support.

The amount of physical and financial assistance that parents can provide for the music educator and the music program is limited only by the ingenuity of that educator.

Types of parents' organizations

There are three types of parents' organizations, with variations. They may be labeled Music Boosters, Band Parents, Symphony Society, or a variety of other names. Regardless of the title or structure of the group, its primary function remains the same: to provide support and assistance to the students for which it was organized.

The one-shot, temporary parents' organization. Booster organizations are often organized on a temporary basis and are then dissolved when a particular project has been completed. Generally, the sole purpose of such an organization is to raise funds for a trip, concert wear, or some major installment or equipment purchase. When a booster group is organized temporarily, it must still be structured with officers, boards, and committees, just as a permanent support group would be. The amount of administrative effort required to establish such a group is by necessity more intense than an organization with a more permanent framework. Planning meetings might be held weekly, and as the project develops perhaps daily attention is required.

This type of support group is acceptable in a situation where a sufficient music budget is provided by the school district but an unanticipated circumstance arises that demands a level of funding beyond that which the school district is willing to provide. A presidential inaugural parade invitation or selection for a performance at a national or state convention of music educators are just two of many situations where a need for increased funding could occur.

Some school administrations prohibit the initiation of a music booster group, but they are likely to support such an organization if it is to be active on a temporary basis with a specific goal in mind. It is not unusual for music parents to organize on a temporary basis, find that they enjoy the interaction that occurs in these groups, and vote, with the blessings of the music educators and administrators, to become a permanent booster organization. The level of involvement required on the part of music educators is generally greater with temporary booster groups than it is with those more permanently structured.

Single performing-group booster clubs. Unfortunately, most booster organizations support only one school performance group, and that performance group is generally the school band. For some unknown reason, many choral and orchestra directors have not seen the need to establish a parent support organization as part of their individual programs. Booster organizations are discussed, if in a somewhat limited fashion, in nearly all undergraduate instrumental music methods textbooks. The same topic is rarely, if ever, discussed in textbooks written for choral music methods classes.

Permanent parents' organizations meet on a regular monthly basis, and their activity level is somewhat determined by the activity level of the school group with which they are associated. One thing is certain: no booster organization will function well if it doesn't have adequate leadership and specific annual goals to meet. This doesn't necessarily mean that a particular educator must provide total leadership for the organization, but he or she must provide direction and assistance in establishing yearly goals. When this action is taken, the leadership within the group will increase.

The comprehensive music booster organization. The most beneficial and educationally sound support group is designed to meet the needs of all music education taking place in a given school. An organization of this type supports the band, choral, and orchestra programs on a basis determined by the needs of each performing group. This support can extend into the junior high school program as well.

It takes skilled and cooperative music educators to combine their talents and efforts in a comprehensive support organization for music education. Part of the inherent difficulty in such a group is trying to balance any fund-raising efforts among affected performing groups. If the members are unable to effectively balance their support for performing groups, they often turn into a booster group with a single focus and purpose. Fortunate are the music educators who have a music parents' organization that is active and effective in the support of the total program. Should a serious crisis ever arise that will drastically affect the music department in a negative manner, there is a large support force already in place that can be a positive voice for the total music program.

Organizing a Parents' Booster Club

Before organizing a parents' booster club, you need to feel comfortable with the idea of working with parents and other community members. You should not feel threatened by the thought of working with individuals outside the school environment. As the music teacher, you are the in-residence community authority, and parents, with very few exceptions, respect someone who shares that knowledge with their children. Be prepared to spend extra time and effort when initiating a parents' organization. In the long run, however, a properly functioning support group will save you countless hours of valuable instructional time. You also must feel that the booster group will be a definite aid to the program, and that the organization will provide assistance in achieving goals and objectives established for the program.

Check with school officials

School officials need to understand the purpose of a booster club. Carefully prepare a parents' organization proposal to present to those school administrators. List the reasons a parents' organization is needed to support the music program and the potential benefits it will offer to that program. It might also be wise to cite area schools that have booster groups as examples in support of the request.

You must be prepared to defend your request to organize a booster group, even though once an administrator offers a negative response to a proposal, it may be very difficult to get that "no" changed to a "yes." If a proposal is well prepared, researched, and documented, most administrators will see the long-term benefits to the music program and, through that program, to the entire school.

Visit with parent leaders

It is easy to determine the influential community leaders who have children involved in the music program. You would do well to visit several of these parents personally to present the plans for a booster organization. Much of the information prepared for school administrators can be shared with them. Enlist their support because they will very likely be the early leaders of the booster club.

Visit area music educators

Music educators from nearby schools can often be of assistance in providing information and practical advice regarding structure, format, and benefits of a new music parents' support group. Possibly the president or some other officer from an area booster club would be willing to come to the first organizational meeting of the new club to discuss what his or her group does to support its school's music program.

Write a letter

With the support of school officials and several parents, you can now draft a letter to be sent to all music parents and other community leaders who are potential supporters. A sample letter is shown in Figure 12.1. The letter needs to be short, but at the same time it must provide enough information to whet the interest of the reader. Be sure to include the starting and estimated ending time of the first organizational meeting. As with overly long concerts, busy parents have no time for marathon meetings.

The meeting

The extent to which you plan the organizational meeting will have a direct effect on the outcome of that meeting. Parents are willing to give of their time in support of a program that is guided by an individual who is upbeat and who can provide a degree of leadership through his or her organizational abilities. A short tape or slide show of a recent or proposed trip or event would certainly be in order,

Figure 12.1. Sample letter for initial contact concerning a new parents' organization

---

Dear Parents and Friends,

I have called a meeting for parents of music students
and other interested people to discuss the possibility
of starting a music booster organization. I am sure
that we all share the common goal of providing the best
possible music program for our students. Such an organization can be extremely helpful in achieving that
goal. The purpose of a music parents' organization
would be to promote and support the entire music program and its activities in the Bea Flat school system.
The meeting will be less than one hour in length.

DATE: Monday, October 14, 1999
TIME: 7:30 PM
PLACE: High School Music Room
AGENDA: 1. Introductory remarks by Superintendent Smart
        2. Need for and purpose of a music parents'
           organization — Mr. Kleff
        3. Open discussion
        4. Election of officers
        5. Date, time, and place of next meeting

Plan now to come to the meeting and let us hear your
ideas. Refreshments will be served.

Sincerely,

John C. Kleff
Music Instructor

---

as would a few words of support from a school administrator, if one can be encouraged to attend the meeting. After the purpose and function of the group have been
explained, the bulk of the remaining meeting time can be spent in open discussion,
perhaps led by one of the parent leaders with whom the project was discussed in
the early planning stages. Election of officers follows the discussion, and the meeting closes with setting the date, time, and place of the next meeting.

Constitution

The parents' organization should draft a constitution or charter that outlines its
function, structure, and intent. A sample constitution and bylaw are presented in

Figures 12.2 and 12.3. This constitution is an example, not a complete document. Check with colleagues for ideas regarding this important facet of booster club development. Keep in mind that as the direction and scope of a parents' organization changes, the constitution or charter must be updated to keep pace with these changes.

Figure 12.2. A sample of articles of constitution for a parents' organization

---

Constitution

Article I — Identification
The name of this organization is _____. Our fiscal year runs from August 1 through July 31.

Article II — Objectives
The objectives of _____, a nonprofit organization, are as follows:
Section 1. To arouse and maintain an enthusiastic interest in the various phases of the music department of ____ High School.
Section 2. To lend all possible support, both moral and financial, to the total music program in the school and to provide social and other programs and awards for music personnel.
Section 3. To cooperate with those in charge of the music department, school administration, and the school board to the end that this department be brought to and kept at the highest possible degree of efficiency; to build and maintain an organization that will help promote the general activities of the _____ music department.

Article III — Membership
Section 1. The membership of this organization shall not be limited. Anyone interested in furthering the aims of the organization shall be eligible to join.
Section 2. Annual dues shall be specified and approved by the membership.

Article IV — Officers
The officers of the organization shall be a president, vice-president, recording secretary, corresponding secretary, treasurer, and music director of the ____ High School.

Article V — Meetings
The regular meetings of the organization shall be held at 7:30 PM on the first Tuesday of each month from September through May. Special meetings may be called by the president.

Article VI — Amendments
The constitution and bylaws may be amended by a majority vote of the members present at any regular meeting. The amendments must have been presented at the preceding regular meeting of the organization and the membership notified of such amendments.

Article VII — Quorum
Ten members shall constitute a quorum for the purpose of conducting meetings.

Figure 12.3. A sample of constitutional bylaws for a parents' organization

Bylaws

Article I — Duties of Officers

Section 1. The president shall preside over all of the organization's meetings, appoint all committees, and be an ex-officio member of all committees.

Section 2. The vice-president shall assume all the duties of the president in his or her absence.

Section 3. The recording secretary shall keep all records of all meetings.

Section 4. The corresponding secretary shall be responsible for all of the organization's correspondence and retain the stamp for bulk mail.

Section 5. The treasurer shall receive all funds accrued by the organization, deposit the same in a federally insured bank, and make disbursements as directed by the organization. He or she shall keep a full and correct account of all money received and expended and make monthly reports at the regular meeting of the organization.

Section 6. The music director shall act as liaison between the _____ band personnel and school authorities.

Article II — Executive Board

Section 1. The executive board shall be composed of the organization's officers, the past president, and such committee chairpersons as deemed necessary by the president at the beginning of his or her term.

Section 2. The executive board shall supervise the affairs of the organization.

Section 3. Elected officers and chairpersons shall not hold the same office for more than two (2) consecutive years.

Article III — Elections

Section 1. A nominating committee of two (2) members of the executive board and three (3) members from the general membership shall be appointed by the president at the February meeting. The past president shall act as chairman with no vote.

Section 2. Nominations may be made from the floor after the report of the nominating committee at the March meeting.

Section 3. Officers are to be elected by ballot at the April meeting, or if a single slate is presented, the secretary is to cast one ballot.

Section 4. Elected officers will be installed at the May meeting, but official duties will not be assumed until July 31 to allow booster activities to be completed.

Section 5. Any elective officer's post that becomes vacant shall be filled by appointment by the executive board to fill the unexpired term, except the president's office, which shall be filled by the vice-president.

Article IV — Disbanding and Funds

If the _____ shall at any time disband, any monies in the treasury shall be turned over to the music department of the high school.

Article V — School Board Approval

No expenditure that adds to the physical properties of the school shall be authorized until first approved by the school board.

264 OUTSIDE THE SCHOOL ENVIRONMENT

Parents' groups and political pressure

It is the right and perhaps the duty of parents to be involved in some manner in the policies established by the school district. It is parents' tax dollars, after all, that support the daily operation of the school. They should be concerned and they should be involved. It is a grave error, however, for any parents' organization to become actively and politically involved as a pressure group to affect change in school policy. The booster group can serve as a forum for discussion of school philosophy and policy that affects the music program, but it must refrain from becoming an official source of pressure for political change within the school system. A well-organized, active, and viable music booster organization can send a strong and positive message to school officials regarding the degree of parental and community support for a particular program. Only when a situation becomes life-threatening for a music program is the active involvement of a booster club as a pressure group justified.

A recommended structure for a booster club

Membership. Booster club membership does not necessarily need to be restricted to parents of student musicians. Businesses associated with the music program should be invited and encouraged to become involved in some way with club activities. Having a child involved in the music program automatically makes that parent a member. If the club is associated only with the orchestra, parents of every string student in the school district, from grade school through high school, are members of the booster club; the same holds true for the choir and band. If the group is a comprehensive, all-school music booster organization, the parents of all music students are considered members.

Structure. The usual panel of officers is elected, and they in turn select a board of between fifteen and thirty members who indicate a willingness to become actively involved in the organization. The board meets monthly. Various project committees are made up of members of the organization at large and are chaired by a board member. Separate standing committees can handle fund-raising, publicity, concert attendance, awards, membership, and community events. Other committees can be established by the board as the need arises, with the committee chair in charge of keeping accurate records of committee work and providing progress reports to the panel of officers and the board.

Not all parents are willing to be actively involved on a long-term basis in a music organization. For this reason, a board of fifteen to thirty key members is the best that can be expected for active participation. But many others will gladly give a little of themselves over a short period of time, and in doing so are freed from the obligation of attending all monthly meetings.

Activities. The booster organization's activities should include the printing and distribution of a newsletter to its membership three or four times a year. Included in the newsletter could be a calendar of events, individual school activities, feature activities, club projects, and news of other innovative projects. Fund-raising in support of the music program need not be the major consideration of the parents' organization, but very often it will be. Other projects can be to promote concert attendance for school and community cultural events, support budget requests, support and assist Music in Our Schools Month (see chapter 11 for a discussion of this MENC-sponsored program), organize classroom visits, and encourage community musical efforts. It must be kept in mind that a music teacher's obligation to the school is to *teach*. The organization of a booster club and the eventual assuming of responsibility for a variety of activities by that club can allow the dedicated and concerned music educator to devote maximum effort to his or her students.

Determining a name. Some common titles for school music booster groups were mentioned earlier and would certainly be satisfactory for this organization. The author, however, suggests a title such as Friends of Music, because it promotes an image of professionalism that carries beyond the doorstep of the local school and promotes a feeling of comprehensiveness. Ultimately, however, the parents themselves must select the organization's title. The title of the group provides a degree of identity, and that fact should be taken into consideration when selecting a name for the organization.

Music educators willing to try this structure will find themselves with a streamlined, effective, and efficient organization with which to deal. Always keep in mind the importance of a charter or constitution. It is a requisite for group stability. The membership makeup and leadership of a booster organization may change, but its scope and direction remain intact when the group is guided by a charter or constitution.

A final thought concerning booster club organization: Music educators should make every effort to solicit and promote the involvement of all members of a community's musical family. Parents often possess the banking, business, publicity, and promotional skills needed to run an effective organization and support a school music program. One-parent, two-parent, same-sex partners, and multi-parent families should all be involved in children's education.

FUND-RAISING

Much has already been said about budget reductions resulting in increased fund-raising efforts by the music department, other entities within the school, and in some cases, the school district itself. Moneys raised by students and/or their parents should be used only for those things not covered by the school district funding. In many cases funds that are raised are used for travel purposes. Concert wear, large equipment items, awards, music camp scholarships, clinicians, and guest conductors are often paid for by money raised through the efforts of a performing organization or its support group. However, even in times of the tightest budget restrictions, the school district still has the obligation to provide new and replacement equipment, equipment maintenance and repair, festival and contest fees, music and instruction books, and printing. In situations where even the basic obligations of the school district to the music program cannot be met, resourceful music educators generally find some way in which to maintain a program's integrity for the mutual benefit of the students and community.

Need for fund-raising

Before initiating any fund-raising campaign, a genuine need for that campaign must be established. Neither parents nor students are motivated toward achieving a financial goal unless a genuine need for fund-raising is demonstrated. Some teachers feel that simply declaring a need to raise funds will touch off frantic activity. Instead, you must set financial goals and demonstrate the need to meet them.

Approval for fund-raising

It is always a good idea to keep administrators informed of any fund-raising project to be undertaken by the music department. When a project involves students, permission should be received from the appropriate school officials. Fund-raising projects undertaken solely by a parent support group generally do not need administrative approval, but informing school officials of this action is a courtesy and a good administrative practice.

Getting organized

In most successful fund-raising campaigns, many people are involved. Chairpersons should be appointed to address various aspects of the project, including the overall project, publicity, civic relations, and sales.

The project chairperson oversees the total effort and coordinates the work of the other leaders. This chairperson should have a winning and positive attitude. The publicity chairperson is responsible for getting news releases to the media and for any advertising associated with the campaign; an ideal candidate will possess appropriate writing abilities and will have the energy and time to carry out these functions. The civic relations chairperson coordinates a group of parents who will visit every civic and service organization in the community. These organizations are always in search of programs for their meetings. With enough advance notice, an informational program can be developed about the group doing the fund-raising and how the proceeds of the drive will be used.

The sales chairperson works closely with the music educator in selecting fund-raising products and activities and in developing the campaign approach. In a typical campaign structure, five or six student musicians and their respective families are grouped into teams under the leadership of a team captain. Five or six team captains are grouped under an area chairperson, and all area chairpersons report directly to the sales project leader. This type of organizational structure is effective in the world of business and industry and can be used, at its simplest level, to manage a short but intense fund-raising effort.

Activity guidelines

Music department projects should entail only limited student involvement. Fund-raising campaigns that involve a great deal of student time are generally not successful and, if they are, are difficult to justify from an educational standpoint. A one-week campaign with one month of preparation time preceding the effort is usually sufficient. Students and parents alike thrive on the intensity of a short campaign and the feeling that there's a job to be done.

Check the competition

Become aware of other school, church, and civic organizations that schedule annual fund-raising campaigns. A sure way to guarantee failure and perhaps create feelings of ill will is to schedule a music department fund-raising effort in direct conflict with other school or community campaigns.

Selecting a product

When selecting a product for sale, the product should return a minimum profit level of forty, and more ideally, fifty percent. Sell a product that is useful, not something that people buy just to support the group. Pick a product that meets both the group's and your criteria. Remember that enthusiasm sells. It's difficult for individuals to communicate enthusiasm if they don't like a product. Fund-raising company representatives are willing to provide samples of their products. Comparison shop for similar products to compare both quality and price.

Beware of a product that is overhyped by a company representative; if the profit margin or product appears to be too good to be true, it probably is. It's best to select products that have sold well in the past, but be sure to allow plenty of time between campaigns. If a sales item was successful in previous years but suddenly fails, the fault may not lie in the campaign approach. Seek out a different product.

When selecting a product or service to be sold for fund-raising purposes, consider these five questions:

1. Do the customers get something of value for their money?
2. Is it a better value than they can get somewhere else?
3. Is a service being provided?
4. Is there a need for the service or product?
5. Is the service or product unique?

How you answer these questions can directly influence your product or project selection. Some consumable products can be sold several times a year on a telephone reorder basis. The simplicity of a telephone reorder campaign is often attractive to participants and customers alike. Food products, if they are of high quality, are particularly appealing for that reason.

Preselling a product is an advantage that must be considered. A brief description of the product, perhaps in a brochure, and an explanation of how the profit will be used are generally sufficient to sell a quality product. With a good brochure, student salespeople need not take samples with them when making sales. The customer pays for the product when it is ordered. After the shipment arrives at the school, students can deliver presold orders in a very short period of time. A classic example of this technique is the annual Girl Scout cookies campaign.

Many campaigns providing products for use in fund-raising also have prize programs designed to motivate students toward and beyond their sales goals. If such a plan is not part of a campaign's fund-raising program, you may wish to initiate one at the local level. By the same token, just because a prize program happens to be available through a company does not necessarily mean that you must adopt that portion of the program. In some cases, a higher profit percentage can be negotiated in lieu of the motivational prize program.

Activity guidelines

Keep the campaign short, and if selling a product, be sure it is backed by a solid program of sales and distribution through a professional consultant who will actually come into the school. There are enough fund-raising representatives who are willing to call on individual schools to explain their programs and products that it is simply not necessary to take the risk of dealing with fund-raising campaigns on a mail-order basis.

Develop an advertising budget

The public must be prepared in advance for a major fund-raising drive to succeed. Annual United Way campaigns are an example of advance advertising. Developing a theme or logo is another way to build an identity for a successful effort.

Student accounts

One of the problems with any fund-raising program has been the equitable dispersion of benefits in direct proportion to the amount of effort invested by student participants. This problem is particularly true when travel is involved. Students, parents, and teachers alike have been concerned with the inequity of a system that allows students who put forth very little effort toward achieving a group's financial goal to receive the same benefits as other students who achieved or exceeded the goal that was established for them.

An approach that has been developed by a number of successful music educators, and is recommended by this author for use, is to establish an individual account for each member of a performing group. Profits raised by individual students as part of a fund-raising campaign or series of campaigns are credited to each individual's account. For example, perhaps an invitation to perform at a national convention has been received by a high school choral director. The total cost of the trip for meals, lodging, and transportation is $48,000. Perhaps the school district was able to provide $8,000 in the form of a special allocation, and gifts from local businesses and service clubs total $4,000. With a choir enrollment of eighty-four students, and with a total of $36,000 yet to be raised, the resulting cost per pupil figure is approximately $430.

Fund-raising projects are then designed to allow students to easily meet that cost per pupil goal. When the predetermined funding deadline arrives, those students with full funding in their accounts make the trip at no additional expense to themselves or their families. Those students with deficiencies in their accounts must make up the difference between their account balance and the $430 trip cost.

When sufficient advance notice is given to students and their parents that this procedure is being followed, there is no confusion as to how money is allocated, and all parties can agree that the system provides parity for all involved in the project. The old "all for one and one for all" system, in which every member of a group contributed his or her efforts to whatever level is adequate to support a project, is certainly an alternative to the preceding system. The account system, however, removes much of the pressure from the music educator to maintain equity, and the danger that hard feelings may replace exuberance upon successful campaign completion is eliminated.

Fund-Raising Ideas

As indicated in chapter 5, ninety-six percent of school music programs in this country are involved in some type of fund-raising. Those programs annually raise on average nearly $12,000 through these efforts, a significant portion of their yearly budget. Because of this significance, music educators are encouraged to read periodical literature associated with their performance areas in an attempt to keep abreast of new fund-raising ideas. Another source of ideas is the efforts of colleagues. Music educators are always happy to be able to share their fund-raising successes and failures with one another.

The following products and projects are offered as examples of items and ideas that have proven to be successful over the years. The geographic region in which a school is located must be considered when deciding on a fund-raising project. For example, a frozen fish sale, for obvious reasons, is going to be more appropriate in Minnesota in March than it will be in Phoenix, Arizona. Other concerns to bear in mind when making decisions regarding fund-raising projects are maintaining the integrity of the music program and promoting credibility, which will establish standards for future fund-raising projects. Above all, find fund-raising projects that you personally like and feel comfortable with, then stick with them for a few years. The public will notice this type of stability and actually come to anticipate a particular fund-raising effort.

Sales

For some readers who have promoted the sale of everything from birthday calendars to toilet paper, the following list may appear to be rather mundane. The items on the list, however, have been successful in the past. When choosing a product, past success should be a determining factor.

Candy can be considered the original fund-raising product, and candy sales still account for a major portion of annual revenue raised by school music groups. It is especially popular when funding requirements are not too extreme.

Popcorn, lightbulbs, candles, Christmas ornaments, cleaning agents, and shampoo sales, while quite popular in the 1980s, have lost ground to other types of consumable sales products. One advantage of these products is that they have long shelf lives and are not perishable. These and similar products still have potential to earn hundreds and perhaps several thousands of dollars in a disciplined campaign. Along with candy products, they are usually provided on a consignment basis, which means that unsold, unopened cartons of merchandise can be returned. Beware of using any products in a fund-raising campaign from a company that has in place a no-return policy on items supplied for sale as part of that campaign.

Sausage and cheese products as fund-raisers have become quite popular over the past few years. The success of these items perhaps lies in the fact that the quality of the product has been maintained, and the American public has grown more attracted to that type of product. The total funding potential for sausage and cheese products remains somewhat higher than other items because they are consumable food items and also make attractive and welcome gift packages.

Citrus fruit and pizza sales have become the foundation for many school music programs that need to raise tens of thousands of dollars annually. Both products must be presold and delivered to the customers upon receipt of the shipment at the school, and have the potential to raise anywhere from $5,000 to $12,000 with each project. The goal of such fund-raising drives is to create sales sufficient to place truckload orders. This effort pays dividends through reduced freight costs. Citrus fruit and pizza products are also attractive as fund-raisers because they can develop a clientele for reorder purposes.

Frozen food sales have also been successful and are certainly worthy of consideration if fresh products are unavailable in your area. In addition to fish, frozen product lines include caramel and cinnamon rolls, breads, a variety of pies, cookies, soups, chicken breasts and strips, and more. The top-selling frozen food items will vary from one geographic area to the next, but chicken breasts, cinnamon rolls, and pizzas generally head the bestseller lists.

While the profit percentage is less than with several other fund-raising products, the total dollar value of sales and the reorder possibilities make frozen food sales an attractive fund-raising possibility. When dealing with frozen products, check out the qualifications and background of the parent company, and carefully follow prescribed receipt and delivery policies relating to any perishable items. Frozen items are presold to consumers. They must be happy with their purchase or future sales efforts are doomed.

Magazine sales are another source of substantial income that can be earned on an annual basis. Nearly every household subscribes to at least one magazine. But the recent development of multi-million-dollar prizes associated with clearing house companies' promotion of magazine sales has made the sale of magazines at the school level less attractive as a fund-raising agent.

School administrators are often reluctant to allow fund-raising efforts that permit large sums of money to leave the community. For example, if a school band raises $20,000 through the sale of some product, that means that another $20,000 to $25,000 leaves that community as income for a company in some distant state. Some administrators encourage local promotions if fund-raising is a necessity. Once again, seek administrative approval before initiating a fund-raising campaign.

"Nonproduct" projects

Any number of fund-raising projects can be developed that do not necessarily involve the sale of a product. Very often these projects are annual affairs, and once established, build a faithful clientele. Other nonproduct projects can earn large amounts of money for a music program, but their success very often depends on promotional efforts. An example of a successful project is an annual pops concert with a guest artist. Through creative organization, promotion, and performance, such a project can become an anticipated annual event. Turkey suppers and soup and pie dinners have become popular fund-raisers in smaller communities across the country, with the food often donated and prepared by parents and supportive community members. Meals of this nature often precede a concert and help increase the audience for the performance. Dinners can generate anywhere from $3,000 to $5,000 profit for a music program. School carnivals and big-name entertainment can be very successful moneymakers, but they require an up-front investment and hold an element of financial risk for the sponsor.

With the interest in running, mini-marathons (6K and 10K races) have become a popular and fun way to raise money. Assistance in organizing the event and helping with locating sponsors is often available through a local track or athletic club. Some music groups are able to secure the concession and refreshment contract with the local school system. Such an arrangement can provide thousands of dollars in annual income.

Rent-a-kid programs and car washes are sources of quick funding that require a minimum of student and teacher effort. Pledges may be generated from the public on the number of cars to be washed in one day. Caution is urged when soliciting pledges that contributors understand the approximate amount of their financial obligation when the car wash is completed. One publicized car-wash scheme had music students securing pledges from the citizenry at the rate of $.01 per car to be washed by that group. What appeared to be a rather insignificant sum mushroomed when the 100-member ensemble washed a total of 5,000 cars in twenty locations in the city. The amount of the individual pledge totaled of $50, far more than any benefactor could have imagined, and created some hard feelings. People being asked for donations need to understand in advance the extent of money pledged.

Auctions and raffles

Auctions have a proven history of financial success with little or no investment and offer profits of nearly 100 percent when auction items are donated by community members and local businesses.

In schools and communities where they are permitted, raffles can be a source of substantial funding as well. They involve a minimum of effort and generally last for about a month. There are several ways to operate a raffle project, but perhaps the most successful involves a variation of the account method, described earlier: a fixed dollar amount to be raised per student is established, and the students and their parents have the option of selling or buying the raffle tickets. A $5 ticket price is suggested rather than the usual $1 per ticket, particularly if the prize to be awarded is at least $1,000 cash. If the figure of $200 per student is established, forty $5 tickets must be sold, as opposed to 200 of the $1 tickets. The $5 price makes the process much more expedient. If a student sells only twenty tickets, then either the student or his or her parents understand that they must purchase the remaining twenty tickets. A raffle can be especially productive when older students are involved. A critical aspect in preparing for a raffle is that students and parents understand their role in the project. On a national level, fund-raising efforts involving auctions and raffles reach an average profit level of nearly $6,000.

Using scrip as a fund-raiser

In some parts of the United States, creative PTA organizations, music booster groups, and other support organizations have developed an extremely successful means of raising funds for their particular causes through the use of scrip. *Webster's Collegiate Dictionary* defines *scrip* as "a temporary paper to be exchanged for money, goods, land, etc."

Generally speaking, the manner in which a scrip program works is that, on a weekly or biweekly basis, customers (more often than not, parents of student musicians) order their scrip certificates through an individual representing the parents' organization. The certificates are most often in $10, $25, or $50 denominations. The scrip is redeemable at specific retail outlets, usually large grocery stores. A personal check in the amount of the desired scrip accompanies the certificate order form that is submitted by the customer. After all orders are received and totaled, scrip certificates are ordered and distributed to the customers to use when they make future purchases.

The parents' organization pays each retail outlet five percent less that the actual dollar figure of the scrip that was ordered, thereby creating a five percent profit for the group. For example, if the amount of scrip on a particular order totals $5,590, the check from the organization to the vendors would be in the amount of $5,310.50, a profit of $279.50.

The program continues throughout the calendar year, not just the academic year, and becomes an integral part of the business activities of the organization. Booster clubs actively using a scrip system for fund-raising in their communities report profits of more than $10,000 annually. Consider this: 100 families participate on a regular basis in a scrip program and make all of their annual grocery purchases using scrip. The amount of groceries purchased by the group will total between $300,000 and $400,000, creating a five percent profit margin of approximately $20,000.

Fund-raising through scrip certificates demands a chairperson who can handle accounting and detail work. There are several companies nationwide that handle all the project details relating to using scrip for fund-raising, such as dealing with

retailers and printing scrip certificates. They collect the funds from the group placing the order and provide the proper scrip certificates for that order, thereby sim-
plifying the entire process. However, using an outside scrip company reduces the
total profit from each scrip order that is available to the booster club.

THE ROLE OF THE MUSIC EDUCATOR IN FUND-RAISING

While music program fund-raising projects are conducted by parents' organizations, it is still the responsibility of the music teacher to be involved, if only re-
motely, in the process. These responsibilities could include serving as a source of
informational leadership for the group and providing a sincere rationale for a fund-
raising project. A music educator must also be prepared to answer honestly all
questions and doubts about club projects and to provide leadership in screening
and selecting quality fund-raising projects.

Whether fund-raising projects involve parents or students alone, the results of a
project and the quality of the experience for the participants is determined by the
music educator's integrity, dedication, and administrative abilities. A good administrator is also a good delegator. Working with fund-raising projects offers numerous opportunities to demonstrate that skill.

The reader must understand that the intention of this chapter is not to necessarily advocate fund-raising by music students, their parents, or both. Nor is it advo-
cating the establishment of parents' organizations where none presently exist. The
purpose is to provide experienced and inexperienced music educators with enough
information and support material to allow them to deal with one or both subjects as
effectively and professionally as possible should the need arise. A poorly structured
parents' organization is far worse than no support group at all, and poorly organized, inadequately administered, unsuccessful fund-raising projects reflect negatively on the music program and the music educator in charge of that program.

Finally, readers are urged to avoid being negative about raising funds for their
music programs. Both positive and negative attitudes are contagious when dealing
with students and their parents on fund-raising projects.

SUGGESTED ACTIVITIES

1. Using the model constitution presented in Figures 12.2 and 12.3, draft a set of
   constitutional articles and bylaws for a Friends of Music parents' organization.
2. Discuss fund-raising with a local music educator with some experience in such
   projects and determine a best and a worst actual fund-raising experience. Discuss in class.

3. Review twelve consecutive recent issues of a music education periodical and determine the total number and variety of products offered for sale. Discuss in class.
4. Invite a fund-raising company consultant to class and discuss the do's and don'ts of sales-oriented fund-raising projects.
5. Invite an area booster club president or other officer to class to explain the structure and purpose of the club, the student benefits derived, the level of adult participation, and other pertinent information. Before the scheduled visit, compile a list of questions to ask the club officer.
6. By researching periodical literature, determine ten additional ideas for fund-raising projects not presented in this chapter.
7. Determine the most popular fund-raising product in your geographical area. Why is it so popular? What, if any, negative aspects can be associated with the sale of that product for fund-raising purposes?
8. Interview the manager of a local food store about his or her feelings on the scrip certificate plan discussed in this chapter. Report your findings to the class.

Toward Broader Horizons

CHAPTER THIRTEEN

HISTORICAL

INFLUENCES ON

MUSIC EDUCATION

INTRODUCTION

This chapter is devoted to a survey of the people and events that have affected the development of music education as a viable part of America's public school curriculum. It is interesting to note that the early development of music education in this country was people-oriented, with easily identifiable leaders making valuable contributions. In the first forty or fifty years of this century, conventions, contests, and the music industry assumed a role of increased significance. In the last few decades, projects, seminars, and conferences have assumed leadership responsibilities, along with the emergence of the Music Educators National Conference (MENC), as a stronger and more unified voice for all of music education. It is not the intent of this chapter to provide an in-depth study of the history of music education in the United States. A comprehensive investigation of the topic justifiably belongs at the graduate level.

It is the author's most sincere desire that the historical survey presented in this chapter will engender the readers' interest and promote further study of the development of music education. Both current and future music teachers can look with pride at the music education movement, aware that their profession has an honorable three-hundred-year history of outstanding and dedicated achievement.

Undergraduate students in music education rarely have an opportunity to study with any depth the people and events that have contributed historically to their chosen career field. In most music schools in this country, the study of the history of music education is reserved for graduate school. Prospective music educators need to have a basic understanding of their specialty's evolution prior to entering the profession. To see their chosen career as a true profession, they must approach it to a certain degree from a historical perspective. Having done so, music educators are in a better position to understand why school districts support music education to the extent they do, as well as how such an extensive system as public school music education came into existence.

What follows is an attempt to acquaint readers with the events and circumstances, as well as the pioneering individuals, that contributed to the goal of the Music Educators National Conference, "Music for every child, every child for music." That statement, which was made in 1923 by Karl Gehrkens and subsequently adopted as the MENC motto, is as true today as then. Knowledge of the historical roots of music education can lead to a feeling of professional pride and allow young music educators to administer their music education programs with confidence.

Early Foundations of Music Education

The *Bay Psalm Book*

The Puritans who settled in Boston brought to this country a book of psalms called the *Ainsworth Psalter.* There were no melodies included and over the years it became increasingly difficult for the colonists to remember the tunes. In 1640 three colonial ministers prepared a metrical, revised version of the psalms entitled the *Bay Psalm Book,* which was the second book published in America (the Bible was the first)—an indication of the important role that music played in the seventeenth century. The publication of the *Bay Psalm Book* marked the beginning of American-made songbooks.

The *Bay Psalm Book* went through numerous editions and was published in many countries. It appeared in twenty-six different editions in this country by 1774, and there were probably seventy in all, including both European and American versions. The number of tunes in the book rarely exceeded five or six until the late seventeenth century. The ninth edition, in 1698, was the first edition with musical notation, but it had bars only at the end of each line. This very crudely printed book is the oldest existing printed music in America.

In 1721 the Rev. Thomas Walter produced a singing book, which was the fourth book published in America, entitled *The Grounds and Rules of Music Explained, or an Introduction to the Art of Singing by Note.* Walter's book is said to be the first printed music in America to have bar lines. It was written in choral style and some tunes had three parts.

The singing school

Singing in the church before the middle of the eighteenth century was uncultivated and was said to be "distressing to the ear." Rev. Walter said, "It sounded like 500 different tunes roared out at the same time" (Sunderman 1971, p. 19). From 1620 to 1700 the musical sensitivity of the colonial people was dulled by the terrible state of singing in this country. The early colonial times saw little part singing, and if church members did possess tune books, they were certainly not able to read them. During the 1600s, many churches allowed only the "saved" to sing, with the congregation joining in on the "amens." When the entire membership was allowed to sing, the pastor would sing a line and the congregation would answer in rote fashion. This was called the "lining out" method.

The development of singing schools was a direct result of the desire to improve singing in church, and it gave public school music its first methods and all of its first teachers. Singing schools were basically instructional sessions organized by the clergy or other individuals possessing some degree of musical skills. The schools rarely lasted for more than twenty-four sessions and the students paid the instructor a prearranged fee. For example, an advertisement in an early Ohio paper promoted a singing school for a fee of $1 for thirteen nights, two hours per night, and the students had to "bring their own wood and candles" (Sunderman 1971, p. 20). The first recorded singing school was in Boston in 1717. From 1720 to 1775, the primary concern of the singing school was not the theory of music, but rather to get people to sing the melody correctly and to approximate the correct rhythm. By 1800 the movement had found its way to Maine, the Carolinas, and Georgia, but singing by note was still not universally adopted. The advent of note singing as brought about by the singing school was the first great step toward attempting "music for all."

Everything about the singing school is characteristically American. For example, it was supported by fees paid by the participants, not through the use of tax monies, and the music taught was popular and socially useful. The singing school remained eclectic, never adopting one method, but using bits and pieces from all available materials. Singing schools also produced their own textbooks and music, thus creating an element of independence. The schools promised both musical and moral benefits for their students. As the schools improved singing, for instance, they also provided an element of recreation for the young. Those particular aims are still a force in music education today (Britton 1966, pp. 15–16).

In its time, the singing school was as universal and as much a part of daily life as the country store or the post office. The singing school undoubtedly laid the foundation for the high level and rapid rise of music within this country. At the time singing schools were being organized, Bach had already completed much of his vast offerings of choral and instrumental music in Europe. Handel and Haydn began and ended their productive musical careers while Americans were still learning to sing psalm tunes. The foundation laid by the singing school movement played a significant role in the progress of music in this country.

The decline of the popularity of singing schools began around the middle 1800s. Contributing to the decline was an increase in singing societies and other musical societies, along with the growth of music programs in public school curriculums. Also, students began traveling to Europe to study privately with teachers or to study in America with European-trained teachers.

Singing societies

The early singing schools and singing societies were almost synonymous with one another. The singing school, however, primarily taught people how to sing, while the singing societies provided opportunities for musical performance. In this country, the oldest singing society still in existence is the Stoughlan Musical Society in Stoughlan, Massachusetts, which was organized in 1786. One of the greatest and most influential societies of its time was the Handel and Haydn Society of Boston. Organized in 1815, this singing society was dedicated to the performance of music composed by the two great masters from whom the society took its name. Singing societies were important in that they provided an outlet for musical talent and, through their performances, set standards for musical attainment. Additionally, they were able to bring outstanding musical works before the public, and in doing so provided impetus to the singing school movement.

The Pestalozzian principles

John Heinrich Pestalozzi was born in Zurich, Switzerland, in 1746, the son of a middle-class surgeon. Almost all pre–Civil War vocal music in American public schools was guided and patterned according to Pestalozzian principles of teaching. Pestalozzi ranks high as an individual who inspired and greatly influenced American education. He was probably the first person to insist that music be included in the course of study in public schools.

Pestalozzi was not so much interested in rote instruction; he believed that it was important for students to appreciate the differences in melody, rhythm, harmony, and dynamics. He felt that they should eventually be able to translate notation and characters into a familiar language, as if they were reading the letter characters of a language.

Pestalozzi's educational principles were adopted for music instruction by Lowell Mason. (A detailed study of Lowell Mason's contributions to the progress of music education appears later in this chapter.) In 1834 Mason published the *Manual for Instruction,* the first formulation of modern principles of teaching music. In the following list of pedagogic principles, Mason drew from Pestalozzi seven key ideas for the teaching of music to children:

1. To teach sounds before signs—to make the child sing before he or she learns the written notes or their names.

2. To lead children to observe, by hearing and imitating sounds, their resemblances and differences, their agreeable and disagreeable effects, instead of explaining these things to him—in short, to make them active instead of passive in learning.

3. To teach but one thing at a time—rhythm, melody, expression being taught and practiced separately before the child is called to the difficult task of attending to all at once.

4. To make children practice each step of each of these divisions, until they are masters of it, before passing to the next.

5. To give the principles and theory after practice and as an induction from it.

6. To analyze and practice the elements of articulate sound in order to apply them to music.

7. To have the names of the notes correspond to those used in instrumental music (cited in Birge 1928, p. 38).

Mason's adaptation of Pestalozzi's educational principles was the first formulation of theories for teaching music in the United States.

CONFERENCE/CONVENTION MOVEMENT

Musical conventions began to appear in the early 1800s and were designed to provide training for singing school teachers. They generally lasted two or three days. The first recorded convention of this kind took place in Concord, New Hampshire, in 1829.

The Boston Academy of Music was founded in 1832 by the mayor of Boston, Samuel E. Elliot, and some of his associates. By 1834 it had become the focal point of the convention movement. Lectures at the 1834 convention presented the academy's method of teaching music as outlined in the *Manual of the Boston Academy of Music*. This event was so successful that participants voted to return the following year, a trend that continued for eighteen years. Due to the enthusiasm and efforts of Mason, another of the academy's founders, the annual gathering became a source of significant influence for years to come (Birge 1928, p. 38). In 1840 the group adopted as its name the National Music Convention.

As one might expect, a controversy developed between those individuals who wanted to maintain a lecture approach to the convention and those who wanted the performance of great works to be the main emphasis of the event. A compromise was realized and a second organization was formed, the American Musical Convention, which maintained the lecture format.

The convention movement spread as associates of the Boston Academy of Music traveled away from that city to hold conventions in the West. The format and curriculums of the conventions continued to diversify. Lectures were developed on a variety of musical topics, such as singing-class pedagogy. Those supervisors attending the conventions spent a great deal of time in a rehearsal setting, and the sessions always closed with a concert. Also included in convention curriculums were such topics as sight-singing, reading of new music, trying new methods, and performing new works by the great masters. As time went on, conventions became very commercial. Convention directors became heavily involved in the promotion and sale of their own musical materials, conductors circulated their own methods texts, and publishers were able to sell merchandise. Convention critics questioned whether the sessions were held for commercial or musical purposes. In spite of this criticism, the attendees went home with new ideas on teaching music and revitalized enthusiasm for the instruction of music in their own communities.

In 1906, Philip C. Hayden invited music supervisors from the Midwest to a meeting in Keokuk, Iowa, to observe and provide feedback for a rhythm-based approach to note reading. Those attending the 1907 Keokuk Conference were totally unaware that they were marking one of the milestones in school music history. Over a hundred supervisors attended, and of those, sixty-nine became permanent members of the conference.

However, no one considered the possibility that this organization would become permanent. At that time, the music section of the National Education Association was regarded as the official representative of school music teachers. In 1910, at a meeting in Cincinnati attended by 150 members, the name of the organization was established as the Music Supervisors National Conference. At their 1915 meeting in Kansas City, more than 3,000 music educators attended; by 1920, conference membership had risen to a total of nearly 2,000 music instructors (Keene 1982, p. 249). In 1926 a National High School Orchestra was organized to perform for the conference. The orchestra was made up of school musicians from over thirty states, consisting of 246 players from 121 different schools. Joseph Maddy, later of Interlochen Arts Academy fame, conducted the orchestra.

At their meeting in 1934, the conference members voted to change the organization's name to the Music Educators National Conference (MENC). Thus an organization originally made up of supervisors became one representing every aspect of music as taught in public schools. Music education has gained recognition as part of the school curriculum largely because of MENC's work. This organization has grown to a total membership of nearly 67,000 (14,000 of them are collegiate members), a significant voice for music education throughout America.

THE PUBLISHING INDUSTRY

As the influence of the singing schools gradually spread to the public schools, American publishers were quick to realize a new market was being established for educational materials. From 1850 to 1860 over sixty-five different music books were published. Sales of music books in the nineteenth century totaled millions of copies, very few of which were used in the public schools, but all had some indirect effect on the music education movement. Just one example of a successful publishing effort was *Carmina Sacra,* a popular 1841 effort of Lowell Mason, which sold over 400,000 copies in a ten-year period. Between 1840 and 1880 the Oliver Ditson Company bought the rights to a large number of music books, and by the late nineteenth century it had become the largest publisher of tune books in the country. The John Church Company in Cincinnati, Ohio, became the largest music book publisher in the Midwest. In 1861 Ditson published a text by Joseph Bird in which the author strongly disagreed with Lowell Mason's rote-learning approach. His book, *Vocal Music Reader,* was the first step in the multiple book, or series, concept. When music was introduced in the elementary schools of Boston in 1864, the need for a graded series of instructional texts was created. Lowell Mason, who was instrumental in making music part of the curriculum of the Boston schools, published the first and second in a series of music books, entitled *Song Garden,* in 1864, with the third and fourth book appearing in 1866 (Keene 1982, p. 189).

Hosea Edson Holt also became disenchanted with the rote approach to teaching vocal music. He took charge of the elementary school music program in the Boston schools in 1859 and developed the *Normal Music Course,* which was a series of five graded books first published in 1863. The Silver Burdett Company purchased the rights to these works two years later and began their publishing efforts with Holt's series.

In response to Holt's books, Luther Whiting Mason's series, entitled the *National Music Course,* was written between 1870 and 1875. Because it set the standard for similar books for the next fifty years, this series will be discussed in greater detail in the next section of this chapter. The *National Music Course,* along with Holt's *Normal Music Course,* became the most popular of all the music series published between 1850 and 1900.

During the latter part of the nineteenth century, competition between publishing companies was intense. They soon discovered it was to their distinct advantage to offer institute classes whereby classroom teachers could be trained in the use of their published materials. For example, in 1887 the Ginn Company initiated institute classes using Luther Mason's *National Music Course,* with the author and eight of his associates as faculty. The Silver Burdett Company offered institutes, beginning in 1889, that promoted Holt's opposing view on teaching music presented in his *Normal Music Course.* These institutes grew very popular, as well as extremely profitable for music publishing companies.

National Music Course

Luther Whiting Mason's series for elementary music instruction enjoyed a fifty-year period of popularity. It consisted of seven books, five readers, and two supplementary texts. Mason included charts as instructional visual aids. The music incorporated into the series was taken largely from German folk tunes, and, perhaps thanks to this content, the series was translated into German and used in that country. The *National Music Course* was the first completely planned method for teaching music and was adopted by the Japanese government after Mason's visit to that country. School music in Japan came to be known as "Mason-song." In this country, the *National Music Course* was by far the most popular and progressive book of Mason's time.

Modern Music Series

Published in 1898, the *Modern Music Series* was the result of a joint effort by Robert Foresman, who did the planning and general psychology of the series, and Eleanor Smith, who did much of the editing, translating of verses, and song-writing. The Silver Burdett Company acquired the rights to the series in 1901. It became very popular, especially in the Midwest, and it introduced a new era in music education and established new instructional standards. The pedagogy of the series was experimental and offered suggestions only, leaving much of the teaching process up to the imagination and skill of the teacher. The *Modern Music Series* was among the first to insist that only songs of the highest quality be used to teach reading technique, rather than merely relying on exercises specifically written to teach technique. In this respect, the series was definitely a pioneer.

CONTESTS AND FESTIVALS

The role that contests and festivals played in advancing the cause of school music is of unquestionable importance, particularly for instrumental music. Little documentation exists regarding contests in the nineteenth century. One of the earliest known events was a convention of fifteen cornet bands held in Portage, Wisconsin, in 1877. That same year eight brass bands competed before large audiences in Port Huron, Michigan. Each band was judged on the basis of its parade marching and concert performance. In 1897, at a choral competition in Ottawa, Kansas, a $400 first prize was awarded to the winning choir (Keene 1982, p. 294). In 1912, the first contest devoted to a competition between public school musicians was held: the All-Kansas Music Competition Festival. The early Kansas contests included competitions for organ, piano, voice, strings, wind instruments, and girl's glee clubs.

The entire contest movement greatly appealed to the energetic and competitive American citizenry. The states of Kansas, Missouri, and North Dakota were front-runners in the movement. The Welsh immigrants residing in these states brought with them their inherent love of music and the *isteddfods,* traditional musical exhibitions held in their homeland, a concept on which early music contests in this country were based. The North Dakota contest, which was organized in 1919, grew so large by 1921 that elimination contests became necessary. In 1922, 600 students from forty-four schools participated in the finals of that event. The first national band contest was held in Chicago, June 4 through June 6, 1923. This contest gave a national focus to school bands and brought them to a position of prominence during that time. The original contest was organized by a Chicago music dealers' association with some help from the Conn instrument manufacturing company. The thirty bands that participated ranged in size from twenty-five to eighty-five members. This competition was greatly criticized by the participating schools because there was only one adjudicator, the adjudication standards were different from those being used at the state level, and there were no required pieces and no size or instrumentation requirements.

The success of this first "band tournament" caught the attention of the instrument manufacturing industry. Prior to this time, industry leaders saw little future in the sales of instruments to schools. In fact, some manufacturers considered projects aimed at school sales to be "wasteful." The success of the 1923 contest was a turning point in the industry's history.

Because the market for musical instruments for professional and amateur adult bands was greatly reduced by the end of World War I, instrument manufacturers determined that the survival of the industry was directly related to the development of a new market large enough to sustain mass production. Thousands of former military musicians assumed teaching positions as band directors at the close of the war, creating a tremendous increase in the number of band programs in schools throughout this country. The industry decided to support financially a national contest. A 1924 event was planned, also to be held in Chicago, complete with a repertoire list that accentuated many school bands' inadequate instrumentation. An effort was made to ensure that the scope of the contest was truly national by securing participating bands from every section of the country, and the meeting was given the grand title of the Schools Band Contest of America. Interest in the event grew rapidly during the late 1920s. Railroads offered reduced fares for participants, and communities throughout the country raised funds to support a trip to Chicago for the local school band. The band became a great source of community pride. Even during the Depression years, only one Schools Band Contest was canceled. This national contest accepted orchestras in 1926, and the event eventually became so large that competition for band and orchestras had to be held on alternate years.

The national contest played a large role in the success of instrumental music in the public schools, and it was a natural public relations vehicle for those programs. Another result of the national contest was that state and national associations for instrumental teachers were developed as a forum to discuss problems associated with the contest movement and as a medium to raise performance standards. They also dealt with instrumentation problems. The "one-half woodwind and one-half brass" instrumentation concept was a source of controversy as soon as it was introduced. As a result, a "blue ribbon" committee was established to develop a standard instrumentation for school bands. Members of the panel included John Philip Sousa, Edwin Franko Goldman, and Herbert L. Clark, and the panel's instrumentation recommendations became the standard for American bands and is used to this day (Keene 1982, p. 304).

By 1940 the contest movement served a total of 10,000 bands and orchestras, 7,500 vocal and instrumental ensembles, and 15,000 instrumental soloists, a total of over a half million student participants (Keene 1982, p. 305). The advent of World War II saw the end of the national contest, but the effects of the contest movement established the meteoric rise in stature of instrumental music in public schools throughout the United States.

EARLY LEADERS AND EDUCATORS

John Tufts. Almost a century after the Mayflower's arrival in New England, a Boston bookseller offered for sale a book by a relatively obscure, 42-year-old minister, the Rev. John Tufts. *Introduction to the Singing of Psalm Tunes* was the first American music textbook. Its sale marked the beginning of organized music education in the United States. For notation, Tufts used only F, S, L, M (fa, sol, la, and mi), and note lengths were indicated by various punctuation signs following each note. There were thirty-seven tunes on twelve pages. Tufts called his approach "learning to sing by rule" (Lowens 1964, p. 39).

The New England singing school movement was developed from Tufts' book. By 1744 it had gone through eleven editions, and it was still in use in the nineteenth century. After Tufts, there was no musical step of comparable magnitude until Lowell Mason came on the scene in the early part of the nineteenth century. Tufts was unknown when his book was published; for that reason, early advertisements of *Introduction to the Singing of Psalm Tunes* did not include his name. Tufts can be considered a pioneer in the movement to improve church singing, and his work left a permanent mark on our culture (Howard and Bellows 1967, p. 47).

William Billings. William Billings was the first native, self-taught American composer to meet the challenge of the advent of singing by note. In 1770 (the year Beethoven was born; Bach had been dead for twenty years) Billings's first work appeared: *The New England Psalm Singer or the American Chorister.* One of his best works was a collection called the *Singing Master's Assistant,* published in 1778.

Fuging tunes were not Billings's creation, but he was so successful at using them that many people through the years have thought that they were his own discovery.

Billings's music is important because it appeared at a time when singing the old union psalms was going out of style, and his tunes were easy to memorize.

Billings was as much a force in America's democratic upheaval as was the Boston Tea Party, because he aroused a musical response from the people. One of his tunes, "Chester," was also called the "Battle Hymn of the Revolution"; it was the only tune the Continental pipes used when on the march. A devoted patriot and a friend of Samuel Adams, Billings was very popular in his time. He was blind in one eye and had a withered arm, legs of different lengths, and a rasping voice that added color to his slovenly appearance. Although he was highly respected, his deformities are thought to have occasionally made him the brunt of practical jokes (Howard and Bellows 1967, p. 46). While little of his music is alive today, Billings made a lasting contribution to our musical life through his activities, which included forming singing societies and church choirs. He improved the quality of church performances by introducing the pitch pipe and advocated the use of the violincello in church music, a move considered daring at that time. He brought New England's musical interest to life.

Lowell Mason. The individual who is believed by many music educators to have made the greatest contribution to the advancement of music education in the public schools is Lowell Mason. He was the first teacher of school music in the United States and the first supervisor of vocal music in the Boston schools.

Mason was born in Medfield, Massachusetts, in 1792, the son of a hat manufacturer and part-time mechanic. During the early years of his life, he learned to play a variety of musical instruments. When he was 20, he moved to Savannah, Georgia, where he took a full-time position in a bank, but he still found time to organize a band and direct church choirs. While in Savannah, Mason became involved with the Handel and Haydn Society of Boston and composed a collection of church music for them, which they published. He didn't want his name associated with the publication because he still wanted to be known as a banker, not a musician. The Handel and Haydn Society encouraged him to accept an appointment with three Boston churches so that he could become more involved in the society. In 1827 he was elected president of the Handel and Haydn Society and made sweeping innovations designed to improve the quality of its performances (Keene 1982, p. 48). In 1833, influenced by Mason's work, the mayor of Boston and some of his associates established the Boston Academy of Music to give greater scope to Mason's efforts. This was the first school of music pedagogy in the United States. In 1837 Mason began teaching music classes, without pay, in elementary schools in Boston. In 1838 he was appointed supervisor of music with an annual budget of $130 for each school he supervised. Of this fee, $90 went to training teachers and $20 to piano rental. There is some disagreement as to how long Mason served as supervisor of music, but he was probably dismissed in 1845. At that time, the school board accused him of showing religious favoritism in selecting his teaching associates (Sunderman 1971, p. 50).

After severing relations with the Boston schools, Mason immersed himself in writing, lecturing, and teaching at the Boston Academy of Music, activities that resulted in his being recognized as an outstanding proponent of music education. Mason was definitely America's first important public school music educator. Among his accomplishments are

1. Revised music instruction materials according to the Pestalozzian principles.

2. Collected innumerable psalm, hymn, and school music books.

3. Taught so successfully that he had few peers.

4. Organized and instructed educational conventions.

5. Originated the study of the rudiments of music in American public schools.

6. Worked for improved singing schools.

7. Established a precedent for the type of song material to be included in nineteenth-century church songbooks (Sunderman 1971, p. 54).

Charles Aiken. The most striking pioneer figure in music education history, with the exception of Lowell Mason, is Charles Aiken. In 1839 Aiken met Reuben Mussey, a famous surgeon who was also a fine cellist, while both were living in Cincinnati. Mussey initiated a singing class in the basement of a Presbyterian church, asking Aiken to be its leader. Aiken taught temperance songs and used the new movable Do system of instruction in that school. All types of people took these classes, free of charge, and learned music using techniques based on the teaching methods of Lowell Mason. Aiken next went to Europe to study and gather facts about the German schools and their music education techniques. His seventy-page report on his findings there had an immediate effect on music education in Vermont and Ohio, and subsequently that of the entire nation.

In 1842 Aiken taught music without a salary in the Cincinnati schools. During the following years, he continued to instruct public school students, but did a great deal of teaching outside the school. Aiken was appointed superintendent of music for the Cincinnati schools in 1871 and was responsible for introducing music into the elementary grades of that city. In addition to teaching and administration, he assisted in the writing of several texts and edited *The High School Choralist.* During the eight years he served as the superintendent of music, Aiken made numerous improvements in the system, such as establishing a means of systematizing music instruction—using exams to measure and improve instruction—and he wrote the first edition of the multi-volume *Cincinnati Music Readers.* These books used the works of the great masters and were considered to be remarkable for their time (Keene 1982, p. 170).

Aiken retired in 1879. His son, Walter H. Aiken, who was considered a brilliant choral director, was appointed superintendent of music in Cincinnati in 1900. He was active in music education for a period of fifty-four continuous years. The work of the father and son combined amounts to eighty-six years of service to the students and public of Cincinnati.

Luther Whiting Mason. Luther Whiting Mason, a distant relative of Lowell Mason, began teaching in Cincinnati in 1857. He initiated a thorough study of available music instruction books, including the materials of Johann Nageli, an associate of Pestalozzi in Swiss and German schools. He published a translated version of the materials that had formed the basis of Lowell Mason's songbooks written for young voices. Luther Mason became known for his rote-note approach to music instruction.

In 1864 Mason accepted a position in Boston to organize and teach elementary music. In doing so, he established a precedent for elementary music instruction, because before this time, music had only been offered at what we know as the junior high school level. He recognized a pressing need for teaching materials at the elementary school and wrote the *National Music Course,* a series that became very popular. Luther Whiting Mason is considered the founder of school music methodology. Not only was his *National Music Course* the first series of its kind to receive national recognition, but it became the prototype of most music instruction books that followed. Mason is recognized for his formulation of instructional materials for early grades (Birge 1928, p. 98).

Sterrie Weaver. Sterrie Weaver was born in New London, Connecticut, in 1853. He studied music at evening singing schools, later attended the New England Conservatory, and eventually studied music education in Germany. In the late 1800s he became music supervisor of three schools in Connecticut. He also found time to edit the periodical *The Music Courier.*

In 1900 Weaver opened a school to train music supervisors and had a great influence on music education in a short period of time. He successfully applied the scientific method to the problem of reading music, and through his addresses, articles, and personal actions he encouraged others to take a more scientific approach to their work. When he died in 1904, his work was just becoming nationally known. Weaver stood out among his contemporaries. Edward Birge pointed out his distinctness:

> Like the prophet Elijah of old, he suddenly appeared on the scene of school music, delivered his message, completed his work, and suddenly departed. His character was strong, self-reliant and ruggedly honest. His personality was simple, and vibrant with energy and deep feeling. His intellect was keen and penetrating, and he was a born teacher. It was his mission to evolve a method of teaching sight-reading that was de-

void of all the paraphernalia of the period and to prove that every child can be taught to read music (Birge 1928, p. 124).

Birge concluded that Weaver was the first exponent of tests and measurements in music sight-reading: "This stands out as his main contribution to school music and, in the writer's opinion, the main contribution of the period" (Birge 1928, p. 128).

Philip C. Hayden. Born in Brantford, Ontario, in 1854, Philip Hayden studied at New York University for one year and Oberlin College for five years. He served as supervisor of music in Quincy, Illinois, and Keokuk, Iowa. He taught music in public schools for a total of thirty-five years. Hayden founded the *School Music* magazine in 1900 and published a series of articles about his method of teaching music through a progressive series of rhythmic forms. In 1906 he sent a letter to thirty Midwest music supervisors inviting them to Keokuk for a meeting and an opportunity to observe and investigate his work. The response was so great that, in January 1907, *School Music* published a nationwide invitation, this time signed by twenty-six music supervisors who indicated their belief in the value of holding a meeting at Keokuk. They pledged their attendance and requested that their colleagues from across the country join them. Hayden had originally hoped that at least fifteen supervisors would attend. In the end, more than 100 music supervisors from around the nation participated in the first meeting of what was to eventually evolve into the Music Educators National Conference.

Frances Elliot Clark. Born in 1860 in Angola, Indiana, Frances Elliot Clark studied organ and voice at a singing school. With only an eighth-grade education, she passed the necessary exams and began teaching in 1884. During the summers she attended Tri-state Normal College. There she studied voice, sang in choirs, and became recognized as a soprano soloist. For training as a music supervisor, she attended the Ginn Institute in Detroit, Michigan, where she learned the note-rote approach.

In 1891 Clark accepted a position in Monmouth, Illinois. It was here that she developed the abilities that would take her to the top of her profession. She became very active in women's music clubs, both locally and on the national level. In 1896 she moved to Ottumwa, Iowa, a town with a history of excellent music programs. She organized three choirs there, the best of which was said to be able to read and sing such music as Handel's *Messiah* and Mendelssohn's *Elijah*. Clark recognized the need to relate the history of music to performance. Although there were no books on the subject, she developed ten-minute talks about opera, Bach's life and works, as well as the lives and works of other recognized composers. Her efforts represented one of the first attempts at including music appreciation in public school instruction (Keene 1982, p. 246).

Clark left Iowa in 1903 to accept a music supervisor's position in Milwaukee. Music was highly regarded in that city, but there was little of it in the public schools. In the grade schools Clark organized a new and very successful music program, which included ear training and music in kindergarten classes. Clark was vice president of the music section of the National Education Association when she presided over the 1907 meeting of the soon-to-be Music Supervisors National Conference in Keokuk, Iowa. She offered guidance and provided stability during the early meetings, which were at times somewhat confrontational.

Clark's greatest contribution to music education was her early recognition of the educational value of the "talking machine." By 1906 records were being pressed, and Clark was excited by the educational value of the machines, though many others considered them only toys. She arranged for the first demonstration of a Victor Talking Machine as a teaching tool for grade school children from Milwaukee. The school principals in attendance were very impressed and immediately ordered some of the machines for their schools. Clark later joined the Victor Talking Machine Company, where she organized an educational department. Victor published its first educational catalog in 1911; by 1924 the catalog was classified into subjects by grade and contained almost 3,000 selections. The use of the Victrola spread throughout the country and became one of the all-time greatest teaching aids for the instruction of music, bringing good music within the reach of every child (Keene 1982, p. 246).

Will Earhart. Will Earhart was one of the first people to expand the high school curriculum beyond choral music. He established classes in harmony, music appreciation, and various instruments, as well as forming an orchestra and a band. He is particularly known for his contribution to the music appreciation movement. Earhart wanted his students to know about a composer, his place of origin, his successes, and his place in the world. He wanted them to understand musical form. Earhart's efforts to establish music appreciation courses in Richmond, Indiana, were later accepted by many as a model.

Earhart organized an orchestra in Richmond, Indiana, in 1898 and was an enterprising and innovative leader prior to World War I in organizing orchestras where they had not previously existed. In 1921 he conducted a performance of an orchestra made up of members of the Music Supervisors National Conference in St. Joseph, Missouri. This concert led to the formation of a committee on instrumental instruction by the conference in 1922 (Birge 1928, pp. 261–263).

CONTEMPORARY MUSIC EDUCATION

The contemporary period in music education began in the mid-1950s. Music education found itself caught up in the sweeping changes occurring throughout the

American educational system. Dramatic curricular changes in American public school education were being initiated based largely on the work and recommendations of James B. Conant (1959). As previously indicated in chapter 7, Conant's findings pointed out the need for increased student involvement in art and music at the public school level. In several curricular areas at this time, change was initiated and nurtured by industrial philanthropic foundations. The music education profession is indeed fortunate that the Ford Foundation elected to financially support projects in public schools that directly affected music education.

What follows is a brief survey of five important projects and seminars that have influenced music education over the past thirty-five years. Together they represent the movement toward quality contemporary music education. There are several printed sources from which information can be obtained relating to events affecting music education in the last fifty years. Perhaps the most thorough treatment of the subject can be found in *Contemporary Music Education* by Michael L. Mark (1996), and it is that source that serves as the basis for the material that follows. For more in-depth study of this interesting topic, readers are encouraged to refer to Dr. Mark's work.

YOUNG COMPOSERS PROJECT

Between 1959 and 1962, thirty-one American composers were placed in school systems across the country through sponsorship of the Ford Foundation. The young musicians, all under 35 years of age, served as composers in residence for students in their representative schools. From an original Ford Foundation grant of $200,000, the composers were selected by a committee chaired by Norman Dell Joio, and received a stipend of $5,000 per year to write music for choruses, orchestras, bands, and other ensembles in the public schools to which they had been assigned. The stipend was approximately what music educators were receiving in annual wages at that point in time. This was a tremendous opportunity for young composers in that their compositional efforts were very likely to be studied and performed, and the prospect of immediate rehearsal and performance feedback was professionally rewarding and stimulating.

CONTEMPORARY MUSIC PROJECT

In 1963 the Ford Foundation awarded a grant to the Music Educators National Conference to organize the Contemporary Music Project for Creativity in Music Education. Through the project an additional forty-six composers in residence were placed in public schools by 1968. The five-fold purpose of the Contemporary Music Project, as stated in the proposal accepted by the Ford Foundation, was:

1. To increase the emphasis on the creative aspect of music in public schools.
2. To create a solid foundation or environment in the music education profession for acceptance, through understanding, of the contemporary music idiom.
3. To develop a close relationship and better understanding between members of the composition and music education professions.
4. To cultivate taste and discrimination on the part of music educators and their students for the quality of contemporary music used in the schools.
5. To discover, whenever possible, creative talent among students (Mark 1996, p. 30).

In addition to continuing the Young Composers Project (retitled Composers in Public Schools), the Contemporary Music Project sponsored numerous workshops and seminars across the country. The Seminar on Comprehensive Musicianship, held on the campus of Northwestern University in April 1965, focused on the improvement of college and university training of music educators. Particular attention was given to the breadth of required theory courses in music schools and the adequacy of these courses in preparing music teachers to deal competently with creativity and contemporary music concepts. The seminar established basic principles for comprehensive musicianship, and while relatively few colleges have integrated it into their teacher-training programs, the concept has had a great impact on elementary and secondary school performing ensembles.

Pilot projects were the third result of the Contemporary Music Project and were also sponsored in cooperation with public school systems. Objectives of the pilot projects were to:

1. Identify suitable approaches in the presentation of contemporary music.
2. Experiment with various techniques for providing creative musical experiences for children.
3. Identify contemporary music suitable for use with students at several grade levels.
4. Provide in-service training for teachers (Mark 1996, pp. 28–34).

The Contemporary Music Project ended in 1973. According to Mark, the project gave direction, issued challenges, developed contemporary methods and materials, and created an atmosphere of open-mindedness toward change and innovation on the part of the music education profession (Fitzgerald 1966, p. 491).

THE YALE SEMINAR

From June 17 to June 28, 1963, thirty-one musicians, teachers, and other scholars gathered on the campus of Yale University to consider the problems facing music education in the United States. Concern had developed among leading music educators that, although students participating in large ensembles in public schools were enjoying the audience appreciation of their performances and the satisfaction derived from striving for high contest and festival ratings, they were perhaps missing out on the musical aspects of the experience. Educators were starting to ask, "Have students really learned anything about music?" It was the task of those individuals gathered for the Yale Seminar to examine the kindergarten through twelfth-grade music education curriculum, with the object being to bring the subject matter and methods of teaching in line with contemporary knowledge and culture. It was determined that the development of musicality should be the primary aim of music programs throughout the country.

The seminar found that classroom materials were lacking in relevance and that student exposure to both non-Western and early Western music was being neglected almost entirely. Music teachers were also failing to share music from the jazz, popular, and folk idioms with their students.

The seminar noted that weak musical arrangements were being used by both large and small ensembles. The same problem existed with the songbook series used by many general-music classroom teachers. They concluded that the music selected for use in music programs directly reflected the skill level of the teachers involved as well as their lack of interest and/or ability to work to improve the listening and hearing skills of their students. Instrumental music was found to have been successful in contributing to the overall musical growth in the country, but the seminar participants expressed concern that vocal music repertory appeared to be primarily aimed at audience appeal and was being programmed so as to offend the least possible number of listeners. Their report concluded that materials used in music classrooms and rehearsals had not changed appreciably over the previous thirty years. The recommendations of the Yale Seminar participants included:

1. The basic goal of the K–12 music education curriculum should be to develop musicality through performance, movement, creativity, and listening.

2. The music education repertory should be broadened to include jazz, folk, and contemporary popular music.

3. A sequence of guided listening to worthwhile music should be developed.

4. Performance activities should include large ensembles for which an authentic and varied repertory would exist; small-ensemble participation by student musicians should be of particular importance.

5. Advanced theory and literature courses should be available to students who could most benefit from them.

6. Performing musicians, composers, and scholars should be brought into schools to provide students with insights as to how professionals think and work.

7. Music programs in the public schools need to take greater advantage of community and national human and material resources.

8. Audiovisual aids and individualized instruction programs need to be developed and used in music classrooms.

9. A plan must be developed to train and retrain teachers so as to enable curriculum revision to be successfully implemented (Mark 1996, pp. 36–37).

These recommendations were already in place in some existing school music programs, but other programs have benefited from them. School music repertory has improved significantly, although artificial and synthesized music is rapidly influencing that repertory. Whether that influence will eventually be judged positive or negative has yet to be determined. The training of music teachers has improved in the United States due in part to upgraded state certification requirements and to the fact that institutions of higher education have enhanced their efforts to provide their students with the proper tools to become good teachers.

THE MANHATTANVILLE PROJECT

The Manhattanville Music Curriculum Project (MMCP) was initiated in 1965 and was based on a grant from the United States Office of Education. The project drew its name from the fact that it originated at the Manhattanville College of the Sacred Heart in Purchase, New York.

The primary objective of this project was to develop a music curriculum and associated methods and materials for a sequential music program, grades K–12. Some experimental music programs were already in existence in the United States; therefore, the project began with an exploratory study of ninety-two of these programs, which were located in thirty-six states. Fifteen of the experimental programs were selected for in-depth study.

The MMCP was divided into three phases. Phase I involved determining student-learning potential, studying problems relating to curriculum reform, and drafting a series of classroom procedures. Phase II involved refining information gained from studies and organizing that information into a workable curriculum. Phase III entailed the refinement and field testing of the music curriculum developed as a result of the study. It also investigated separate curriculums for early childhood education; addressed the problem, the need for, and the approach to teacher retraining; and developed a testing instrument for the assessment of the level of completion of program objectives.

The MMCP approach to music instruction was used in a small number of schools over a period of time. The most common use in today's schools is the adaptation by traditional music programs of its strengths, namely its emphasis on creativity and compositional activities. The lack of a high level of implementation and application of the resultant MMCP curriculum is more than likely due to its requirement that teachers work within a framework far removed from traditional music education. Proponents of the MMCP approach to music instruction were largely unsuccessful in convincing administrators and parents that music education need not necessarily justify itself based on performance. The informal, self-motivated approach that is a requisite of the MMCP approach corresponds closely to the philosophical foundation of open education, a philosophy that has not to date gained wide acceptance in educational circles in this country.

THE TANGLEWOOD SYMPOSIUM

Convened at Tanglewood, Massachusetts, in July and August 1967, the Tanglewood Symposium was a venture sponsored by the Theodore Presser Foundation, the Berkshire Music Center, and Boston University of Fine and Applied Arts. The symposium brought together scientists, sociologists, musicians, labor leaders, educators, corporate and foundation representatives, and government leaders. The symposium was entitled "Music in American Society," and it centered on three broad issues:

1. What are the characteristics and desirable ideologies for an emerging postindustrial society?
2. What are the values and unique functions of music and other arts for individuals and communities in such a society?
3. How may these potentials be attained? (Mark 1996, p. 39)

Committees were formed and addressed the following:

The wide divergence between "school music" and what children listen to away from school.

How higher personal income levels, along with increased leisure time, provided more opportunity to participate in and enjoy the arts.

The need to recognize the value and necessity of the study of African and Asian music during this country's struggle for racial equality.

Why contemporary or "new" music is aesthetically valid.

The importance of music education's role in helping students "know" as opposed to "appreciate" a musical work.

The need for the music education profession to anticipate future social conditions and develop different kinds of teaching and performance techniques, as well as to be prepared to work with more sophisticated students.

The role of music education in adult education.

The need to explore the roles of such individuals involved in the process of music as the creators, distributors, consumers, and educators.

Recommendations resulting from the Tanglewood Symposium included the following:

1. Elementary music education curriculums should place more emphasis on elements of musical experience, such as (a) understanding many types of music through listening and performance; (b) studying music by singing, playing, and movement; (c) arranging and composing music; and (d) being able to understand and use musical notation.

2. All junior high school students should be required to take one general music class.

3. All senior high school students (even those in performance groups) should be required to take one arts course.

4. Social musical instruments should be taught at all levels.

Another committee recommendation was that a means should be established to identify potential future music educators while they are still in high school, and that the MENC should prepare a set of materials that could assist high school counselors in such an identification process.

The Tanglewood Symposium provided the profession with a brilliant basis for an aesthetic philosophy of music education and called for music to be placed in the school curriculum core. The symposium also called for music of all periods, forms, styles, and cultures to be included in that curriculum (Mark 1996, pp. 38–45).

It is interesting to note that, some twenty-five years later, multicultural education was a primary focus of the 1990 MENC biannual meeting in Washington, D.C. In 1989 MENC published *Multicultural Perspectives in Music Education* as a teaching resource for this important topic. The organization offers other books and videos on the topic. Contact MENC for a copy of the Professional Resources Catalog.

AT THE CLOSE OF THE MILLENNIUM

The 1980s saw many heated discussions relating to the need for educational reform in this country. The subject became politicized when then-President Bush and his advisors announced a plan for education reform entitled "Goals 2000." The short-sighted document omitted reference to the arts as part of an educational reform recommendation package. The narrow and incomplete view of education outlined within it had a polarizing effect on the educational community. There were ex-tremely vocal advocates and opponents of Goals 2000 in its original form. Advo-cacy groups for the arts became very active and motivated in their lobbying efforts to include a goal for the arts in this curriculum.

National Coalition for Music Education

The most prominent, active, and vocal advocacy group to come out of this stressful time for the arts was the National Coalition for Music Education. It was spearheaded by officials from the Music Educators National Conference, the Na-tional Academy of Recording Arts and Sciences, and the National Association of Music Merchants. The National Coalition formed a National Commission on Mu-sic Education, which eventually consisted of numerous major performing artists, members of both the U.S. Senate and House of Representatives, presidents of the three founding organizations, prominent actors, music industry representatives, a variety of education professional organizations, and presidents and chief executives from many major corporations. The National Commission was perhaps the most prestigious grouping of individuals in the support of any facet of the arts in this country's history.

The National Commission on Music Education conducted public forums in Los Angeles, Chicago, and Nashville. The purpose of the forums was to provide opportunities for information exchange on the local and national levels and to sur-vey public opinion. Additionally, the forums were to provide a platform for the deeply rooted concerns about what the commission termed "the dangerous omis-sion of music and the other arts from the nation's educational priorities" (MENC 1991, p. xi).

The National Coalition also sponsored a National Symposium in Washington, D.C., in 1991 to discuss the commission's concerns under the organizing idea "America's Culture at Risk." The symposium's final report was presented to mem-bers of Congress and distributed to most government agencies as part of its activi-ties. It helped consolidate the views of the national forums as to the value and importance of music and the arts as a part of the total learning process. The actions taken originally by the National Coalition along with the subsequent national campaign of support for music education by the National Commission in the 1990s have played a very important and dramatic role in securing a place for the arts in the long-term goals for educational reform in the United States.

The National Coalition's credo simply and eloquently states its philosophy: "Just as there can be no music without learning, no education is complete without music. Music makes the difference" (MENC 1991, p. viii). The "Music Makes a Difference" action kit, based on the work of the National Coalition, is available from MENC and can be a valuable resource for all music educators.

The National Standards

In March 1994 a piece of legislation was passed into law that set into motion a remarkable chain of events that resulted in what many people consider to be the single most significant accomplishment in the history of public school music education in the twentieth century. The legislation, entitled "Goals 2000: Educate America Act," was the result of an effort led primarily by MENC. It stipulated that music and the other arts be included in a national educational reform movement to develop world-class standards and assessments.

MENC received grants totaling $1 million from the Department of Education, the National Endowment for the Arts, and the National Endowment for the Humanities to develop voluntary national standards for grades K–12 for each of the four arts disciplines: music, visual arts, theater, and dance. The standards that resulted describe the knowledge, skills, and understanding that all students should acquire in the arts as part of their public education, providing a basis for assessment of program success, as well an aid in the development of curriculums.

For the first time in their professional lives, music educators have a set of guidelines on which they can qualify their music programs: guidelines that they can share with parents, administrators, and their community as to what should be included in a music education program and what results can be expected to be demonstrated by students enrolled in that program.

There are those who question the need for such standards. They express concern that course content will be dictated by government bodies and worry that time is not available in typical daily teaching schedules to cover what they feel needs to be taught. They pose the questions, Where will the money come from for materials? Who will teach all these classes? The good news is that the standards are voluntary. They exist as an aid to instruction in music, not as a hindrance. In many cases, the standards describe what music educators are already doing in their music classes. They affirm the quality of work already being done. Music teachers also can use the standards to support their requests for more time, more help, improved facilities, and so on.

THE CHALLENGE

In the new millennium, music educators must become involved in getting the national standards adopted in their own individual states. In some cases this step may be a difficult one, because numerous state departments of education already have in place standards for the arts they have developed themselves and may be reluctant to become involved in anything with the word "national" attached to it. Adoption of the national standards is only the first step; implementation must follow. Determination and design of curriculum and the accompanying instructional activities necessary to achieve the standards are the responsibility of the states and the local school districts. This in itself is a formidable task. This process will be an evolving one that can eventually lead to changes in the way music educators are trained at the college and university levels, enabling them to better promote curriculum design and instructional activities favorable to achieving the goals established by the national standards. MENC has numerous aids available to music educators wishing to become more involved in implementing the national standards in their own school districts.

SUGGESTED ACTIVITIES

1. Research the attendance at the first Keokuk Conference, select an individual not previously discussed in this chapter, and report to the class that person's contributions to the history of music education.
2. Determine who were the three ministers responsible for the compilation of the *Bay Psalm Book* and report to the class on their motivation for the project.
3. Compare the lives and contributions to the education movement of John Tufts and the Rev. Thomas Walter.
4. Select a significant twenty-five-year period in the history of music education in the United States and compare it with what was taking place musically in Europe during the same period. What was the status of education in general in both locales? What were the social and political factors associated with the status of music and music education in the United States and Europe at that time?
5. Interview a veteran music educator regarding the format of contemporary music conventions and compare these conventions with those held during the time of Lowell Mason.
6. Research and present a report to the class on how music education in this country was affected by the 1957 Soviet launch of the first space satellite.
7. Research and report to the class on what is known as the "shaped note" or "buckwheat" music notation system.

8. Conservatories played an important role in the progress of music education in the nineteenth and early twentieth centuries in the United States. Compare the early music conservatory concepts and approach to education with the programs used in music education in today's colleges and universities.

9. Discuss in class the effect the National Band Contest movement had on the vocal music programs in the United States.

10. Examine the guidelines for teaching music established by Pestalozzi. Which, if any, of the guidelines are still in use today?

11. Compile a report to be submitted in class on the development and purpose of the normal school in the United States and how it affected music education.

12. Develop a half-hour instructional project based on Manhattanville Music Curriculum Project principles and present it to the class.

13. Assemble a panel of local music educators for the purpose of discussing their views as to the direction music education has taken in the last ten years. Prepare a list of questions in advance.

14. Lead a class discussion on the extent that Goals 2000 and the national standards have influenced the music education curriculum at the college or university you attend.

CHAPTER FOURTEEN

TOWARD A
PHILOSOPHY OF
MUSIC EDUCATION

INTRODUCTION

This chapter offers a down-to-earth and understandable approach to developing a philosophy of music education. The subject of "philosophy" has been approached with a great deal of apprehension through the years by undergraduate college and university students. However, exploring philosophical foundations can be made enjoyable as well as rewarding. The information included here can only serve as introductory material to a somewhat more complex, yet not overwhelming, effort to accommodate the need for a philosophy of music education. The author hopes that this chapter will whet the appetite of prospective teachers to examine in greater depth their involvement in music education: what they do, how they do it, and, perhaps more important, why they do it.

The chapter begins by discussing how a new music educator can develop a philosophy. Then, the need for a philosophy of music education is explored. Common schools of philosophy—including idealism, realism, pragmatism, and experimentalism/instrumentalism—are described, as well as their strengths and weaknesses and relation to music education. Aesthetic education is addressed separately as an important contributor to music education philosophy. Finally, the chapter returns to the concept of building a philosophy of music education to show how a justification for the inclusion of music in the school curriculum can be developed.

If educators are to administer successfully complex music programs, the development of an individual music education philosophy is not an option, but a mandate. Through investigation of the traditional schools of educational philosophy, as well as an examination of current philosophical visions and aesthetic theories, educators can satisfy that mandate. Philosophy can then become both a collection of ideas and a way of thinking as music educators approach their important work.

DEVELOPING A PHILOSOPHY

The most common approach toward the development of a philosophy of music education has been to relate music education to one of the more traditional educational philosophies, such as idealism, realism, or pragmatism. This practice, while offensive to some music educators and philosophers, is perhaps one of the most effective procedures presently available to music educators.

Bennett Reimer, Charles Leonhard, and Abraham Schwadron are some of the most active and vocal exponents of a comprehensive philosophy of music education. All three are prolific writers and lecturers on the topic of the philosophy of music education and are highly respected for their views on the subject. Reimer, Leonhard, and Schwadron argue that a comprehensive philosophy should be based on aesthetic theories. They feel that only through a serious study of aesthetics are music educators able to develop the background necessary to enter into a productive partnership with educational philosophers, one in which the philosophers could assist the music educators in examining their beliefs and principles. The music educators, in turn, could provide new data and concepts for the philosophers. Reimer, in his book *A Philosophy of Music Education* (1989), has provided music educators with a model for associating music education with several aesthetic theories. Reimer's book is the most recent in-depth effort to relate aesthetic theories to music education and should be on the "must read" list of all serious students of music education philosophy.

Leonhard defines a philosophy of music education as a "system of . . . beliefs which underlies and provides a basis for the operation of the musical enterprise in an educational setting. A philosophy should serve as the source of insight into the total music program and should assist music teachers in determining what the musical enterprise is all about, what it is trying to accomplish and how it should operate" (1965, p. 59). Developing a philosophy of music education must involve building a theory that relates to the meaning and value of music and the role of music in life.

In medieval times, philosophy was referred to as the total of all knowledge represented by the arts and sciences. Educational philosophy today can be both speculative and prescriptive, and, as previously mentioned, music teaching in general is aligned with prevailing educational philosophies. The two main streams of philosophical thought in American education are pragmatism and realism. Most educational beliefs appear to be associated with one or the other, or a philosophy somewhere in between. Pragmatism has profoundly affected music education texts and methods in the last fifty years. The idea of "learning by doing" dominates current music education thought as it relates to music methods. A more detailed presentation of the effects of traditional educational philosophies on music education appears later in this chapter.

The Need for a Philosophy of Music Education

Successful music education programs have always attempted to achieve a balance between student concerns and what music educators deem to be important subject matter concerns. Unfortunately, there are also many examples where the balance was never reached, or for that matter even sought. Some programs present the knowledge of music without an actual musical experience, while others provide extensive opportunities for students to make music without allowing them the opportunity to develop an understanding of why they are doing it. A solid philosophical approach to music education should not permit such unbalanced teaching.

The development of a solid philosophical approach must begin at the undergraduate level. This is a demonstrated weakness in the training of music education teachers. Generally speaking, colleges and universities have been woefully negligent in exposing undergraduate students to material relating to the evolution of a philosophy of music education. Only a few music departments currently offer an undergraduate class in music education philosophy. Many of those same schools offer a unit on the subject as part of a broader music education class. The prevailing thought in higher education appears to be that any serious study related to the philosophy of music education should be reserved for the graduate level. The education of undergraduate music students, then, must necessarily revolve around the development of skills, methods, and techniques, at the expense of encouraging critical thinking on the part of those students. This approach to the training of teachers in the music education profession is indeed unfortunate and serves as the prime motivating factor for the inclusion of this chapter in a book dealing with the administration of school music programs.

It is essential that college students preparing to enter the music education profession develop an understanding of the importance of their career field. This is the time in an individual's life when the need for self-justification is the highest, as he or she is preparing to become a contributing member of society. Students need to develop meaning for their professional lives. They need a mission! This is especially true in music education, because the value of the career field is often not fully understood by its own members and is generally even less understood by professionals in related fields. In Bennett Reimer's words, "The individual who has a clear notion of what his aims are as a professional, and who is convinced of the importance of these aims, is a strong link in the chain of people who collectively make a profession" (1989, p. 4). The profession will become more solid, more secure, to the degree that music educators are able to formulate a persuasive, forceful, and compatible philosophy.

Individuals need to feel that their chosen profession is important and that they can enrich society. If music educators cannot develop these feelings, their resulting contributions will be of questionable value: "The understanding a person has about the value and nature of his profession inevitably affects his understanding of the value and nature of his life" (Reimer 1989, p. 4).

In addition, music educators can turn to their philosophical foundations for appropriate solutions to problems when they arise. A responsible, well-tested philosophy enables teachers to react rationally and confidently to a situation rather than spontaneously and perhaps recklessly.

A philosophy supplies the most important and specific objectives of music education. As Reimer points out:

> It is the function of a philosophy to provide broad objectives under which specific behaviors and behavior clusters can be chosen intelligently and influenced effectively. Without the synthesizing, directing force of a philosophy, education can only be indiscriminate and diffuse. Every aspect of the teaching and learning of music is similarly influenced by a philosophy. If problems of method, of program, of organization and administration, of evaluation, even of research are to be dealt with in ways which are relevant to the nature and value of music education, that nature and value must clearly be understood. A philosophy, then, provides the foundation on which the entire structure of music education rests. (1989, p. 11)

Problems in the organization and administration of a music program can be facilitated, accommodated, and guided by an individual's philosophy of music education. This philosophy is of the utmost benefit in decision-making. Decisions based on a philosophical foundation are made quickly, with ease and confidence.

A philosophy of music education should evolve from a variety of experiences and be in keeping with contemporary social philosophies. It should also be dedicated to the developmental growth of students and teachers alike. This philosophy must have survived the test of practice and time and be able to withstand current debate and examination. If a philosophical approach to music education is sound, it will stand up to close scrutiny.

A strong philosophy of music education is not totally acquired from academic investigation. It is also developed through classroom experience and administrative opportunities. It must be flexible to adjust to changing times; as situations change, certain characteristics of one's philosophical position will mature and adjust to the change. Music education philosophy is founded on mistakes as well as successes (Klotman 1973, p. 5).

The academic preparation for developing a philosophy of music education is of great importance, and as mentioned earlier, it is in somewhat of a state of neglect in institutions of higher learning. Work at the undergraduate level should build a foundation for philosophical principles and serve as the framework for the future "on-the-job" developmental processes.

SCHOOLS OF PHILOSOPHY

Present-day philosophies relating to music education stem from traditional philosophies of education. Rightly or wrongly, this relationship has resulted from the lack of any other basic source that can serve as a philosophical foundation for music education. Reimer, Schwadron, and Leonhard have all voiced a need to base music education philosophy on the study of aesthetics and aesthetic theories, and Reimer's book (1989) is a brilliant effort in that direction. Others voice the opinion, however, that music education philosophy is not just about the aesthetics of music and how people respond to it, but rather represents a series of tightly reasoned arguments for the need for teaching music (Jorgenson 1990, p. 18).

Most music education philosophies, therefore, are closely tied to traditional education philosophy. For that reason, a general presentation of traditional philosophy is included here. It is important for music educators to have some understanding of the philosophical evolution of their profession. In the following section, several educational philosophies are described, along with their application to education in general, and more specifically to music education.

Idealism *Spiritual*

An idealist believes that reality is governed by a permanent, uniform, and absolute spiritual mind. Physical objects are simply imperfect reflections of the ideas they represent. For example, the pencil an individual may have in hand is only an imperfect representation of the "ideal" pencil. Idealism does not greatly concentrate on ideals for living, but rather on ideas as the necessary elements of reality. Idealists feel that objects of the so-called external world exist only as ideas. For example, it is not so much that a tree or painting has reality, but it is an idea of a tree or painting that is conceived within the mind (Brown 1966, p.78).

Strengths of idealism. The greatest strength of idealism is its conscious, intellectual approach to reality, along with the stability of the philosophy. What is true is true, always was true, and always will be true. Idealism is more systematic and specific than other philosophies (Abeles, Hoffer, and Klotman 1995, pp. 43–44).

Weaknesses of idealism. Although "what is true is true" according to idealism, it is difficult to arrive at what is "the" truth. Logic has proven to be a less precise philosophical tool than idealists like to admit. For example, people tend to make judgments according to personal values rather than on the basis of logical reasoning. Furthermore, idealists have difficulty accounting for new developments and changes.

Idealism and education. The process of education is very serious and very purposeful for the idealist. The idealist music teacher poses as both an inspiration and a model for student imitation. Thus the teacher's personality is very important, and a good teacher makes a conscious effort to develop himself or herself as a proper model for students. The idealist tends to teach aspects of music that are considered to be of great and lasting worth. The *Messiah,* Beethoven's symphonies, Tchaikovsky's *Romeo and Juliet,* and the piano music of Brahms are all examples of music that would qualify for inclusion in a music curriculum based on idealism.

In Abraham Schwadron's (1967) words, "The idealist holds to the mutual companionship of mind and feelings, for true taste and aesthetic enjoyment require exposure, objective mastery, and finally understanding" (p. 19). The objective of an idealist education is to arouse an emotional response by means of exposure, followed by careful study of the characteristics of the music and the background of the composer. Exposure (hearing music) followed by study (learning about music) leads finally to understanding, which an idealist equates with aesthetic pleasure. Music's expression of meaning beyond itself is explained in the writings of idealist philosophers such as Susanne Langer and John Dewey, who argued that music aroused or expressed feelings without the need for words. One person may listen to a piece of music and find it sad; another may find the same piece pensive. This is not important. What is important, however, is that the music has expressed something to each.

The idealist teacher primarily uses the discussion method in the classroom setting and presents worthy models of creative work for student imitation, as well as stimulation of student interest and initiative. The idealist teacher has a strong interest in evaluating the level of student learning and is concerned that students gain a comprehensive understanding of classroom work and the ability to apply that knowledge. The capacity of the student to grasp the "big picture" of the material studied is also of great importance.

The idealist teacher sees discipline as a part of teaching, not as an end in itself but rather as a pattern of behavior that will eventually benefit the student. The idealist attempts to show students the effect of misconduct on the rest of the class. The teacher asks the misbehaving student what would happen if everyone behaved in a similar manner. Infractions of discipline are therefore seen as demonstrations of selfishness in ignoring the obligations to fellow class members and members of the community (Kneller 1964, p. 38).

Realism

Realism is a belief in the reality of matter, independent of opinions and desires. When compared with idealism, the realist's position is more material and less spiritual. Realists feel that all physical things or objects are real in themselves and exist independently of the perceiver. For example, if there were no human perceivers, the objects would still exist and still be real. Plato felt that to understand an object or concept is to comprehend its form and structure. This is the basis for the theory that education should have a central core of subject matter that will help students experience the physical and cultural structure of the world in which they live. Realists consider liberal education to be the focal point of all education. Liberal education refers to education that pertains to a wide range of subjects and activities, such as mathematics, science, literature, and the arts. The realist is interested in knowledge as it relates to all humanity (Glenn, McBride, and Wilson 1970, p. 30).

Strengths of realism. The principal strength of realism is practicality. Realists take what they have and work with it. They don't spend time wondering if a wall in front of them is "real," but they know if they bump into it, the result will be real. Realism deals with reality as it can best be known (Abeles, Hoffer, Klotman, 1995, p. 49).

Weaknesses of realism. The practicality that is the primary strength of realism is also one of its weaknesses. Knowledge of reality as perceived through the senses is subject to error. Realism relies on the opinion of experts, and this creates the problem of who should decide, and what will happen if the experts disagree. A case in point is that there is much disagreement in music education. Determining the correct embouchure, the best way to teach rhythm, the value of music contests, the problems surrounding the inclusion of jazz or multicultural studies in college curriculums, and the content of music theory courses are all widely debated by educators.

Realism and education. To the realist, ordered and organized forms are similar to mathematical relationships; thus musical works of profound structure and design qualify as artistic products. Pedagogically the study of construction precedes the emotional dimension of a musical work. The realist feels that playing an instrument is important for the development of mature appreciation and cultural taste.

Realists believe in teaching what the authorities in an academic discipline feel is worth knowing, and they place a great deal of emphasis on direct experience, such as actually singing a song rather than talking or reading about it. The realist teacher likes the objectivity of the scientific method and uses an objective approach to learning. Realists tend to see students objectively or impersonally, and they are not concerned with personality or character development. They are primarily interested in the acquisition of specific information and skills considered necessary to function in society. For example, a piano teacher might have a student learn all the Beethoven concertos because they are seen as essential repertoire for successful concert pianists.

Realists have no respect for the "inspirational value" of history because history is something to be viewed objectively. They favor the "whatever works" policy as an objective means of transmitting knowledge to students. Realists see lecturing and reading as part of the learning process and are quick to include computers and individualized instruction methods in the classroom approach. These teachers see themselves as central to the educational process. If they cannot provide a given piece of information, they will tell the students where to find it.

Realists tend to be impatient with distracting behavior. They feel that "life is too short for fooling around." The realist teacher feels that children should be taught to live by absolute moral standards. Acquiring good habits is essential because virtue does not come automatically; it must be learned (Abeles et al. 1995, p. 49). The idea of accepting what can be known and working with that knowledge as best one can seems defensible, practical, and reasonable.

Pragmatism

Dating back to the sixth century BC, pragmatism did not come into its own until the late nineteenth and early twentieth centuries, and then it flourished primarily in the United States. It is, therefore, a philosophy generally regarded as being indigenous to the United States, although it is deeply rooted in the British tradition of "we know what we experience." Charles Sanders Peirce, William James, and John Dewey were leading exponents of the pragmatic point of view. Pragmatism is concerned with questions of practical usefulness. Pragmatists feel, for example, that ideas, beliefs, and attitudes are important, particularly for their formation and functioning in social interaction. Thus pragmatism assumes that the principal function of knowledge is to guide action.

Pragmatists uphold the value of examining particulars in order to see how those particulars might work in practice. They feel that all things are in a state of flux, creating a need for experimentation. Dewey proposed five steps of thinking: activity, awareness of the problem, observation of the data, formulation of a hypothesis, and testing of the hypothesis. This scientific method of gaining knowledge is the basis of pragmatic philosophical thought. Pragmatists believe that the only knowledge that really matters results from successful testing of hypotheses.

Pragmatists greatly emphasize education and feel that the function of the school is not merely to prepare students for life, but also to provide a suitable environment for actual experiences.

Strengths of pragmatism. One of the great strengths of pragmatism is the dedication to the process of uncovering the truth and determining reality through the application of the scientific method. Pragmatism is not burdened with the problem of "who is the expert." The scientific method satisfies that question. The process, not persons, determines the truth, and the meaning of an idea resulting from that process lies in its consequences after it has been put into operation.

Weaknesses of pragmatism. Perhaps the greatest weakness of pragmatic thought is its devotion to a relatively simple means of determining truth. Pragmatism tends to work well in small, controlled situations, but many questions in life are too large and unwieldy to withstand experimental examination. Unfortunately, the scientific method cannot answer questions of value any better than can logical thinking. Pragmatism provides information that can be useful in making decisions, but pragmatism cannot distinguish which is the right decision. Without lasting values and goals, teachers have little guidance as to what should be taught (Abeles et al. 1995, p. 50).

Pragmatism and education. Pragmatists tend to place a great deal of importance on learning how to acquire skills and gather information. Because what needs to be learned is always changing, the pragmatic educational emphasis is on the process rather than the product. A music educator following this philosophy would teach students how to sing or play an instrument but not emphasize a specific repertoire; if students know how to do something, they can adapt to the specific, individual needs (i.e., perform specific pieces) that they might encounter as musicians. "Pragmatism views teachers as agents who impart to the young techniques for living, and acquiring knowledge" (Abeles et al. 1995, p. 58).

The pragmatic teacher is interested in the nonmusical result of music study. He or she feels, for example, that it's acceptable if music study contributes to improved student citizenship and health, even if that's not a part of the subject matter. The pragmatist provides classroom opportunities for social interaction and believes that group work is an important ingredient in the teaching approach. That same teacher wants the facts presented in class to be useful to the student. Pragmatist teachers want their students to be active in the classroom rather than merely passive listeners. Those same teachers are constantly alert to the need for change and are ready to adapt to new situations as they arise.

The pragmatist teacher is less interested in evaluation than is the idealist or realist. This teacher is not so much concerned with the content that has been learned, but rather how the material was learned. The strict conventional idea of discipline is not of great importance to pragmatist teachers, but unusual disruptive behavior is not tolerated. To the pragmatist, the results of the learning experience assume the greatest importance. For this reason, pragmatists have at times been accused of being too lenient in structuring music classroom activities. Pragmatist music teachers feel that music education is not a product taken home after leaving school, but rather a process that goes on partly in school and partly in all informed social communications and liaisons occurring throughout a lifetime.

Experimentalism/Instrumentalism

Experimentalism, formerly known as instrumentalism, stems from the writing and work of John Dewey and is characteristically twentieth-century American in origin. The experimental philosophy is closely related to pragmatism in that experimentalists believe in learning by doing and in the importance of direct experience.

The experimentalist wants an active school with active learners. Experimentalist teachers have the responsibility to organize, select, and direct learning activities toward meaningful goals, but they also feel that they must arouse student interest, so that students are led to knowledge that will help them deal with the problems of life. These teachers stress thinking through problems rather than memorizing meaningless answers and feel that human relationships are developed in a democratic classroom atmosphere. A variation of this philosophy has been used for many years in an attempt to justify music programs in public schools; music education, it has been argued, benefits students in ways that are essentially unrelated to music. Phrases such as music education "contributes to better health," "develops wholesome conduct and good citizenship," and "promotes good work habits" are examples of statements often offered in support of music education. Such declarations "may convince some reluctant administrator to more fully support the music education program, but those values can't stand close scrutiny because they are not directly related to music and not unique to music. In fact, many other areas of the curriculum are in a position to make a more powerful contribution to these values than is music" (Leonhard 1965, p. 59). Bennett Reimer cited the writings of Susanne Langer and John Dewey when he challenged educators to put aside their nonmusical objectives and look to aesthetic qualities for a foundation on which to build a philosophy of music education (Reimer 1959, pp. 29–32).

AESTHETICS AND MUSIC EDUCATION

It was mentioned earlier in this chapter that there are those who feel that a new and comprehensive philosophy of music education must relate to the study of aesthetics and to aesthetic theories. The purpose of this section is to clarify the meaning of "aesthetics," what is meant by "aesthetic experience," and what constitutes "aesthetic education."

Aesthetics

The *Harvard Dictionary of Music* defines *musical aesthetics* as the study of the relationship of music to the human senses and intellect. Schwadron (1966) interpreted aesthetics as the "philosophy or study of the beautiful, resulting in the establishment of criteria which help one to determine whether or why one particular composition is beautiful while another is not" (p. 187).

Aesthetic experience

According to Reimer, an aesthetic experience includes some level of involvement with expressive qualities rather than simply with symbolic designations. He believed that an example of how this "aesthetic attitude" is cultivated are the elaborate steps taken to create an encouraging atmosphere in concert halls, theaters, and museums: in other words, providing a setting that makes people receptive to an aesthetic experience (Reimer 1989, p. 103).

Charles Leonhard and Robert W. House felt that the aesthetic experience can be any that has qualities of both undergoing and doing, and involves a balance between struggle and fulfillment. They pointed out that ordinary experiences have two components: the practical and the intellectual. The authors used the following example to make their point. A farmer who transforms uncultivated land into a field undergoes a practical experience. At the same time, the experience involves an intellectual process. The farmer determines the need for a crop and reflects on how to best clear and plow the field, then uses his knowledge, based on years of farming experience, concerning climate, soil, and the market to determine which crop to plant and when to plant it. Leonhard and House (1972) concluded: "He is conscious of the results of his efforts, can conceive of the finished product and anticipates the consummation of his experience. These constitute the aesthetic element of his experience. . . . An experience is aesthetic when resistance, tension, excitement and emotion are transformed into a movement toward fulfillment and completion" (p. 93).

In the simplest terms, an aesthetic experience can also be expressed as "an individual's response to something beautiful." The key word here is *individual's*. What could be an aesthetic experience for one person may be something entirely different for another. Reimer (1989) used the analogy of four people viewing the same scene from a lookout point along a mountain road. All look at the same scene, but each one perceives something different and reacts accordingly. The first viewer, a geologist from a nearby university, notes the interesting examples of glacial movement and wonders if she should bring her graduate seminar class to the location to view the scene. The second person, a farmer (undoubtedly the one who just cultivated the previously unbroken land), looks at the field below, worries about the lack of moisture, and decides to raise chickens instead of farming. The third viewer, a clergyman, is awed by the grandeur of the scene, and because he sees this as an instance of divine creation, begins to recite a prayer. The fourth person to view the scene is a music educator. Reimer, with tongue somewhat in cheek, describes the probable reaction:

> The music educator (aesthetic to the core) perceives the interplay of colors, of shapes, of the texture of the clear sky against the roughness of forest and sparkle of water, of the mass of mountains against the horizon, framing the entire valley. The perceived aesthetic qualities of the scene are enjoyed for their intrinsic loveliness. The scene is felt to be beautiful—to give a sense of pleasure, of significance, of immediately present import. "How lovely," he thinks. And in wordless absorption he "loses himself" in the qualities presented to his vision. His experience is aesthetic. (p. 105)

Individuals bring different backgrounds and points of reference to the same experience and will most naturally react in varied and somewhat unpredictable manners. How boring it would be to exist in a world where everyone reacted in a similar manner to parallel experiences or sets of circumstances.

Aesthetic education

An aesthetic experience is not founded on universal material responses, but rather is developed in abstract fashion through education. In music, if the aesthetic experience occurs as an interaction between the listener and the musical work, the resulting experience depends largely on the preparation of the listener to perceive the aesthetic, as well as the capability of the object (or piece of music) to produce the aesthetic. It is in the cultivation of attitudes and the application to the learning process of the experiences that occur through contact with aesthetic objects that education makes its contribution. "The purpose of aesthetic education is to develop the ability of people to perceive the embodied, expressive quality of things and to react to the intrinsic significance of those qualities" (Reimer 1989, p. 106).

BUILDING A PHILOSOPHY OF MUSIC EDUCATION

Four traditional philosophies of education have been explored in this chapter, along with their respective implications for music education. It is tempting to consider taking the best points of each view and combining them into the "perfect" philosophy: an eclectic one. Some philosophers caution against this practice and suggest rather that music educators explore in-depth each philosophy to find the one that comes closest to their actual beliefs and classroom practices. Teachers are then encouraged to build from that accepted philosophic viewpoint and adopt the entire doctrine as theirs, thus creating teaching techniques and a classroom environment based on that philosophy. These philosophers urge this course of action, because in times of trouble or program justification it is difficult, if not impossible, to fall back on a philosophy developed eclectically. They believe that a single, educationally sound philosophy is a far more practical and defensible approach for teachers to follow in developing an individual philosophy of music education.

Undergraduate courses can provide students with only a basic foundation on which to build a philosophy of music education. The first few years of new music educators' professional lives are spent experimenting with and sorting out the multitude of methods and teaching procedures presented to them as college or university undergraduate music students. They will retain the practices that work for them and discard those that don't; thus each will formulate a personal philosophy of music education. Perhaps the least desirable course of action a music educator could take would be to select a particular philosophical approach to teaching in advance of classroom involvement and then attempt to become that type of teacher without the benefit of the actual teaching experience. If the foundation is properly and carefully laid at the undergraduate level, the prospective music educator will find many options available to build a philosophy of music education based on experience as well as theory.

There are some educational philosophers who believe it is perfectly legitimate and logical to build a single philosophy based on the exploration of several. As Kneller (1964) stated, "This is the way of the eclectic, and it is a reasonable first step toward the building of a systematic philosophy of education" (p. 127). Some music educators and prospective music educators will be attracted in different ways by all forms of the traditional philosophies presented in this chapter. If one is to develop an eclectic philosophy, however, caution must be exercised to ensure that each element selected is related logically to the rest. Kneller feels that all philosophies start eclectically. Each reader will have to begin by selecting from the philosophies he or she has read and, based on life's experiences, draw upon those ideals that best represent the reader's own thoughts and feelings.

Whichever method is used to build a philosophy of music education, it is necessary as well to consider building from the aesthetic theory approach discussed earlier in this chapter. Music educators need to examine their philosophical lives to determine (1) what purpose they have in life, (2) what it is they value most highly, (3) what they consider to be worthwhile knowledge, and (4) whether or not they really "love" children. Whatever the outcome, this self-analysis cannot help but be beneficial. In any walk of life, individuals must have philosophies of their own to understand where they are going. If music teachers or their administrators cannot develop philosophies of education, students will have no alternative but to follow aimlessly or put youth's important questions to someone else (Kneller 1964, p. 128).

MUSIC IN THE SCHOOL CURRICULUM

Through the development of a personal philosophy of music education, music educators are in an authoritative position to examine the place of music in the curriculum of today's schools. When asked as part of a job application process to articulate, either verbally or in writing, their philosophy of music education, music educators must necessarily respond with what they believe is the place of music in the school curriculum. This response can be carefully shaped by one's personal philosophy, regardless of that philosophy's stage of development. School administrators are not so much concerned with whether a prospective teacher relates to the realistic or pragmatic schools of philosophical thought, for example, but rather how the teacher views the role of music education in that particular school system. From a historic standpoint, as early as 1959, at a joint meeting with the Music Educators National Conference (MENC) in Atlantic City, New Jersey, the American Association of School Administrators passed a resolution that stated:

We believe in a well-balanced school curriculum in which music . . . and the like are included side by side with other important subjects such as mathematics, history and science. It is important that pupils, as a part of general education, learn to appreciate, to understand, to create, and to criticize with discrimination those products of the mind, the voice, the hand, and the body which give dignity to the person and exalt the spirit of man. (Korvall 1966, p. 195)

Three decades later, both houses of Congress passed the "Goals 2000: Educate America Act." For the first time in the history of this country, the arts have been included among the various educational disciplines in which every young American should be able to demonstrate competence. MENC established a task force to develop criteria through which competency could be assessed in music education. The resulting work of that task force was published in the form of the National Standards for Arts Education. The national standards that relate directly to music education appear in the MENC publication *The School Music Program: A New Vision*. This publication presents nine national voluntary standards in music for grades K–4, 5–8, and 9–12. They are

1. Singing, alone and with others, a varied repertoire of music.
2. Performing on instruments, alone and with others, a varied repertoire of music.
3. Improvising melodies, variations, and accompaniments.
4. Composing and arranging music within specified guidelines.
5. Reading and notating music.
6. Listening to, analyzing, and describing music.
7. Evaluating music and music performances.
8. Understanding relationships between music, the other arts, and disciplines outside the arts.
9. Understanding music in relation to history and culture.

These standards are designed to reflect a national consensus concerning the highest-priority skills and knowledge young people should have acquired on exiting grades four, eight, and twelve. They apply to every student through grade eight and to every student enrolled in music beyond grade eight. Although music instruction in school is important in the development of those students who are talented in music, its primary purpose is to improve the quality of life for all students by developing their capacities to participate fully in their musical culture (MENC 1994, p. 2).

The national standards for music must necessarily influence the vision of music educators as to what their students should be learning in the classes and rehearsals under their supervision. Will this vision affect one's philosophy of music education?

Undoubtedly and justifiably so. Figure 14.1 is an example of a response that could be presented to school administrators concerning the role of music education in the school's curriculum, based on the National Standards for Music Education.

Figure 14.1. Statement of the role of music education in the curriculum

The music education program in the curriculum of today's schools should provide every student with the opportunity to develop intellectual, technical, aesthetic, and social goals. These goals represent a basic minimum for performers and nonperformers alike. The school should attempt to achieve as much depth and understanding in these skills as the resources of the school and community will permit.

Intellectual. Students should possess an awareness of the logical organization of musical works and develop the ability to listen attentively and follow with understanding their performance. The ability should be developed to appreciate good standards of musical performance and to value such artistic principles as unity and coherence, variety and contrast, and structural balance and architecture.

Technical. Students should be able to use the singing voice as a means of self-expression and develop the ability to make music on instruments, either in exploration or as part of in-depth study. Students should be able to read musical notation and use that ability to participate in group and community singing. Children of all ages should be given many opportunities to explore music through composition.

Aesthetic. Students should develop a sharpened sense of beauty in sound through the development of musical listening abilities, so that musical listening experiences can be meaningful, creative, aesthetically significant, and satisfying. Students should be provided the opportunity to develop an awareness of their musical heritage relating directly to human aesthetic history and theories. Student consciousness should be encouraged concerning the level of aesthetic and cultural values present in their own communities.

Social. A sense of belonging should be achieved by student participants, as well as a feeling of identification through association with successful performance groups. The social qualities of music need to be recognized. Both listening to and making music lead to enjoyable associations with people of like interests. Students also need to become aware of the contributions that artists have made to their own cultural enjoyment.

The statement of the place of music education in today's schools given in Figure 14.1 results from the process of philosophy of music education development and is offered as a model approach to music education curriculum.

Developing a philosophy is a demanding, yet necessary, process that frees the teacher's imagination and allows the mind to be applied systematically to issues of importance. Kneller summed up the process this way: "An educator who does not use philosophy is inevitably superficial. A superficial educator may be good or bad—but, if good, less good than he could be, and if bad, worse than he need be" (Kneller 1964, p. 128).

SUGGESTED ACTIVITIES

1. Carefully examine the suggested program in the curriculum of today's schools given in Figure 14.1. Briefly list the suggested requirements that support each goal and determine which traditional philosophy is compatible with each particular requirement and why.

2. How can you justify including music in a high school curriculum? Draft a statement that would convince a school principal and parents.

3. Select two secondary school or college music teachers you remember well and sketch their philosophic orientation according to classroom techniques and attitudes toward music and music students.

4. Think about music education as you know it in the last ten years. How do you feel it has improved? How has it failed? Make a comprehensive list of improvements and failings.

5. List the ways in which your education has been most successful to this point and why. In what respect has it been less than successful and perhaps even frustrating?

6. Recall and describe in writing a learning experience that involved an aesthetic experience.

7. Discuss in writing the differences and resulting causes and effects of musical athletics and music aesthetics.

8. In 200 words or less, respond in writing to the question "What is aesthetic education?"

9. Write a five-minute speech to be presented to a general meeting of parents and staff regarding what you do as a music educator, why you do it, and why the program is important to the school, and more specifically, to the student participants.

APPENDIX A

REGENESIS
(Song of the Planet)

B♭ TRUMPET 1

JOHN HIGGINS (ASCAP)

APPENDIX B

SBMP 36

And Nature Smiled

Allen Koepke   Allen Koepke

bowed   as   its   pet - als   would   un -   fold.

bowed   as   its   pet - als   would   un -   fold.

bowed   as   its   pet - als   would   un -   fold.

Soon   the weeds did gath- er   'round the rose.   "Share with   us your beau-ty," they

OO

OO

won't need an - y pet - als, you have your dig - ni - ty."_____

won't need an - y pet - als, you have your dig - ni - ty."_____

won't need an - y pet - als, you have your dig - ni - ty."_____

On the hill - side grew a love - ly rose, a

On the hill - side grew a love - ly rose, a

On the hill - side grew a love - ly rose, a

BIBLIOGRAPHY

Abeles, Harold F., Charles R. Hoffer, and Robert H. Klotman. *Foundations of Music Education,* 2nd ed. New York: Schirmer Books, 1995.

"Adjustable Acoustics in Music Performance," *Music Educators Journal,* April 1975.

Althouse, Jay. *Copyright: The Complete Guide for Music Educators.* Van Nuys, CA: Music in Action, 1984.

Anderson, William M., and Patricia Shehan Campbell, eds. *Multicultural Perspectives in Music Education.* Washington, DC: Music Educators National Conference, 1989.

Barresi, Anthony L. "Music Objectives for Choral Festivals, *Music Educators Journal,* March 1979.

Bessom, Malcolm E., Alphonse M. Tatarunis, and Samuel L. Forcucci. *Teaching Music in Today's Secondary Schools.* New York: Holt, Rinehart and Winston, 1980.

Birge, Edward Bailey. *History of Public School Music in the United States.* Washington, DC: Music Educators National Conference, 1928.

Boyle, J. David. "Selecting Music Tests for Use in Schools," *Psychology of Music Education Bulletin,* Fall 1981.

———, and Rudolf E. Radocy. *Measurement and Evaluation of Musical Experiences.* New York: Schirmer Books, 1987.

Brand, Manny. "Putting Our PR Techniques to Use," *The School Musician,* January 1980.

Brian, Keith. "How to Build an Audience," *The Instrumentalist,* March 1979.

Britton, Allen P. "Music Education: An American Specialty." In *Perspectives in Music Education.* Washington, DC: Music Educators National Conference, 1966.

Broudy, Harry S. "Educational Theory and the Music Curriculum." In *Perspectives in Music Education.* Washington, DC: Music Educators National Conference, 1966.

Brown, Andrew F. "Organizing Your Music Library," *The School Musician,* January 1973.

Brown, L. M. *General Philosophy in Education.* New York: McGraw-Hill, 1966.

Buford, Thomas. *Toward a Philosophy of Education.* New York: Holt, Rinehart and Winston, 1969.

Cochran, Kathy H. "Prescription for Discipline," *Music Educators Journal,* December 1983.

Colwell, Richard J., and Thomas Goalsby. *The Teaching of Instrumental Music.* Englewood Cliffs, NJ: Prentice Hall, Inc., 1992.

Comprehensive Musicianship: An Anthology of Evolving Thought. Washington, DC: Music Educators National Conference, 1971.

Conant, James B. *The American High School Today.* New York: McGraw-Hill Book Company, 1959.

Cope, Carolyn O. "Steps Toward Effective Assessment," *Music Educators Journal*, July 1996.

Corcoran, Gary. "Adjudication/Director Relationship," *The School Musician,* March 1983.

Covey, Stephen R. *The Seven Habits of Highly Effective People.* New York: Simon and Schuster, 1989.

Crosby, Philip B. *Leading.* New York: McGraw-Hill Publishing Company, 1990.

Curatilo, Joseph S. "Scheduling Sanity in the Elementary Schools," *Music Educators Journal,* April 1983.

Cutietta, Robert. "Performance Isn't a Dirty Word," *Music Educators Journal,* September 1986.

Daggett, Ron. "Organizing a Parent Booster Club," *The Instrumentalist,* May 1979.

Dempsey, Richard A., and Henry P. Traverso. *Scheduling the Secondary School.* Reston, VA: National Association of Secondary School Principals, 1983.

Deutch, Diana, ed. *The Psychology of Music.* New York: Academic Press, 1982.

Dewey, John. *Art as Experience.* New York: Minton, Balch and Company, 1934.

———. *Democracy and Education.* New York: Macmillan; 1917.

Farnsworth, Paul R. *The Social Psychology of Music.* Ames, IA: Iowa State University Press, 1969.

Fitzgerald, R. Bernard. "The Contemporary Music Project for Creativity in Music Education." In *Perspectives in Music Education,* Washington, DC: Music Educators National Conference, 1966.

Froseth, James O. "Using MAP Scores in the Instruction of Beginning Students in Instrumental Music," *Journal of Research in Music Education,* Spring 1971.

Gagliardi, Frank. "Do We Really Need Competitive Jazz Festivals?" *The Instrumentalist,* April 1983.

Garretson, Robert L. *Conducting Choral Music.* Boston, MA: Allyn and Bacon, 1970.

Garvey, William H. "Marketing: Common Sense Plus," *The Instrumentalist,* August 1979.

Gary, Charles. "What Music Educators Should Know about the New Copyright Law," *Music Educators Journal,* April 1977.

Gates, Terry J., ed. *Music Education in the United States.* Tuscaloosa, AL: The University of Alabama Press, 1988.

Geerdes, Harold P. *Music Facilities: Building, Equipping, and Renovating.* Reston, VA: Music Educators National Conference, 1987.

Glenn, Neal E., William B. McBride, and George H. Wilson. *Secondary School Music: Philosophy, Theory and Practice.* Englewood Cliffs, NJ: Prentice Hall, 1970.

Gnagey, William J. *Motivating Classroom Discipline.* New York: Macmillan Publishing Company, 1981.

Goalsby, Thomas W. "Portfolio Assessment for Better Evaluation," *Music Educators Journal,* November 1995.

Gordon, Edwin. *The Psychology of Music Teaching.* Englewood Cliffs, NJ: Prentice-Hall, 1971.

Harrington, Charles J. "An Investigation of the Primary Level Musical Aptitude Profile for Use with Second and Third Grade Students," *Journal of Research in Music Education,* Winter 1969.

Helwig, Carl, and Michael S. Thomas. "Predicting Choral Achievement through Use of Musicality and Achievement Tests," *Journal of Research in Music Education,* Fall 1973.

Hoffer, Charles R. *Introduction to Music Education.* Belmont, CA: Wadsworth, 1983.

———. "The Music Contest Steps Off in a New Direction," *Music Educators Journal,* January 1976.

Howard, John Tasker. *Our American Music.* New York: Thomas Y. Crowell, 1939.

———, and George Kent Bellows. *A Short History of Music in America.* New York: Thomas Y. Crowell, 1967.

Hunt, James, G. *Leadership.* Newbury Park, CA: Sage Productions, 1991.

Ivey, Donald. "Can We Afford to Deceive Ourselves?" In *Perspectives in Music Education*, Washington, DC: Music Educators National Conference, 1966.

Jipson, Wayne R. *The High School Vocal Program*. West Nyack, NY: Parker Publishing Company, 1972.

Jorgensen, Estelle R. "Philosophy and the Music Teacher: Challenging the Way We Think," *Music Educators Journal*, January 1990.

Kameenui, Edward D., and Darch, Craig B. *Instructional Classroom Management: A Proactive Approach to Behavior Management*. White Plains, NY: Longman Publishers, 1995.

Kassner, Kirk. "Management Systems for Music Educators," *Music Educators Journal*, March 1996.

Keene, James. *A History of Music Education in the United States*. Hanover, NH: University Press of New England, 1982.

Kinyon, John. *The Instrumental Music Directors Source Book*, Sherman Oaks, CA: Alfred Publishing Co., Inc., 1982.

Klotman, Robert H. *Scheduling Music Classes*. Washington, DC: Music Educators National Conference, 1968.

———. *The School Music Administrator and Supervisor*. Englewood Cliffs, NJ: Prentice Hall, 1973.

Kneller, George F. *Introduction to Philosophy of Education*. New York: Wiley, 1964.

Knezevich, Stephen J. *Administration of Public Education*. New York: Harper and Row, 1975.

Kohn, Alfie. *Beyond Discipline*. Alexandria, VA: Association for Supervision and Curriculum Development, 1996.

Korvall, Bonnie, ed. "Music in the School Curriculum." In *Perspectives in Music Education*, Washington, DC: Music Educators National Conference, 1966.

Kouzes, James M., and Posner, Barry Z. *The Leadership Challenge*. San Francisco, CA: Jossey-Bass Publishers, 1995.

Kuhn, Wolfgang E. *Instrumental Music*. Boston: Allyn and Bacon, Inc., 1970.

Langer, Susanne K. *Problems of Art*. New York: Charles Scribner's Sons, 1957.

Lautzenheiser, Tim. "Action: The Key to Motivation," *The Instrumentalist*, October 1985.

Leeder, Joseph A., and William S. Haynie. *Music Education in the High School*. Englewood Cliffs, NJ: Prentice Hall, 1959.

Lehman, Paul R. "Assessing Your Program's Effectiveness," *Music Educators Journal*, September 1989.

———. "Review of Primary Measures of Music Audiation." In *Mental Measurements Yearbook*, edited by James V. Mitchell. Lincoln, NE: University of Nebraska Press, 1985.

———. *Tests and Measurements in Music*. Englewood Cliffs, NJ: Prentice Hall, 1968.

Lemlech, Johanna Kasin. *Classroom Management*. Prospect Heights, IL: Waveland Press, Inc., 1991.

Leonhard, Charles. "Philosophy of Music Education," *Music Educators Journal*, September-October 1965

———, and Robert W. House. *Foundations and Principles of Music Education*. New York: McGraw-Hill, 1972.

Ling, Stuart, and Mark Kelly. "Controlling Rehearsals," *The Instrumentalist*, September 1996.

Lowens, Irving. *Music and Musicians in Early America*. New York: Norton, 1964.

Manlove, Donald C., and David W. Beggs III. *Flexible Scheduling*. Bloomington, IN: Indiana University Press, 1966.

Mark, Michael L. *Contemporary Music Education*, 3rd ed. New York: Schirmer Books, 1996.

MENC. *Growing Up Complete*. Reston, VA: Music Educators National Conference, 1991.

————. *Music Booster Manual*. Reston, VA: Music Educators National Conference, 1989.

————. *National Standards for Arts Education: What Every Young American Should Know and Be Able to Do in the Arts*. Reston, VA: Music Educators National Conference, 1994.

————. *Promoting School Music*. Reston, VA.: Music Educators National Conference, 1984.

————. *The School Music Program: A New Vision*. Reston, VA: Music Educators National Conference, 1994.

Meyer, Leonard B. *Emotion and Meaning in Music*. Chicago: University of Chicago Press, 1956.

————. *Explaining Music*. Los Angeles: University of California Press, 1973.

Mitchell, James V., ed. *Mental Measurements Yearbook* (2 vols.) Lincoln, NE: University of Nebraska Press, 1985.

Moody, William J. "Education and Contest," *The Instrumentalist*, August 1983.

————. "Point of View on Competition," *Music Educators Journal*, October 1983.

Mursell, James L., and Mabelle Glenn. *The Psychology of School Music Teaching*. New York: Silver Burdett, 1931.

Neiman, Marcus. "Fund Raising Without Fruit," *The Instrumentalist*, July 1996.

Palisca, Claude V., ed. *Seminar on Music Education*. New Haven, CT: Yale University Press, 1963.

Pizer, Russell A. *Evaluation Programs for School Bands and Orchestras*. West Nyack, NY: Parker Publishing Company, 1990.

Raessler, Kenneth R. "Warning! The Comprehensive Music Festival," *The Instrumentalist*, December 1983.

Reimer, Bennett. *A Philosophy of Music Education*. Englewood Cliffs, NJ: Prentice Hall, 1989.

————. "What Music Can Do," *Music Educators Journal*, September-October 1959.

Rettig, Michael D., and Robert Lynn Canady. "All Around the Block," *The School Administrator*, September 1996.

Rohner, James M. "Fundraising for Fun and Very Large Profits," *The Instrumentalist*, December 1994

Saville, Anthony. "Programming Advice for the School Schedule," *Clearing House*, May 1974.

Schwab, Alexander M. *School Administrator's Guide to Flexible Scheduling*. West Nyack, NY: Parker Publishing Company, 1974.

Schwadron, Abraham. "Aesthetic Values and Music Education." In *Perspectives in Music Education*. Washington, DC: Music Educators National Conference, 1966.

————. *Aesthetics: Dimensions for Music Education*. Washington, DC: Music Educators National Conference, 1967.

Shuter Dyson, Rosamund, and Clive Gabriel. *The Psychology of Musical Ability*. New York: Methuen, 1981.

Smith, Charles W. "Rotation Scheduling, An Alternative," *The Instrumentalist*, January 1982.

Smith, Janice. "Using Portfolio Assessment in General Music," *General Music Today*, Fall 1995.

Snyder, Keith. *School Music Administration and Supervision*. Boston: Allyn and Bacon, 1965.

Solomon, Ed. "The Night So Silent Menace," *The Instrumentalist*, October 1986, p. 24.

Sprick, Randall S. *Discipline in the Secondary Classroom*. West Nyack, NY: The Center for Applied Research in Education, Inc., 1985.

Sunderman, Lloyd Frederick. *Historical Foundations of Music Education in the United States*. Metuchen, NJ: Scarecrow Press, 1971.

Swanson, Frederick J. *Music Teaching in the Junior High School*. Englewood Cliffs, NJ: Prentice Hall, 1973.

Tait, Malcolm, and Paul Haack. *Principles and Processes of Music Education: New Perspectives*. New York: Teachers College Press, Columbia University, 1984.

Wegner, Michael. *Music Facility Design*. Reston, VA: Music Educators National Conference, November 1996.

Whybrew, William E. *Measurement and Evaluation in Music Education*. Dubuque, IA: William C. Brown, 1972.

Williams, Stanley W. *Educational Administration in the Secondary School*. New York: Holt, Rinehart and Winston, 1964.

Wyatt, Linda. "More Time, More Training," *The School Administrator*, September 1996.

Young, William T. "The Role of Musical Aptitude Intelligence and Academic Achievement in Predicting the Musical Attainment of Elementary Instrumental Music Students," *Journal of Research in Music Education*, Fall 1971.

INDEX